Vocational Education and Tr
Digitization

Research in Vocational Education

edited by
Eveline Wuttke • Jürgen Seifried

Volume 4

Eveline Wuttke
Jürgen Seifried
Helmut Niegemann (eds.)

Vocational Education and Training in the Age of Digitization

Challenges and Opportunities

Verlag Barbara Budrich
Opladen • Berlin • Toronto 2020

Förderung durch den Open-Access-Publikationsfonds der Goethe-Universität Frankfurt

This book is available as a free download from www.barbara-budrich.net (http://dx.doi.org/10.3224/84742432). A paperback version is available at a charge. The page numbers of the open access edition correspond with the paperback edition.

ISBN   978-3-8474-2432-1 (paperback)
eISBN   978-3-8474-1335-6 (e-book)
DOI   10.3224/84742432

Barbara Budrich Publishers
Stauffenbergstr. 7. D-51379 Leverkusen Opladen, Germany

86 Delma Drive. Toronto, ON M8W 4P6 Canada
www.barbara-budrich.net

A CIP catalogue record for this book is available from
Die Deutsche Bibliothek (The German Library) (http://dnb.d-nb.de)

Printed in Europe on acid-free paper by Books on Demand GmbH, Norderstedt, Germany
Jacket design by Walburga Fichtner, Cologne, Germany
Cover picture: BillionPhotos.com, Digital, stock.adobe.com

Content

Section III: Workplace Learning in the Age of Digitization

Section IV: Higher Education in the Age of Digitization

Conclusions and Outlook

Editorial and Introduction
to the Volume

Editorial: Vocational Education and Training in the Age of Digitization—Challenges and Opportunities

In the current discussion on digitization, it is assumed that a technological development thrust is currently taking place that brings with it both—opportunities and challenges. On the one hand, completely new technological usage potentials are opening up; on the other hand, these changes pose major challenges to the skills and competencies of (future) employees and—in the consequence—to education and training. In the case of changing and increasing requirements, vocational education and training (VET), as well as further training, will become decisive in order to continuously develop competencies. However, vocational training institutions themselves are also affected by digital change and must make the best possible use of the potential of new technologies. The task of research is to analyse the changes and support the development of strategies, concepts, and models so that individuals, companies, and national economies can benefit from the potential of digitization and at the same time learn to deal with the increasing ambivalences of the technological and social development.

The contributions in this volume will concentrate on challenges and opportunities of digitization for work and workplace learning as well as for vocational education and (further) training. Theoretical approaches, empirical findings and research-based best practice examples of digitization in workplace-related learning are discussed here. When we planned this book, digitization had already been an issue in science and practice for many years (see the introduction by *Helmut M. Niegemann* in this volume). Both had been discussed for quite a while and in an increasingly intensive manner in the contexts of learning, education, and working. What we couldn't know at the time was how relevant this topic would become in a short while. Now that we are writing this preface, we have been in the pandemic for several months, schools and universities are largely doing without classroom teaching, and in-house trainings in companies are suspended or changed to virtual trainings. Teachers, students, trainers and learners had to adapt quickly. In the last months, we have often heard that the educational landscape will be different in the future. In this context, reference is made to the increasing use and the many advantages of technology-based learning and working. Of course we do not know how much the education and training landscape will change and to what extent technology-based learning and working will increase. The fact is that education and training was already quite digitalised before the pandemic and this will most certainly increase further.

Against this background, the contributions in this volume take up the digitization theme from various perspectives which can be found in four sections of the book (Section I: Vocational Education and Training in the Age of Digitization; Section II: Teacher Education and Professional Competencies of Teachers in the Age of Digitization; Section III: Workplace Learning in the Age of Digitization; Section IV: Higher Education in the Age of Digitization). The four sections are framed by an introduction (*Helmut M. Niegemann*) and a final chapter (*Stephen Billet*).

In the introduction, *Helmut M. Niegemann* looks back at the development of educational technologies. He states that a sustainable and systematic integration of digital media into classrooms is still not the standard today and highlights the potentials of technology-based simulations for training and learning as well as for the implementation of valid methods for the assessment of competencies.

The first section of the volume is dedicated to selected technology related issues concerning initial education and training in the professions. In their contribution, *Michael J. J. Roll* and *Dirk Ifenthaler* discuss the potentials of Learning Factories for the development of digital competencies. They conducted an interview study with 19 teachers from German technical vocational schools and asked them about the impact of digitization and Industry 4.0 for their technical vocational school and the potentials of Learning Factories for teaching and learning. Their findings highlight the importance of structured implementation of Learning Factories and the preparation of all stakeholders for Industry 4.0 processes on organisational and staff level in vocational schools.

Mareike Schmidt, Alina Makhkamova, Jan Spilski, Matthias Berg, Martin Pietschmann, Jan-Philipp Exner, Daniel Rugel, and *Thomas Lachmann* focus on the competence development by using digital learning stations in VET in the crafts sector in Germany. In doing so, they created domain-specific digital learning stations (DLS's in a VR environment) based on core work processes of plasterers, integrated them in master preparatory courses and evaluated learner acceptance and learning transfer. The findings of their evaluation studies highlight the potentials of the DLS-learning environment, but also show some challenges for trainees and trainers.

Within their study, *Christin Siegfried* and *Rico Hermkes* analyse the effects of the use of tablet PCs in economics classes in German Vocational Schools. They focus on the motivational experiences and cognitive load of students and compare the results from a digital and an analogue setting. For more information about learning processes, learners' motivation and cognitive load, they use the continuous state sampling method. Among other results, the analyses show that the use of digital media leads to positive experiences of motivation. *Silke Fischer* and *Antje Barabasch* deal in their contribution with the learning potential of gamification in VET. They put the emphasis on the didactical implementation of 21st Century Skills such as communication and cooperation,

10

creativity and critical thinking in gamification and propose a four steps-approach for VET teachers to support the implementation of gamification in classrooms.

The two contributions of Section II deal with different aspects related to teacher education and teachers' professional competencies. The paper by *Andrea Faath-Becker* and *Felix Walker* is entitled "Development of a Video-based Test Instrument for the Assessment of Professional Competence in the Vocational Teacher Training Course". Based on a discussion of different models of teachers' professional competencies, the authors describe the design of video vignettes and discuss the potential of the video vignette tool for the assessment of teachers' competencies. The video vignettes are designed for the industrial-technical field of teacher training in Germany.

The contribution by *Pia Schäfer, Nico Link* and *Felix Walker* also deals with the assessment of professional knowledge of teachers at vocational schools in the domain of automation and digitized production. They base their argumentation on the TPACK-model (TPACK: technological pedagogical content knowledge) by Mishra and Koehler (2006) and report the positive findings of an evaluation study on the effects of a teacher training on automation technology.

The third section of the present volume focuses on contributions to the relevance of digitization for workplace learning. *Henrike Peiffer, Isabelle Schmidt, Thomas Ellwart* and *Anna-Sophie Ulfert,* discuss digital competencies in the workplace to gain an understanding of what they comprise. They shed light on a specific facet of digital competencies, namely digital competence beliefs. Furthermore, the authors investigate how positive competence beliefs can be promoted through trainings. In doing so, they refer to previous studies that investigated and evaluated different training approaches. The article by *Andreas Korbach* and *Helmut M. Niegemann* deals with the potential of a micro-learning approach (the learning content is available on smartphones) for professional drivers. According to the authors, one of the strongest advantages of micro-content might be its high flexibility concerning individual requirements and time constraints. The design of the learning environment is shown in the paper.

Finally, Section IV is dedicated to higher education. Massive Open Online Courses (MOOCs) have been a remarkable phenomenon in educational technology over the last ten years and attracted a lot of attention. Against this background, *Kristina Kögler, Marc Egloffstein* and *Brigitte Schönberger* first discuss current notions of openness in online education and training and show possible links to generic MOOC models. Then the authors present findings from a review-study comprising about three hundred MOOCs from nine common English-speaking providers. Based on the empirical data, the authors characterise different types of MOOCs with a view to their openness.

Victor M. Hernandez-Gantes and *Edward C. Fletcher* discuss the high school career academy as a model for promoting technological preparation in the United States. The goal of the contribution is to conduct a holistic analysis of the career academy model. The analysis of the authors is based on the results of a three-year study designed to explore how IT career academies with different configurations were implemented, with emphasis on the challenges and opportunities in enabling students to become college and career ready. The results of the qualitative study conducted by the authors are very promising.

Finally, Stephen Billett's contribution entitled "Developing a skillful and adaptable workforce: Reappraising curriculum and pedagogies for vocational education" can very well serve as a kind of summary. Billett argues, that changes in occupational and workplace requirements as well as in working life in the era of digitization prompt a reappraisal of the goals and processes of vocational education. These changes include (1) addressing the specific requirements of workplaces and developing occupational competence, and (2) learning knowledge that is difficult to directly experience (e.g. digital knowledge) required for what is often referred to as knowledge work. Billett stresses that there is a need for vocational education and training to respond to this challenge. This includes preparing students to become active and intentional learners for their initial preparation and ongoing development across working life. The author proposes some ways forward by adopting curriculum and pedagogic practices aligned with achieving these kinds of outcomes. This includes considerations of what constitutes effective educational experiences (within both educational institutions and workplaces), ordering and reconciling these two sets of experiences, the use of educational interventions to secure these kinds of capacities within vocational education, including digitized knowledge. This requires accounting for what constitutes existing and emerging occupational and workplace performance requirements and aligning these with the kinds of curriculum and pedagogic practices that vocational education institutions and educators need to advance in an era of digitization.

The papers in this volume represent different approaches to deal with the potentials and challenges of digitization in different areas of education, learning and training. In this book, theoretical approaches and empirical findings are presented in four sections. Thus, this volume provides both a theoretical as well as an empirical basis. It becomes apparent that the approaches are diverse and include many different aspects. However, the contributions also make clear that the trend towards digitization increasingly requires an alignment of learning objectives (which competences should be promoted?), instruction (how can these competences be promoted?), and assessment (how can these competences be assessed?). All actors in vocational education and training are called upon to take up the challenges of digitization and to develop constructive solutions. We also need more research on the potentials and effects of digitization—an evidence-based debate will help us here.

Last but not least, we would like to thank a number of people and institutions who were very important in the creation of this volume. First, we would like to thank the authors for their contributions. We would also like to thank the Budrich publishing house for the constructive cooperation. Many thanks to the Goethe-University Open-Access-Publication-Fund that finances the open-access publication of our volume. Thanks also to the reviewers, who examined the contributions received in a carefully manner and provided many constructive suggestions for improving the papers. Finally, we would like to thank *Teresa Giek* and *Antonia Steffen* for their efforts in formatting the contributions.

Frankfurt and Mannheim, September 2020

Eveline Wuttke, Jürgen Seifried, and *Helmut M. Niegemann*

1 Introduction—A Look Back Ahead

Helmut M. Niegemann

„Books will soon be obsolete in the public schools. Scholars will be instructed through the eye. It is possible to teach every branch of human knowledge with the motion picture. Our school system will be completely changed inside of ten years". This statement by Thomas A. Edison in 1913 (Smith, 1913) was the first, and perhaps the most prominent forecast on the development of media for education which failed monumentally, but not the last. About sixty years later (1971), Helmar Frank and Brigitte Meder, both internationally renowned scholars in the domain of educational technology, predicted a fast triumph of computer supported teaching and learning during the following ten years; almost 100 percent of lessons in general education system's schools would be supported by computers.

New technologies in combination with the financial interests of the companies producing them seem to produce hypes, which are characterised by excessively high expectations, an initial exponential incline over a short period of time, followed by a harsh decline, and—sometimes, but not always—a rather slow increase more closely associated with realistic expectations.

Taking a look back at the development and propagation of the "new media" of the times we see *visual* and *audio-visual media* (especially the educational film) emerging in first half of the last century, followed by *computer based* or *assisted trainings*, arising in the 1960s, declining in the 1970s and their resurrection since the 1990s. In the 1980s both the *teletext* technology (in Germany labeled *„btx"*, in France *„minitel"*) as well as the *video disc* experienced a short hype.

After the invention of the World Wide Web in 1990 and its unforeseen advancement, which penetrated almost all aspects of society *computer-based trainings* (CBT) became at first just *web-based training*s (WBT). However, new information and communication technologies soon promoted the ideas of *intelligent tutoring systems* (ITS), *simulation systems* and *serious games, virtual* (VR), *augmented* (AR) and *mixed reality* (MR) in the education sector. With the emergence of truly mobile devices, such as smartphones and tablet computers, *mobile learning* could take off after a somewhat bumpy start with notebooks at the beginning of this century.

Nevertheless, a sustainable and systematic integration of digital media into classrooms is, even more than hundred years after Edison and fifty years after H. Franks prognoses, not the standard; even when due to the CoViD19 pandemic in 2020 a considerable amount of instruction through digital media is suddenly taking place almost worldwide. Whether this exceptional event will put digital media sustainably into our classrooms and everyday practice, remains to be seen.

Different from public schools, in vocational education and training (VET) digital media has been implemented continuously since the 1980s when personal computers captured the office desktops in bigger companies and organisations and the costs of information technologies sank steadily while its performance grew. Setbacks in some companies occurred partly due to the poor quality of the instructional design of several products, but still the e-learning market grew steadily. Let us have a more detailed look at some specific technologies and the factors which contributed to their success.

Skinners *programmed instruction* (at first without any idea of computers) profited from the "sputnik shock", the impression that the political and economic enemy had an advantage in technological development due to a better educational system, after 1957. The computer technology of the early 1960s should have helped to overcome the organisational challenges of the instructional technology, especially when *programmed instruction* left the strict theoretical rules of operational conditioning by introducing branching (Crowder, 1959) and other features. This early computer assisted learning, using dedicated connections between central computers and the displays, was quite expensive. So, concerning public schools the hype faded away when alternative political topics (such as the war in Vietnam) prevailed over educational matters and required more and more money. Organisations and institutions dedicated to educational technology research and development were closed at the end of the 1970s. But military and big companies maintained educational technology until the advent of the personal computer in 1980. The new high disposability of the devices opened new opportunities and a new wave of computer-based training and instruction began, using color displays, higher capacities on data carriers, and authoring tools (e.g. Toolbook®, Macromedia Director®) to develop e-learning programs by vocational trainers without the help of professional programmers. A not negligible part of the success may be due to the need for training in the new office application software (text processing, spreadsheet calculation etc.). Some ideas originating from that time actually succeeded albeit at a much later time (e.g. electronic performance support systems—ePSS; a combination of short computer-based explanations or training units, and tools to facilitate work, e.g. pre-organised Excel sheets).

The next emerging condition fostering instructional technology was the internet. Since 1990 and the world wide web, which initially allowed for the communication of an increasing amount of data to many recipients, then the two-way communication including the streaming of video data companies have been able to adapt and correct E-learning units just in time. As companies are no longer forced to send CDs and DVDs with e-learning units by mail to their foreign subsidiaries in all continents in order to convey new features of their software releases (e.g. SAP SE).

While video conferencing has been possible earlier via rather expensive satellite channels, the technology became inexpensive and available for everybody, not only could students learn from Youtube videos, blended learning formats like "flipped classroom" were introduced in continuous education and trainings. Video communication reached a peak in 2020 when the corona crisis forced millions of people worldwide to communicate, negotiate and teach at home, as offices, schools and universities began using these tools extensively.

The same technology also allows to distribute lectures of renowned experts from elite universities (e.g. computer scientist Sebastian Thrun from Stanford University in 2011) to a very large audience and to establish the massive open online courses (*MOOCs*), becoming an initially hyped movement ,which seems to have found some stable structures within specialised companies. The acceptance and effectivity of MOOCs soon proved to be better using short video units (*"mini-lectures"*). Although we do not have clear results from psychological research concerning the endurance or depletion of learners listening and studying in front of a display, everyday experience shows, that 60- or 90-minutes video lectures are generally less accepted than mini-lectures of 10 to 20 minutes.

With the rise of the laptop, and later notebook computers (market-relevant since the 1990s, booming around the turn of the millennium), then smartphones and tablets (market-relevant since 2007 resp. 2010) *mobile learning* became a trend. Despite hopes and expectations that tablets would replace the bundle of heavy textbooks, pupils have to carry daily to school (especially in German speaking countries), even in most developed countries there are only scattered "tablet classes" or even "tablet schools". Smartphones, which are owned by more than 95% of students in Germany, are often forbidden during lessons due to fears of undesirable use. Again, the use of the mobile instructional technologies took root in business and industry. Especially smartphones became an important tool for *MOOCs* and other forms of micro-learning offers. The rather small displays barely allow for listening to long lessons or to read long texts but are well accepted for quick lessons and video resp. multimedia instruction.

Rather early in the history of the personal computer users liked to use it not only for work, but also for playing games. This fact led soon to the idea to use games for the purpose of learning, especially to foster a kind of motivation transfer from the joy of playing to learning. Indeed, a lot of studies show that *digital games for learning ("serious games")* can convey important ideas from several curricula in schools, in business and in the military. In case of specific psycho motoric as well as problem solving skills, it is evident that exercises in simulated, more or less authentic situations work as exercises and therefore foster learning. Many science issues, coding skills, mathematical, technical, economical abilities and even historic knowledge can be learned through well-designed games for learning. But there are limits to their usage, which game-based learning enthusiasts (e.g. Prensky, 2001) seem to neglect: *Serious games* take a lot of time to convey a specific subject matter, much more time than most other formats of instruction and the development of high-quality games for learning are expensive. The loss of time is a consequence of the cover story, in which the subject matter in good cases is integrated, or in worse cases is just associated in some way. Thus, the use of games for learning in schools is uncommon.

Mostly at the core of a serious game is a simulation, even if the simulated reality is more or less fictional. Decisive for the efficiency of learning is the similarity of the cognitive and/or the psycho motoric operations executed in the simulated environment and the operations to be executed in real situations. Hence, classical simulation devices (flight simulators, truck simulators, boat simulators, etc.) as well as business games try to immerse the learners into an environment as authentic as possible. Although all newer realisations of these simulations use electronics, the really new ways to use simulated experiences for instruction are via Augmented Reality (AR), *V*irtual Reality (VR) and Mixed Reality (MR), especially for vocational education and training in technical and medical domains. The challenge here is on the one hand the amount of authenticity—a technical problem—and the instructional design of valid learning tasks and exercises on the other including the quality of the feedback for the individual learners. Individualisation means adaptivity and requires interactivity. Two of the big promises of digital learning over the last sixty years are the ability to individualise the learning experience and the ability for participants to set their own learning pace due to the flexibility and lack of time restrictions.

Similar to the individualisation in commerce by finding patterns of individual consumer behavior based on data from online shopping or customer cards there are some possibilities to get information from learners' online behavior: time variables, clicking behavior, input, navigation etc. are used for *learning analytics*. Until today it is still not clear whether this *artificial intelligence (AI)* technology will succeed in the domain of learning as long as the human-computer communication is mostly restricted to mouse clicks, fingertips on a touch screen or the input of words or numbers. Domains in educational technology where AI has proven itself to function technically and psychologically are *intelligent tutoring systems (ITS)*, e.g. "Active Math" (Melis & Siekmann, 2004) or "Autotutor" (Nye, Graesser, & Hu, 2014), and *automatic grading systems* (Landauer, Graham, & Foltz, 2000), but unfortunately both areas are up until now not successful in the market.

Last but not least the domain of *technology-based assessment* enabled primarily the area of VET with more efficient and more valid methods to assess complex competencies by methods, such as *adaptive testing* and the use of rather *authentic virtual task environments*.

Overall educational technology has made a lot of progress over the 100 years the discipline has existed. Even though the public discussion was often focussed on the use of technology in schools, the vocational education and training field seems to benefit much more, presumably because educational technology aims primarily to improve the efficiency of learning processes and to foster flexibility, while schools have to strive additionally for objectives, which also need other kinds of support.

References

Crowder, N. A. (1959). Automation tutoring by means of intrinsic programming. In E. Galanter (Ed.), *Automatic teaching: The state of the art* (pp. 109-116). New York: John Wiley and Sons, Inc.

Frank, H. G. & Meder, B. S. (1971). *Einführung in die kybernetische Pädagogik.* München: dtv.

Landauer, T. K., Laham, D., & Foltz, P. W. (2000). The Intelligent Essay Assessor. *IEEE Transactions on INTELLIGENT SYSTEMS, 15,* 27-31.

Melis, E. & Siekmann, J. (2004). ActiveMath: An Intelligent Tutoring System for Mathematics. In L. Rutkowski, J. H. Siekmann, R. Tadeusiewicz, & L. A. Zadeh (Eds.), *Artificial Intelligence and Soft Computing—ICAISC 2004. ICAISC 2004. Lecture Notes in Computer Science. Lecture Notes in Computer Science Vol 3070.* Berlin, Heidelberg: Springer.

Nye, B. D., Graesser, A. C., & Hu, X. (2014). Multimedia Learning with Intelligent Tutoring Systems. In R. E. Mayer (Ed.), *The Cambridge Handbook of Multimedia Learning* (2nd Ed.) (pp. 705-728). New York: Cambridge University Press.

Pappano, L. (2012, November 2nd). Massive Open Online Courses Are Multiplying at a Rapid Pace. *The New York Times.*

Prensky, M. (2001). *Digital Game-Based Learning.* New York: McGraw-Hill.

Saettler, P. (1990). *The evolution of American educational technology.* Englewood, Colorado: Libraries unlimited, Inc.

Smith, F. J. (1913, July 9th). The Evolution of the Motion Picture: VI—Looking into the Future with Thomas A. Edison. *The New York Dramatic Mirror,* p. 24, Column 3. Retrieved from https://quoteinvestigator.com/2012/02/15/books-obsolete/

Section I:
Vocational Education and Training
in the Age of Digitization

2 The Impact of Learning Factories on Multidisciplinary Digital Competencies

Michael J. J. Roll & Dirk Ifenthaler

2.1 Industry 4.0 and the dual vocational training system

2.1.1 Industry 4.0—A brief introduction

The agitation about Industry 4.0 is a very German peculiarity. Outside the German periphery it frequently appears under the name „*Industrial Internet of Things (IIot)*" (Voigt, Müller, Veile, Johannes, & Becker, 2018). Both, in the private sector and in scientific literature, the term Industry 4.0 has no distinct definition. However, it is slowly gaining ground, that there is no fourth industrial revolution behind the politically motivated and artificially proclaimed term Industry 4.0, as it was the case with the previous revolutions (1. Industrial revolution: steam engine, 2. Industrial revolution: electrification and 3. Industrial revolution: automation).

It is rather an evolution that has been linking physical automation of the third industrial revolution bit by bit. The only 'revolutionary' aspect seems to be the holistic view of a fully networked value chain, but the technological tools have been around for many years in practice. Therefore, Industry 4.0 is especially understood as a holistic vision of the future, not only in production, in which people, machines and processes based on the Internet connect with each other. This means real time data exchange vertically within a company (from the management level to the production facility) and links the value chain horizontally. In this context, value-added networks are given preference instead of value chains (Gebhardt, Grimm, & Neugebauer, 2015; Hecklau, Galeitzke, Flachs, & Kohl, 2016).

These networks utilise data exchange between customers, employees, objects, and systems via cyber-physical-systems (CPS) (Acatech, 2016). CPS are defined as integrated systems that use sensors to record physical data and use actuators to capture and influence physical processes in real-time (Spöttl, Gorldt, Windelband, Grantz, & Richter, 2016). The CPS are digitally networked and have user interfaces for human-machine interaction (Vogel-Heuser, Bayrak, & Frank, 2012). Holistic interconnection through Industry 4.0 facilitates adaptations to spontaneous changes of the production environment (Hecklau et al., 2016). This may add advantages for companies like avoidance of redundancies, reduction of storage, and transportation costs.

Through the value-added network and the real-time data transfer, the batch size of one enables an individual mass production (Gebhardt et al., 2015). New business models relying on a more flexible and efficient production could provide a higher customer satisfaction due to possible individualisation of products. Besides the expectation of creating new business models and boosting the economy through individual mass production, there are also some issues which need to be critically reflected:

- Most companies view the digital transformation as the most urgent topic. But at the moment only a few can see themselves in the value-added networks in Germany (Schäffer & Weber, 2018).
- An often-named specific problem for a company while discussing Industry 4.0 is IT-security. It is essential to protect the physical production line but also an herculean task for IT-infrastructure (Thames & Schaefer, 2017). This applies especially to small and medium-sized companies (SMEs) (Sommer, 2015).
- The larger the company, the greater the chance that the complexity of Industry 4.0 can be mastered well by their human resources. For SMEs, the factor of human capital is a critical aspect in investing in Industry 4.0 (Sommer, 2015).
- Suitably trained employees will be the basis for Industry 4.0. But even if companies might know how the digital transformation within Industry 4.0 will affect the work of their employees, the stakeholder in the German dual vocational school system often do not. This will be a critical point for reaching a leading economic position (Gebhardt et al., 2015).

Furthermore, Industry 4.0 may have broad implications for its stakeholders including changes in learning culture (Ifenthaler, 2018; Wilbers, 2017). It especially indicates the change of employee's Multidisciplinary Digital Competencies (Tisch & Metternich 2017; Berger, Granzer, and Lutz 2018).

2.1.2 Multidisciplinary Digital Competence for Industry 4.0

Competence is multifaceted and has been interpreted in great variation (Westera, 2001). For example Hartig and Klieme (2003) define competence as the combination of learnable skills and inherent abilities to behave adequate in non-standardised situations (Westera, 2001). There are numerous concepts of competence in the digital context, which usually differ only in nuances from each other (Meyers, Erickson, & Small, 2013; Ilomäki, Paavola, Lakkala, & Kantosalo, 2014; Fraillon, Schulz, Friedman, Ainley, & Gebhardt, 2015; Vuorikari, Punie, Carretero, & Van Den Brande, 2016; van Laar, van Deursen, van Dijk, & de Haan, 2017).

The concept of Multidisciplinary Digital Competence (MDC) contains the *attitude towards digital devices*, the *handling of digital devices* and the *information literacy* (Fraillon, Ainley, Schulz, Friedman, & Gebhardt, 2014). It includes also the aspect of *digital security* (Ferrari, 2013), *digital collaboration* (Carretero, Vuorikari, & Punie, 2017) and *problem solving* and *reflection* (Eseryel, Ge, Ifenthaler, & Law, 2011) which are also part of the 21st[st] century skills (Ananiadou & Claro, 2009). Roll and Ifenthaler (2020) developed a model of non-subject-related digital competencies especially for technical apprentices. They define this MDC as „*the willingness and ability of an individual to behave adequately, individually and socially responsible in the digital context of professional, social and private situations*".

2.1.3 Learning Factories 4.0 in German technical vocational schools

Heyse (2018) notes that school policy and teaching in general must change in the course of the digital age. This is especially crucial for industry-related vocational schools, where the learners train for their work life. A state-wide initiative supported through the ministry of economy and ministry of education enabled technical vocational schools to install Learning Factories 4.0 which are thought to prepare students for the challenges of Industry 4.0 (Scheid, 2018).

A Learning Factory 4.0 (LF 4.0) is a model-like production line-up being implemented at several technical vocational schools in the federal state Baden-Wuerttemberg since 2017. At the end of 2020 there will be more than 37 technical vocational schools with such a modern production facility in the state of Baden-Wuerttemberg (Ministry for Economic Affairs, Work, 2017, 2018, 2019). Especially students of the metal and electrical industry are learning with the LF 4.0. Scheid (2018) argues that subject-related and not subject-related competencies are developable by teaching with LFs 4.0. However, current LF 4.0 literature does not focus on competence development in technical vocational schools nor exist empirical studies documenting the benefits of LFs 4.0 for learning and teaching.

LFs 4.0 never have the exact same technical structure. This is because the requirements for each LF 4.0 depend on the particular vocational school and its study programs. Some of them focus on control engineering, some on the interface to IT and many focus on manufacturing (Scheid, 2018). The popular term Learning Factory 4.0 includes two different, but similar technical facilities:

1) Modular basic laboratory: There is a modular basic laboratory that allows to teach basic technical content. Individual industry-related topics can be learned at several different subsystems. These modules of a basic laboratory depend on each school's specification. So, the focus of the basic

laboratory can be either automation technology, electrical engineering, mechatronic or robotics. Usually students are allowed to work with the technology. The primary goal of the modular laboratory is to prepare learners for more complex tasks and problems at the large smart facility (Scheid, 2018).

2) Holistic Smart factory: The larger and holistic smart factory is a CPS. It is the second and more popular part of a LF 4.0. In contrast to the modular laboratory, the CPS combines physical production with appropriate control software. The physical production is linkable via Ethernet to Manufacturing Execution Systems (MES) and Enterprise Resource Planning (ERP) software. In contrast to the modular basic laboratory the CPS does not focus on only one subject but combines everything a real smart factory may have. Therefore, it includes components of automation technology, electrical engineering, mechatronic, and robotics. The CPS models complex production lines and batch size one production. In addition, the effects of networked production are shown with the CPS. While the LFs 4.0, especially the CPSs, are different to each other, common elements include a holistic production line combining a chaotic warehouse, the pneumatic conveying systems, one or more automated robots, several quality control elements, pressing modules, and heating modules (Scheid, 2018). However, research focusing on the instructional design of learning environments for Industry 4.0 including LFs 4.0 at (vocational) schools is scarce.

2.2 Research Questions

This chapter seeks to close the research gap of how to design learning environments utilising LFs 4.0 for developing MDC using an explorative qualitative study approach. Hence, the goal of this research is to gain insight into capturing MDC in LFs 4.0 including the following three research questions (RQ):

(RQ1) Which role do digitization and Industry 4.0 have for the technical vocational schools?

(RQ2) What MDC do the technical vocational teachers most value for Industry 4.0?

(RQ3) How do teachers integrate the Learning Factories 4.0 into their teaching?

2.3 Methods

2.3.1 Design

As Scheid (2018) concludes there is no research about the „*teaching-learning arrangements within a Learning Factory*" and which „*required competencies* [are important] *for future shop-floor workers*" (Scheid, 2018, 287). In order to investigate the teacher's perspective on this research gap, a qualitative exploratory research approach was chosen.

2.3.2 Participants

For the present exploratory qualitative study, interviews with a focus on the implementation of LFs 4.0 at German vocational schools have been conducted. The participants are teachers of electrical engineering or mechatronics. The main criteria for selecting the teachers were: (a) They have teaching experience with the LF 4.0 and (b) they were involved in the planning and implementation process of the LF 4.0 in their vocational school. On the basis of these criteria, 28 teachers were selected and contacted by email and phone to explain the research aim and project. A total of 19 interviews were conducted with teachers satisfying the above-mentioned requirements. The sample size should be adequate to investigate and answer the three research questions (Patton, 1990). The interviewees agreed to audio recording, participated on voluntary basis, had the relevant information, and could reproduce it precisely. They were also available on time and were motivated to discuss the topic. Thus, all external conditions for a successful exploratory interview were given (Gläser & Laudel, 2010). Given the general gender inhomogeneity of the technical vocation (Leifels, 2018) it is not surprising, that all interviewed teachers are male. Unfortunately, because not all teachers wanted to provide information about their age, this important demographic information cannot be completely stated here. Based on the information provided, however, the span of the age is between 28 and 54 years. The interviewees teach between 75 and 385 ($M = 220.61$; $SD = 89.26$) students, of the relevant professions, at the LF 4.0.

2.3.3 Instrument

A semi-structured interview guide was designed prior on literature review and consisted of four parts. First, the interviewees were asked demographic and general questions about their school. The second part included questions about the impact of digitization and Industry 4.0 for their technical vocational school. In this section the teachers were also asked which MDC future shop-floor workers should have in general. In the third part, the teachers were asked about the collaboration between their vocational school and regional companies. The fourth part of the interview focused on the pedagogical usage of the LFs 4.0.

2.3.4 Procedure

The interviews lasted from 17 to 37 minutes ($M = 27.15$; $SD = 6.78$). Due to holidays and several exams, the period of conducting interviews stretched between end of April and November 2018. All the interviews were conducted via phone, recorded and afterwards transcribed with the f4transkript transcription software (Dresing, 2019). The gathered material met all six criteria of objectivity (Mayring, 2002).

2.3.5 Analysis

Two trained employees of the University of Mannheim coded the statements ($K = 0.68$) via f4analyse analysis software (Dresing, 2019). The questions of the semi-structured interview guide were open-ended and therefore the statements were coded and recoded inductively (Mayring, 2015). The interviews were held in German. For this article the responses were translated and paraphrased.

2.4 Results

The technology of LF 4.0 is complex and currently one step ahead of the industrial standard a majority of companies use. Therefore, findings highlight the importance of structured implementation of LFs 4.0 and the preparation of all stakeholders for Industry 4.0 processes on organisational and staff level in vocational schools.

2.4.1 Which role do digitization and Industry 4.0 have for the technical vocational schools? (RQ1)

The responses regarding the role of digitization in vocational technical schools revealed two tendencies. Concerning the general technical infrastructure and the integration of digital technology in teaching, the participating teachers emphasised that schools „*recognised the sustainability and necessity of digitization and must now be instructional*" (Interview 15).

The participants claimed the digitization is „*priority no. 1 at our school!*" (Interview 1) and that „*to make our school more effective due to several applications of digitization. This includes also providing fast Wi-Fi, which should be available in every corner of our building*" (Interview 11). While the school administration is organising the acquisition of appropriate infrastructure, the teachers are thinking about the impact of digitization for their teaching. Most of the interviewed teachers interpreted the role of digitization not only in integrating digital devices, but to speak and discuss about the consequences of digitization. „*Our school administration made me discuss the advantages and disadvantages of the increasing role of digitization in our every-days world*" (Interview 16).

The minority of interviewees are still busy with the digitization of their analog materials. This has been expressed in statements like: „*Right now I am concentrating on the digitization of my materials*" (Interview 2) and „*I just started to integrate digital devices into my lessons*" (Interview 7).
Industry 4.0 seems to be on the rise within technical vocational schools. The interviewees told us that „*Industry 4.0 affects every curriculum at our school*" (Interview 14) and „*We have to discuss the chances and threads through Industry 4.0*" (Interview 4).

In relation to the implementation of LFs 4.0 the teachers are aware that these are „*possibilities to teach with the most modern production technology at the time and that means you have to integrate this technology into the class. Otherwise it would be just a big expensive demonstration object*" (Interview 19). While the will to integrate Industry 4.0 topics is present, the teachers warn that „*you have to adapt the new* [Industry 4.0] *content for the varying level of students*" (Interview 13). Even if „*basic topics can be taught with all classes. How deep you can go into the matter depends on the profession of the students*" (Interview 11). However, the motivation to teach with and about Industry 4.0 seems high. Through the implementation of LFs 4.0 these schools have a technological lead in comparison to most companies: „*these vocational schools with a LF 4.0 are technology advanced to several companies*" (Interview 12). To conclude and answer this research question 1: Even if the infrastructure, like fast Wi-Fi, tablets, smartboards is improvable, the teacher are aware to integrate digital devices and topics into their classrooms. LFs 4.0 extraordinary technological standard is currently ahead of that of the companies.

2.4.2 What multidisciplinary digital competencies do the technical vocational teachers most value for Industry 4.0? (RQ2)

The interviewees had many different ideas for the MDC of their students. The interviews revealed: process understanding (nine interviewees with high expectations), problem solving (eight interviewees with high expectations), advanced IT-skills (seven interviewees with high expectations) and broad expertise and holistic thinking (6 interviewees with high expectations each). One example for the last is that *„They must understand the consequences of technology for their individual life. This must be brought more into focus"* (Interview 18).

Digital Communication and Collaboration seemed to be important for the teachers. Six participants express that the students should have basic knowledge of other subjects. Therefore, they can express themselves and understand problems of another profession. Interviewee 14 told: *„They have to learn how to communicate with professionals of other disciplines. For example should a mechatronics' student be able to explain his problem to an IT-specialist and vice versa"*. Seven of the nineteen participants expected students' IT-skills to be more advanced. They explained this exemplary by programming serial ports or handling subject-specific IT-software. The interviewed teachers do not expect that their students should have deep programming skills, but just typical basic programming actions. Interviewee 9, for example explained that *„They must be able to act absolutely safely, especially in interface programming. Because networking in combination with data security and data analysis will become more and more important"* (Interview 9). To have a structured, critical strategy for solving problems seems a general but very important skill for acting safely in Industry 4.0. *„To analyse a problem systematically"* (Interview 6) and to *„develop a creative way to problem solving, if the usual handles did not work"* (Interview 4) seems to be important for future shop-floor workers.

The most often claimed skill students of technical vocational schools should develop to be prepared for Industry 4.0 is an understanding for processes as shown in statements like *„They should be able to understand and analyse processes in general"* (Interview 2). The recognition of individual processes should *„be promoted by their systematic thinking to recognise processes"* (Interview 5).

To summarise the results of RQ2: The interviewed teachers highlighted MDC which are not subject-specific but are needs-oriented and important for young individuals to act adequately, individually and socially responsible in the digital context of professional.

2.4.3 How do teachers integrate the Learning Factories 4.0 into their teaching? (RQ3)

The responses were divided into three different categories: (1) There is no daily usable pedagogical concept, (2) a pedagogical concept is under development and (3) teachers integrate the LF 4.0 daily with functional pedagogical concept.

Before we asked about the pedagogical integration of LF 4.0 we asked for the infrastructure of the LFs 4.0. Most of them were built up by FESTO (Scheid, 2018). The majority of the teachers stated that the installed LF 4.0 works just fine and *„over time you can easily handle minor problems"* (Interview 15). Larger problems, however, can usually not been resolved without external support from the manufacturer. Interview 17 summarises this fact quite well: *„Overall, the system works well, but maintenance and preparation are very time-consuming"* (Interview 17).

Two participants admitted that they cannot integrate the LF 4.0 because they actually have no concept for the pedagogical use of it. However, this is also due to the fact that in these two schools the modules of the LF 4.0 were technically integrated only shortly before. So, Interview 3 revealed *„We have not developed any concepts yet, because we still have to integrate all the modules"* (Interview 3).

By contrast, there are several statements that show a different status quo. These schools are testing and developing different pedagogical concepts right now and so *„[We had] the rough idea for quite a long time. But we are now finally in the actual development phase"* (Interview 2). Many schools developed a concrete idea before they implemented their LF 4.0. But *„conversion and adaptation are part of a bigger process. It took us quite a long time at our school to understand how to integrate our Learning Factory 4.0, especially the CPS"* (Interview 13). Given the complexity it takes a lot of time until teaching at the LF 4.0 works. It seems like teaching with the CPS works best on a project basis, in larger time slots and across class structures, but this requires a high level of school organisation. The interviewees *„have already been able to implement many ideas, but we still see no light at the end of the tunnel. Because the actual development and the actual improvement of the concepts come from experiences and routine"* (Interview 1).

Other participants agreed with Interview 1 and told us that *„there are many small steps but we are slowly going in the right direction"* (Interview 19). But it is not only the pedagogical integration of the CPS, some schools think further and try to integrate a *„virtual twin of the Learning Factory 4.0.* [This] *is our current development task"* (Interview 17). The interviews show that the longer the LFs 4.0 are already installed, the more sophisticated the concepts seem to be. And the more they are already used by the teacher.

This is also reflected in the last category, in which the five affiliated schools already use their LFs 4.0 for a long time and use *„completely elaborated lessons* [which] *could also be used for further education"* (Interview 9). The fact that some schools, after their concepts have already been tested, give further thought shows the following quote: *„We are trying to integrate smartphones and tablets for exploring the Learning Factory. Therefore, we are building up simple AR* [Augmented Reality] *and VR* [Virtual Reality] *functions on our CPS"* (Interview 9). Furthermore, the interviews show a tendency that the higher the level of degree of the students, the more the LF 4.0 is integrated into teaching. Many participants mention that *„for teaching future state-certified technical engineers with the Learning Factory 4.0 there are many elaborated lessons and concepts than for a lower educational level"* (Interview 18). The lower the performance level of the several trained professions, the less concepts are already integrated into daily teaching within the LF 4.0.

2.5 Discussion

In summary, the interviewed teachers understood the necessary of multi-disciplinary digital competence development (Berger et al., 2018; Tisch & Metternich, 2017). For a minority, the focus of digitization of schools is still on providing fundamental responsive digital infrastructure. At a first glance, this seems a bit unexpected, considering that the interviewees work at schools equipped with the latest smart factory equipment. At second glance, it becomes clear that in addition to the LF 4.0, challenges such as the implementation of digital class books, fast and reliable Wi-Fi, which is also available in the entire school, not just in the room with the LF 4.0, or the procurement of digital devices still have to be mastered. Although German vocational schools are usually equipped technically and digitally above average (Krützer & Probst, 2006). But schools are also focusing on how to integrate digitization into their teaching. This means both the pedagogically meaningful usage of digital devices, but also digitally and its effects as a topic (Ifenthaler & Schweinbenz, 2013, 2016).

The complexity of LFs 4.0 and the fact, that most regional companies of the technical vocational schools do not have similar facilities and adequate human resources now (Sommer, 2015), could make it difficult to get help for fixing bugs or further develop pedagogical concepts.

A better orientation could be the universities, which work with their students at Learning Factories (Abele et al., 2015). However, as Scheid (2018) already mentioned, there are major differences between the demands of universities and technical vocational schools. For example, while universities can work with their learners on project level (Baena, Guarin, Mora, Sauza, & Retat, 2017; Schuhmacher & Hummel, 2016), this form is only seldom teachable in the school context because of the often rigid timetables (Scheid, 2018). The digitization of schools and Industry 4.0 as a topic are strongly prioritised in the interviewed schools.

The competencies of RQ2 are not tied to specific training occupations. Therefore, the claimed skills fit in a model of MDC. The ability of understanding processes and holistic thinking could be assigned to *reflection*. To solve problems fits to *problem solving*. Collaborating digital matches with the idea of *digital collaboration*. Advanced IT-skills could be a level of *handling digital devices*. They can therefore be considered part of the required interdisciplinary competences (Wilbers, 2016) to work in an interconnected industry. Only the stated broad expertise of apprentices seems not to fit at a first glance in a specific aspect of MDC. Either it could be part of *reflection, problem solving*, or *digital collaboration* or in none of these (Roll & Ifenthaler, 2020).

Current literature claims that most schools do not have fitting pedagogical concepts, which could help to develop competencies through teaching with the LF 4.0 (Scheid, 2018). But the status quo of integration of LF 4.0 has to be assessed differently. While schools that have implemented a LF 4.0 for some time now have more mature concepts. Most schools are in the developing process. The time factor and the experiences made are to be considered here. It is not surprising that the use of LFs 4.0 varies, considering that many students in vocational schools have a lack of basic knowledge, like math, grammar, and languages (Scheid, 2018). While Scheid (2018) points out that various additional technologies such as augmented reality (AR) and virtual reality (VR) should complement the pedagogical concepts of the LFs 4.0, the findings show that some schools have already left the planning stage and are developing concepts on how to integrate AR and VR into their lessons with the LF 4.0. The biggest difficulty is breaking down the complexity to a level appropriate for each technical student. In five cases of our sample, this seems to work pretty well. The findings of RQ3 reflect the opinion of Kotter and Schlesinger (2008) that major technological implementations and change processes need to be very well prepared. The difficult and unsolved question here is how the teachers could have been better prepared for the complexity of the Learning Factories 4.0.

2.6 Implications and further research

The findings may be of interest to organisations that have identified Industry 4.0 as a major topic of their technical vocational education. School authorities should have detailed ideas about the later use of expensive and modern equipment such as LFs 4.0 and the involved stakeholders should have concrete plans on how to prepare teachers. Also, creating new teaching or technical positions which support existing vocational teachers might have accelerated the actual pedagogically thought-out usage of LFs 4.0.

Apprentices must be properly prepared for Industry 4.0 in vocational schools and occupational training. In line with Spöttl et al. (2016) and Wilbers (2016), the awareness of which Multidisciplinary Digital Competence should be promoted could also help to consciously integrate them into teaching. The results may help to develop teaching scenarios for other LFs 4.0 in technical vocational schools or to adapt existing ones. The findings with regard to the MDC could be applied to the occupational part of the dual training. The required interdisciplinary cooperation in training of companies (Spöttl et al., 2016) can be more intensively promoted than in the organisational environment of the vocational schools (Scheid, 2018).

This study is limited by the fact, that the statements are subjective personal opinions of the teachers (Flick, 2014; Kidd, 2002). The sample's validity is also limited: The present findings are based on a specific group of 19 respondents. However, given the fact that there are very few technical vocational schools with LFs 4.0, the sample can be called as a broad coverage.

Based on these limitations, existing pedagogical concepts should be scientifically investigated in the next step in order to evaluate the effectiveness of LFs 4.0 as new concepts in vocational schools. In the centre of this evaluation should stand competence tests which will analyse the subject-related but also the Multidisciplinary Digital Competence of apprentices. The fact that the model-based representation of Industry 4.0 can promote competencies is scientifically justified on the university side (Abele et al., 2015; Cachay & Abele, 2012; Cachay, Wennemer, Abele, & Tenberg, 2012), and to prove this also for technical vocational schools is the next step of this research.

Acknowledgements

The authors acknowledge the financial support by Südwestmetall—Verband der Metall- und Elektroindustrie Baden-Württemberg e.V.

References

Abele, E., Metternich, J., Tisch, M., Chryssolouris, G., Sihn, W., ElMaraghy, H., Hummel, V., & Ranz, F. (2015). Learning factories for research, education, and training. *Procedia CIRP*, *32*(Clf), 1-6. https://doi.org/10.1016/j.procir.2015.02.187

Acatech. (Ed.) (2016). *Kompetenzen für Industrie 4.0: Qualifizierungsbedarfe und Lösungsansätze* (acatech Position) (pp. 1-52). München: Herbert Utz Verlag.

Ananiadou, K. & Claro, M. (2009). 21st century skills and competences for new millennium learners in OECD countries. *OECD Education Working Papers*, No. 41. https://doi.org/10.1787/218525261154

Baena, F., Guarin, A., Mora, J., Sauza, J., & Retat, S. (2017). Learning factory: The path to industry 4.0. *Procedia Manufacturing*, *9*, 73-80. https://doi.org/10.1016/j.-promfg.2017.04.022

Berger, R., Granzer, D., & Lutz, L. (2018). Auf dem Weg zu 4.0 im Klassenzimmer. In V. Heyse, J. Erpenbeck, S. Ortmann, & S. Coester (Eds.), *Mittelstand 4.0: Eine digitale Herausforderung* (pp. 167-188). Münster: Waxmann.

Cachay, J. & Abele, E. (2012). Developing competencies for continuous improvement processes on the shop floor through learning factories—Conceptual design and empirical validation. *Procedia CIRP, 3,* 638-643. https://doi.org/10.1016/j.procir.-2012.07.109

Cachay, Jan, Wennemer, J., Abele, E., & Tenberg, R. (2012). Study on action-oriented learning with a learning factory approach. *Procedia—Social and Behavioral Sciences, 55,* 1144-1153. https://doi.org/10.1016/j.sbspro. 2012.09.608

Carretero, S., Vuorikari, R., & Punie, Y. (2017). *The digital competence framework for citizens with eight proficiency levels and examples of use.* European Union. https://doi.org/10.2760/38842

Dresing, T. (2019). *audiotranskription.* Retrieved September 23, 2019, from https://www.audiotranskription.de/f4

Eseryel, D., Ge, X., Ifenthaler, D., & Law, V. (2011). Dynamic modeling as a cognitive regulation scaffold for developing complex problem-solving skills in an educational massively multiplayer online game environment. *Journal of Educational Computing Research, 45*(3), 265-286. https://doi.org/10.2190/EC.45.3.a

Ferrari, A. (2013). *DIGCOMP: A framework for developing and understanding digital competence in europe.* (Y. Punie & B. N. Brečko, Eds.), *Borrador. INTEF.* European Union. https://doi.org/10.2788/52966

Flick, U. (2014). *An Introduction to qualitative research.* Los Angles, London, New Delhi, Singapore, Washington DC: Sage Publications.

Fraillon, J., Ainley, J., Schulz, W., Friedman, T., & Gebhardt, E. (2014). *Preparing for Life in a Digital Age.* Heidelberg: Springer Science + Business Media. https://doi.org/10.1007/978-3-319-14222-7

Fraillon, J., Schulz, W., Friedman, T., Ainley, J., & Gebhardt, E. (2015). *International computer and information literacy study: ICILS 2013 Technical report.* Amsterdam: IEA. https://doi.org/10.15478/uuid:b9cdd888-6665-4e9f-a21e-6156-9845ed5b

Gebhardt, J., Grimm, A., & Neugebauer, L. M. (2015). Developments 4.0—Prospects on future requirements and impacts on work and vocational education. *Journal of Technical Education, 3*(2), 117-133.

Gläser, J., & Laudel, G. (2010). *Experteninterviews und qualitative Inhaltsanalyse: Als Instrumente rekonstruierender Untersuchungen.* Wiesbaden: Gabler Verlag.

Gronau, N., Ullrich, A., & Teichmann, M. (2017). Development of the industrial IoT competences in the areas of organization, process, and interaction based on the learning factory concept. *Procedia Manufacturing, 9,* 254-261. https://doi.org/-10.1016/j.promfg.2017. 04.029

Hartig, J. & Klieme, E. (2003). Kompetenz und Kompetenzdiagnostik. In K. Schweizer (ed.), *Leistung und Leistungsdiagnostik* (pp. 127-143). Berlin, Heidelberg: Springer.

Hecklau, F., Galeitzke, M., Flachs, S., & Kohl, H. (2016). Holistic approach for human resource management in industry 4.0. *Procedia CIRP, 54,* 1-6. https://doi.org/-10.1016/j.procir.2016.05.102

Heyse, V. (2018). Mittelstand 4.0 im Spannungsfeld des digitalen Wandels. In V. Heyse, J. Erpenbeck, S. Ortmann, & S. Coester (Eds.), *Mittelstand 4.0: Eine digitale Herausforderung* (pp. 9-15). Münster: Waxmann.

Hummel, V., Hyra, K., Ranz, F., & Schuhmacher, J. (2015). Competence development for the holistic design of collaborative work systems in the logistics learning factory. *Procedia CIRP, 32*, 76–81. https://doi.org/10.1016/j.procir.2015.02.111

Ifenthaler, D. (2018). How we learn at the digital workplace. In D. Ifenthaler (Ed.), *Digital Workplace Learning—Bridging formal and informal learning with digital technologies* (pp. 3–8). New York, Berlin, Heidelberg: Springer. https://doi.org/-10.1007/978-3-319-46215-8

Ifenthaler, D. & Schweinbenz, V. (2013). The acceptance of Tablet-PCs in classroom instruction: The teacher's perspectives. *Computers in Human Behavior, 29*(3), 523-534. https://doi.org/http://dx.doi.org/10.1016/ j.chb.2012.11.004

Ifenthaler, D. & Schweinbenz, V. (2016). Student's acceptance of tablet PCs in the classroom. *Journal of Research on Technology in Education, 48*(4), 306-321. https://doi.org/http://dx.doi.org/10.1080/15391523. 2016.1215172

Ilomäki, L., Paavola, S., Lakkala, M., & Kantosalo, A. (2014). Digital competence—an emergent boundary concept for policy and educational research. *Education and Information Technologies, 21*(3), 655–679. https://doi.org/10.1007/s10639-014-9346-4

Kidd, S. A. (2002). The Role of Qualitative Research in Psychological Journals. *Psychological Methods, 7*(1), 126–138. https://doi.org/10.1037//1082-989X.7.1.126

Kotter, J. P. & Schlesinger, L. A. (2008). Choosing strategies for change. *Harvard Business Review, July*, 130-139.

Krützer, B. & Probst, H. (2006). *IT-Ausstattung der allgmeinbildenden und berufsbildenden Schulen in Deutschland*. Bonn, Berlin: BMBF.

Leifels, A. (2018). Erster Azubi-Zuwachs seit 2011—Gendergap bei Berufswahl und Gehalt. *Volkswirtschaft Kompakt, 165*, 2018.

Mayring, P. (2002). *Einführung in die qualitative Sozialforschung: Eine Anleitung zu qualitativem Denken*. Weinheim: Beltz.

Mayring, P. (2015). *Qualitative Inhaltsanalyse: Grundlagen und Techniken*. Weinheim: Beltz Pädagogik.

Meyers, E. M., Erickson, I., & Small, R. V. (2013). Digital literacy and informal learning environments: An introduction. *Learning, Media and Technology, 38*(4), 355-367. https://doi.org/10.1080/17439884.2013 .783597

Ministry for Economic Affairs, Work, and Housing of Baden-Wuerttemberg (2017). Förderung von „Lernfabriken 4.0" in Baden-Württemberg. Stuttgart. Retrieved from https://wm.baden-wuerttemberg.de/fileadmin/redaktion/m-wm/intern/Dateien_Downloads/Innovation/Liste_Lernfabriken_4.0.pdf

Ministry for Economic Affairs, Work, and Housing of Baden-Wuerttemberg (2018). Wirtschaftsministerium fördert 21 „Lernfabriken 4.0" an beruflichen Schulen. Stuttgart. Retrieved from https://wm.baden-wuerttemberg.de/de/service/presse-und-oeffentlichkeitsarbeit/pressemitteilung/pid/wirtschaftsministerium-foerdert-21-lernfabriken-40-an-beruflichen-schulen/

Ministry for Economic Affairs, Work, and Housing of Baden.-Wuerttemberg (2019). Wirtschaftsministerium fördert 21 „Lernfabriken 4.0" an beruflichen Schulen. Retrieved February 7, 2019, from https://wm.baden-wuerttemberg.de/de/service/-presse-und-oeffentlichkeitsarbeit/pressemitteilung/pid/wirtschaftsministerium-foerdert-21-lernfabriken-40-an-beruflichen-schulen/

Patton, M. Q. (1990). *Qualitative evaluation and research methods.* Thousand Oaks, CA: Sage Publications Inc.

Roll, M., & Ifenthaler, D. (2020). Lernortübergreifende Kompetenzentwicklung in der Industrie 4.0: Die Entwicklung digitaler Handlungskompetenz in der dualen Berufsausbildung aus der Ausbilderperspektive. *Zeitschrift für Berufs- und Wirtschaftspädagogik, Beiheft 29,* 185–209.

Schäffer, U. & Weber, J. (2018). Digitalisierung Ante Portas. *Controlling, 30,* 4-11.

Scheid, R. (2018). Learning factories in vocational schools: Challenges for designing and implementing learning factories at vocational schools. In D. Ifenthaler (Ed.), *Digital workplace learning: Bridging formal and informal learning with digital technologies* (pp. 271-289). New York: Springer.

Schuhmacher, J. & Hummel, V. (2016). Decentralized control of logistic processes in cyber-physical production systems at the example of ESB logistics learning factory. *Procedia CIRP, 54,* 19–24. https://doi.org/10.1016/j.procir.2016.04.095

Sommer, L. (2015). Industrial revolution—Industry 4.0: Are German manufacturing SMEs the first victims of this revolution?. *Journal of Industrial Engineering and Management, 8*(5), 1512-1532. https://doi.org/10.3926/jiem.1470

Spöttl, G., Gorldt, C., Windelband, L., Grantz, T., & Richter, T. (2016). *Industrie 4.0: Auswirkungen auf Aus- und Weiterbildung in der M+E Industrie. bayme vbm Studie.*

Thames, L. & Schaefer, D. (2017). *Cybersecurity for industry 4.0.* New York: Springer.

Tisch, M. & Metternich, J. (2017). Potentials and limits of learning factories in research, innovation transfer, education, and training. *Procedia Manufacturing, 9,* 89-96. https://doi.org/10.1016/j.promfg.2017.04.027

van Laar, E., van Deursen, A. J. A. M., van Dijk, J. A. G. M., & de Haan, J. (2017). The relation between 21st-century skills and digital skills: Asystematic literature review. *Computers in Human Behavior, 72,* 577-588. https://doi.org/10.1016/j.chb.2017.03.010

Vogel-Heuser, B., Bayrak, G., & Frank, U. (2012). Forschungsfragen in „Produktionsautomatisierung der Zukunft". *Diskussionspapier Für Die Acatech Projektgruppe „ProCPS – Production CPS".*

Voigt, K.-I., Müller, J. M., Veile, Johannes, W., & Becker, W. (2018). Industrie 4.0 – Risiken für kleine und mittlere Unternehmen. In W. Becker, B. Eierle, A. Fliaster, B. Ivens, A. Leischnig, A. Pflaum, & E. Sucky (Eds.), *Geschäftsmodelle in der digitalen Welt* (pp. 517-534). Wiesbaden: Springer Gabler.

Vuorikari, R., Punie, Y., Carretero, S., & Van Den Brande, L. (2016). *DigComp 2.0: The Digital Competence Framework for Citizens. JRC Science for Policy Report.* https://doi.org/10.2791/11517

Westera, W. (2001). Competences in education: A confusion of tongues. *Journal of Curriculum Studies, 33*(1), 75-88. https://doi.org/10.1080/00220270120625

Wilbers, K. (2016). Berufsbildung 4.0: Berufsbildung im Zeitalter der großen Digitalisierung. *Berufsbildung, 70*(159), 7-10.

Wilbers, K. (2017). Industrie 4.0 und Wirtschaft 4.0: Eine Chance für die kaufmännische Berufsbildung. In K. Wilbers (Ed.), *Industrie 4.0: Herausforderungen für die kaufmännische Bildung* (pp. 9-52). Berlin: epubli GmbH. https://doi.org/10.1007/-978-3-658-04883-9_4

3 Competence Development with Digital Learning Stations in VET in the Crafts Sector

Mareike Schmidt, Alina Makhkamova, Jan Spilski, Matthias Berg, Martin Pietschmann, Jan-Philipp Exner, Daniel Rugel & Thomas Lachmann

3.1 Introduction

Digitization and the increasing use of new technologies do not only influence our daily life but have an impact on workflows in the modern working world. Particularly, in the crafts sector digital transition is challenging since it requires much effort to keep up-to-date besides the daily routine. This situation also affects education and demands new skills of students who will be the employees of the future, as well as it requires a rethinking of educational institutions and trainers on how to change instruction methodology and course design. VET faces the challenge not only to bridge the gap between theory and practice but additionally to train students how to use digital tools efficiently and to adapt to changes in traditional processes.

The research project D-MasterGuide (DMG) addresses these challenges with an approach that is suitable for inter-company vocational training centres of the building and renovation trade. In this domain, apprentices are encouraged to not only acquire necessary expert knowledge but also methods expertise, media literacy, and self-competence. The latter includes skills to reflect on own behaviour and to document gained knowledge. Therefore, we create eight domain-specific digital learning stations (DLS's) based on core work processes of plasterers, integrate them in master preparatory courses and evaluate learner acceptance and learning transfer.

DLS's contain anchored instructions, work orders or exercises in order to augment blended learning lessons with situated learning experience. Students and trainers switch between digital learning sequences and activities in the workshop to review and discuss their results afterward in meetings. This scenario enables new learning dynamics and competence development of the participants. Moreover, it enriches the lessons with virtual reality tours (VR), video animations of the working area, role-playings, open exercises, and a self-organised learning environment. Finally, self- and external assessments are the basis for deeper discussions as well as for an increase of self-reflection.

The technical basis of our approach is the Smart Guided Learning System (SGLS) which combines a learning management system (LMS) with a process guidance component. The architecture is enriched by different devices, applications, and services providing optimal tools depending on task and place of action. Our *participatory development process* involves apprentices and trainers to give direct feedback and derive improvements for the next implementation stage.

In the next section, we shortly introduce the current situation as prerequisites of the DMG approach and briefly describe its main goals and principles in section three. Then, section four explains in more detail the project workflow, its phases and their related outcomes. Finally, we subsume the gained results in the conclusion and give a brief overview of future work.

3.2 Prerequisites

Digital communication becomes more important in small and medium-sized craft enterprises (SMEs), on the one hand during contact with customers and suppliers on the other hand due to internal communication. As a result of a market study to promote digitization efforts in the craft sector, a majority of companies replied that they understand digitization referred to their company mainly as communication and the area of office-optimisation, organisation, and planning (Heil, Fröder, & Spilski, 2018, 55). According to (Brolpito, 2018, 13) the European Commission „highlights that today 90% of jobs require some kind of digital skills, while almost half (44%) of the EU workforce has low basic digital skills, of which 22% has no digital skills at all". Also, in a study about the digitization of trade (Bitkom, ZDH, 2017) a majority of participants are open to digitization (81%). However, more than half of them see the transformation process as a big challenge and more than two-thirds consider the lack of digital literacy as the main obstacle.

The DMG consortium perceives the main reasons in the self-competence of acting persons on how to handle innovations. Self-competence is the ability to act responsibly for oneself and comprises characteristics like autonomy, critical faculties, confidence, reliability, sense of responsibility and duty. Therefore, partial competences like self-reflection, self-efficiency, motivation, and target orientation should be strengthened already in the vocational training. Moreover, a neutral consideration of digital techniques and tools should be achieved since digitization increases and changes the craft-related world of work (Spilski, Heil, Schmidt, Schwertel, & Mayerl, 2017, 39). Although, nowadays the young generation grows up and spends a lot of time online, „they are media-related, they are not media-literate" (Dehne, Lucke, & Schiefner-Rohs, 2017, 78). Thus, VET should not only strengthen the practical and theoretical skills of apprentices but also develop competences to deal with technologies and media usage.

Schmid, Goertz and Behrens (2016, 21) state that innovation in schools often fails due to insufficient technical infrastructure on the one hand and the lack of resources or competences of the trainers on the other hand. The first issue can be resolved by using the given financial aid and invest it into a solid technical infrastructure and tools. The latter relies on different reasons: trainers are often lost in various confusing information, they usually are not given space for the necessary additional work and try to achieve the related competencies by self-studies. Furthermore, some of them fear embarrassing themselves in front of their class if some students are more experienced with digital devices and technology. The German education system established the dual system with cooperation between publicly funded vocational schools and SMEs. Typically, the training lasts two to three and a half years and the trainees spend alternately parts of their time at school and the other part at a company. Learning at inter-company vocational training centers of renovation trade traditionally has focused on practical actions in cabins or movable walls. In master craftsman training (e.g. preparatory courses) many trainers still use teacher-centered instruction to impart construction knowledge. Learning with projects and open issues hardly takes place.

The DMG project proposal focuses on participants of preparatory courses for the master craftsmen in the plastering trade. In this phase students still have enough learning resources and thus, positive effects like self-competence and neutral consideration of digital techniques and tools are most likely reachable. Most of the participants are between 18 and 25 years old and aspiring owners or future second-level managers with a highly personal interest in leadership and management issues.

3.3 The DMG Approach

As we learned before, digitization in education requires not only money to buy technologies and hardware but also needs increased competences for both students and trainers, strategic development to change the attitude towards digital learning and rethinking of learning and pedagogical concepts.

The DMG project develops concepts to encourage students to think and work independently. They should be supported individually based on their prior knowledge, learning level and speed. Alternatively, self-reflection can be used as a developmental possibility to strengthen confidence and to enhance learning motivation. Finally, apprentices should use digital technologies to increase various competences—theoretical knowledge, practical skills and digital and media literacy to simplify their professional life.

Moreover, the DMG project aims to support trainers in the transformation process and strengthen their confidence. Some of them are afraid that their work will be replaced by digital technologies. This fear is unfounded: (Schneider & Preckel, 2017, 30) revealed that „educational technology is most effective when it complements classroom interaction". Trainers can do more than presenting basics in lecture style. They often have a lot of experience of the working environments and are able to enrich lessons as experts in a variety of topics. Thus, digital systems might be useful tools to assist trainers in their everyday life: learning data can be used to focus flexibly on competences, strengths and weaknesses of the group and adapt the results to versatile possibilities of course design.

The DMG approach integrates different principles to a didactical-methodological concept. The DMG approach combines the method of *learning stations* (similarly to *learning islands*, Dehnbostel, 2008, 531ff.) as part of an overarching setting with the principles of *process-oriented learning* (Howe & Staden, 2015, 26ff.). Hence, processing of an order is divided into domain specific steps with related tasks that are assigned to different stations.

The core of the DMG framework comprises eight digital learning stations (DLS) that are mainly used in a *blended learning scenario* within the classroom. These DLS contain amongst other content anchored instructions, work orders or exercises to enrich the lessons with a situated learning experience. Learners and trainers switch between digital learning sequences and activities in the workshop to review and discuss their experiences and results afterward in meetings. This enables new learning dynamics and competence development of the participants. Extended media types support students to change from consuming to active learning behaviour in order to achieve sustainable learning success. Hence, anchored instructions are designed as virtual tours (VR) or video animations of the working environment, whereas open exercises enable students to create solutions with text, images, tables or attached documents. Self- and external assessments provide variety in the everyday learning situation and are the basis for deeper discussions as well as for an increase in self-reflection. Trainers profit from the blended learning scenario with roleplayings, discussion or feedback sessions to enter into dialogue with their students.

Additionally, the DMG approach considers heterogeneous learning groups with divergent learning levels, speed and prior knowledge. Each DLS includes learning sequences for three different learning levels (novice, advanced or master)—similarly to *developmental tasks* described in (Becker, 2013, 17). Thus, teachers can react flexible to the knowledge of the class and select appropriate level.

Besides the core framework, an easy-to-use and self-organised digital working environment might help to encourage students to increase their learning progress and motivation outside of the class. Therefore, we include preconditions and prior knowledge of the learners, derive requirements and suggest individual incentive measures via digital assistance.

Finally, we include teachers in the testing process and coach them how to use DLS in the classroom. The direct involvement of trainers and students in these phases increases the acceptance of using the technologies afterwards since their requirements and needs are addressed by design.

3.4 DMG Workflow Phases and their outcomes

The *participatory development process* of the DMG project demands close collaboration within the extensive consortium consisting of technology partners, end-users and scientific partners (see details on https://d-master-guide.de). Based on concrete issues, we elaborate on conceptual designs and implement solutions that are tested and evaluated continuously. The DMG workflow can be divided into three phases which are repeated in several iterations for the entire duration of the project:

- **Specification Phase:** In this period requirements of the target group are collected, analysed and provided as a specification for the following phase.
- **Realisation Phase:** Based on the documents of the previous phase the requirements are technically realised either as new developments, customised configuration or content creation.
- **Testing and Evaluation:** Students and trainers test the result of the former phase in trails on-site and return direct feedback and evaluations. Thereafter, the data are analysed and interpreted to serve as input for the Specification Phase of the next iteration.

The following subsections describe briefly the phases of an iteration with their main results.

3.4.1 Specification Phase

Each iteration of the DMG workflow starts with collecting and analysing requirements derived from the DMG approach and the last evaluation phase. The resulting specification does not only affect the content and curriculum of our framework but also the technical infrastructure of the underlying learning environment. In the following subsections, we will explain in detail the initial requirements we derived for both aspects.

3.4.1.1 Curriculum Concept

Digital Learning Stations (DLS). The DMG framework consists of eight process-based DLS oriented towards the renovation trade. They include curricula for three learning levels (novice, advanced or master) with an increasing complexity of the related scope of work (simple task orders, advanced customer orders or extended project orders). The curricula with a blended-learning approach involve micro-processes to support understanding, working and using digital tools in overlapping typical occupational situations. Although we implemented all DLS prototypically for the specific topic insulation, the concept can be used for any other topic since the processes remain the same.

A curriculum comprises real actions in presence as well as blocks of preparing and follow-up exercises within the learning sequence. Figure 1 shows the realised syllabus of DLS 1 on the novice level. It offers clusters of several exercise types to encourage learning in various manners. The sequence consists of a mix between individual work (could also take place from home/distance) and guided group work. It comprises general information, anchored instructions, self-checks as preparation or follow-up tasks, open exercises and reflection in discussion panels. The following paragraphs describe several elements in more detail:

Figure 1: Curriculum of DLS 1, novice level

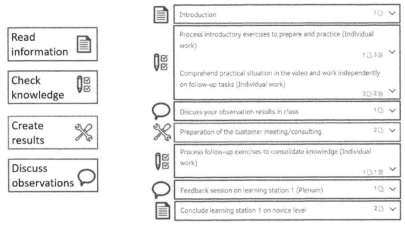

Source: own representation

Anchored instructions (AI). Each DLS starts with impulses in the form of AI to describe the current issue. AI is a technology-centred learning approach and a form of situated learning that emphasises problem-solving within an integrated learning context, which can be examined from multiple perspectives. A complex story encourages students to solve realistic problem formulations actively and independently. The relation of stories with further knowledge helps learners to apply new knowledge and to overcome the theory-practice gap.

As we already live in an era where VR training is being used to prepare students, employees, to operate remote equipment, let alone entertainment and retail purposes, VR experience instances were conceived as a special case of AI. It is necessary to sensitise prospective masters to this medium given that the scope of their future work could include uses of different artificial realities (e.g. client consulting situation, giving a hint of the final result of plasterworks). The VR experience was designed as an introductory unit to the DLS by assuming learners being novices of that type of experience. Thus, the requirements included natural methods of interaction and a detailed tutorial designed to familiarise the learners with virtual reality in general and the actual gameplay in particular. The VR experience instances were designed to give the possibility of practice-based learning experience rooted deeply in the real-world context. A narrative with a real-world problem behind the learning content was also supposed to spark interest and give awareness about the following content of the DLS.

Self-checks and competences. One relevant part of the level-based curriculum of a DLS is so-called self-checks where students can test their knowledge on their own or in small groups sharing one user account. The questions related to the mapped process are clustered around several competences (social, professional and media competences) and rely on the learning level of the corresponding curriculum. Self-checks are used as a block of introductory or follow-up exercises including practical knowledge. This knowledge is a prerequisite for the successful completion of a DLS as prior knowledge in commercial-technical professions is assumed to be important for learning progress (Nickolaus, Abele, & Albus, 2015, 24).

Working with documents. Our framework also aims to support the use of new technologies comprising theoretical and practical knowledge. Students should not only consume media and read books to be tested afterward but create meaningful media in artisanal context. Therefore, we included trainings where practical tasks are combined with exercises to use digital tools, e.g. by documenting their crafted work, prepare checklists for consultation meetings with customers or create tables to insert measured data. Hence, students learn how to work with several tools on the one hand and gain knowledge about the different necessary steps of a process on the other hand.

Challenges and benefits for trainers. The DMG approach relieves trainers from the classical and commonly used teacher-centred instruction. Students can gain and repeat basic knowledge either in the form of distance learning or independent work in silence. Then, trainers may spend their time answering open questions directly with single students or the entire class, enlarge and deepen the topics by open discussions, exchanging experiences or interactive role-plays. Giving students individual feedback within the learning system on open exercises enables tutors to simultaneously document their assessments. Finally, the recommendation and additional statistics about the students' progress within the DLS give tutors a brief overview of their competences and support them in adapting their lesson planning to the current class situation.

3.4.1.2 Architecture Plan

The DMG architecture realises the concept of *smart learning environments (SLE)* (Koper, 2014) that augments physical learning locations and situations (e.g. classroom, lab, workplace) with digital, adaptive and context-sensitive services, devices and content to organise learning in a better and more efficient way. Thus, we set up a so-called ***Smart Guided Learning System (SGLS***, see Figure 2*)*, that relies on an LMS extended by the necessary components, functionalities, and interfaces to other services or tools (e.g. VR Apps).

Figure 2: DMG Architecture

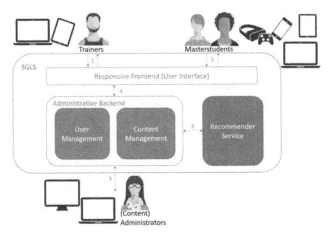

Source: own representation

The LMS comprises two components: the responsive frontend supports a mobile-first approach and offers students and trainers a user-friendly learning environment. The administrative backend provides powerful tools for administrators to set up complex learning scenarios.

Students switch between several devices (e.g. VR headsets, smartphones, tablets or laptops) depending on their tasks with specific requirements or their current learning environment (e.g. workshop, classroom). SGLS provides them with learning material, work assignments, and information and stores the students' activities and results (2). The most suitable devices for trainers are laptops and tablets (1). They provide data by giving individual feedback and assessments and therefore document the development of their students. SGLS, in turn, delivers statistics and reports to trainers such that they might use the information for their lesson planning. The content- and user management components support administrators to create and structure material for the DLS, import users and assign roles, permissions or content. PCs or laptops serve best to pre- or post-process data and exchange (3) it with the SGLS. An internal data transfer (4) between the frontend and the backend component ensures the mapping of complex learning scenarios to a comfortable user-experience.

Based on the consideration that learners would be overwhelmed with the amount of learning content, it was conceived to incorporate a process guidance component in form of a recommender service (RS) into the LMS with the aim of achieving media competences. Ultimately, the goal of RS is to assist the process of content discovery without being overloaded with information and

47

to provide tailor-made recommended content. RS exchanges relevant user data (5) with the LMS: it receives activity-based data of a user and returns a list of relevant content data after its computations. This might be exercises of a higher learning level, suggestions to repeat content related to certain competences or unworked tasks to catch up on the work progress of their class.

For the VR experience we varied the hardware between Oculus Rift, Go and Quest. The choice of these technologies relied mainly on the affordability of the mentioned hardware and, consequently, their potential use within the educational setting. Oculus Rift is wired to a PC and benefits of the quality of images and precise positional tracking. Hence, trainers can use it perfectly to demonstrate specific scenarios with an additional screen in the classroom. On the contrary, Oculus Go and Quest can be used wireless with their head-mounted displays and are well suited for self-learning experiences. Currently, VR components and SGLS are loosely coupled: information in the curriculum gives instructions to switch to the VR environment, explains the task or gives general instructions on how to use the headsets. Results of the VR tour can be stored manually within the SGLS system if desired.

3.4.2 Realisation Phase

In the realisation phases, we setup the digital learning stations (DLS) and extend the SGLS and Apps with necessary functionalities. The next sections describe three implemented examples in more detail: the realisation of an anchored instruction (AI) as VR experience, the setup of a DLS with open exercises and finally the entire environment with a recommender guiding students how to proceed.

3.4.2.1 Introductory Impulses

The VR environment was grounded in the story of a house inspection. The learners virtually walk around a house that was captured with the help of a 360° camera as on-site inspection. Ultimately, their goal is to identify the scope of work and proceed to plan the repairment and finishing. To do this, they start by finding all the problem areas on the exterior of the house. Every correctly identified spot is followed by a multiple-choice question to eliminate false positives and to deeper introduce the learners to the learning material as gamification approach. Figure 3 shows an overview of the user interface of the VR learning environment.

Figure 3: Interface of the VR application

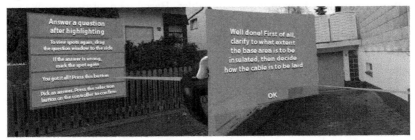

Source: own representation

The VR environment enables learners to switch between three levels of difficulty which correspond to the three competence levels. Completion of a VR component of the DLS takes around 25 minutes on the medium level. Upon completion, the results are shown with the option to export them as a report. Besides, the learners have the possibility to replay their walkthrough with the additional analysis of the viewing direction and dwell time in form of heat maps, enabling them to identify their blind spots and moments of doubt.

3.4.2.2 Process-oriented Practice

As already described in section 4.2, admins use the LMS to setup DLS, whereas students and trainers access the different materials and required workflows of the DLS in an easy-to-use learning environment. DLS map available content in level-based curricula to support a teaching structure: Thus, AIs are available directly within a DLS (e.g. Web-based-trainings) or given as instructions on how to proceed with external devices (e.g. VR application with glasses). Self-checks are realised as tests with various question types like single-, multiple choice or matrix questions, drag & drop, image selection or sorting tasks that can be evaluated automatically by the system. Students can work on self-checks independently and develop their competences. Hence, trainers do not have to lecture fundamental knowledge and can focus on topics which are most relevant for the class (e.g. main interest or specific support).

In the craft sector particularly tables play an important role since almost every step within a process relies on lists, e.g. requirement lists for customers, measurement lists, item-, capability- or stock-lists, checklists documenting the sequence of work or the criteria of work packages. Thus, we extended exercises so that tables can be created, filled, edited and displayed directly within the learning environment. The workflow allows to submit solutions such that the trainer can evaluate each contribution individually. We also created an exercise to introduce how to work with tables. Based on a curriculum vitae in tabular form students learn stepwise to fill, extend and finally style tables for their own purposes and train their media literacy.

3.4.2.3   Supporting Self-competence

Besides DLS, the learning environment provides additional support for students and trainers. Immediately after login a notification reminds users about their last activity and provides a direct link to continue. A help page comprises several information how to use the platform or particular functions. Personal statistics and reports help students to reflect on their learning progress. Trainers benefit from this information about their class to improve and adapt their lessons based on the student's strengths and weaknesses.

An integral part of the SGLS is the embedded recommender service (RS). In a broad sense, RS tries to predict the relevance of items for a particular user based on the assumption that similar users would have related interests and, therefore, would respectively like and dislike similar items. Thus, RS provides the user with a personalised list of recommendations, based on a number of predefined parameters, such as ratings of different items in the past. However, when the list of items highly relevant for the user becomes too long, it may result in a paradoxical situation of choice overload (Bollen, Knijnenburg, Willemsen, & Graus, 2010, 63) where it is difficult to choose from a variety of good alternatives. This assumption led us to consider that only a small amount of the topmost recommended items can be shown to learners unless they explicitly inquire to display more. The learners, however, should be given flexibility in determining what recommendations should be based on.

The initial set of parameters for making recommendations included around ten values which have been reduced and refined during the iterative development process. Based on the predefined parameters, such as previous learning results, search queries, and personal interests, the learner is provided with relevant learning items. The system enables the students to choose from parameters and filters they would like to receive recommendations based on and, therefore, provides more targeted information in an efficient way.

In order to get meaningful recommendations, the learning content (e.g. self-checks) are mapped with metadata reflecting the related learning level and the corresponding process step.

3.4.3 Testing and Evaluation

We used the design-based research approach based on collaboration among researchers and practitioners in real world settings (DBRC, 2003; McKenney & Reeves, 2018). It has been used to analyse the catalysts and barriers in the development of digital learning and optimise our solutions. While conducting several design loops, we applied qualitative interviews, standardised cognitive tests, standardised questionnaires measuring demands, acceptance and self-efficacy, performance measurement, and usability testing of DLS and VR prototypes. In this contribution, we focus on four design loops depicted in Figure 4.

Participants were selected by vocational training institutions in Germany: for loop 1 to 3 the Competence Center for Finishing and Facades in Rutesheim, and for loop 4 the Vocational School for Technology I in Kaiserslautern respectively. In loops 1 and 2, a total of $N = 37$ prospective master craftsmen (three female) were selected from a master preparation class of plasterers (age $M = 27$, $Min = 21$, $Max = 39$). For the third loop, we selected $N = 15$ students in plastering (second year of training) (age $M = 22$, $Min = 17$, $Max = 34$), and for loop 4, we selected $N = 35$ students from the structural engineering department (plasterer, painter and varnisher). Thus, a total of 87 craftsmen and prospective craftsmen (including three teachers) participated until now. The following subsections subsume the results gained from the different design loops.

Figure 4: Design loops

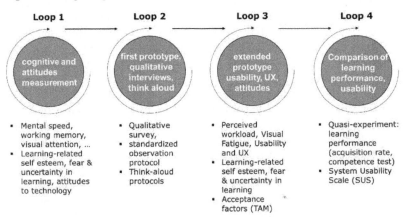

Source: own representation

3.4.3.1 Loop 1: Baseline values

In loop 1, we performed cognition and acceptance measurements by using standardised scales and cognitive tests as far as possible to get the participants' individual baseline values. The following paragraphs have been published elsewhere (Spilski et al., 2019, 4).

Cognitive tests record individual cognitive abilities. The individual processing speed was measured by a number connection test (ZVT, see Oswald, 2016, 1ff. or, for a digital version, Rodriguez et al., 2019, 730ff.), working memory span with the AOSPAN test (Unsworth, Heitz, Schrock, & Engle 2005, 273ff.), the (visual) attention with the Frankfurt Attention Inventory 2 (FAIR 2, Moosbrugger, Oehlschlägel, & Steinwascher, 2011, 1ff.), and the visual spatial imagination with a digital version of the 3DW test (Gittler, 1990, 1ff.).

Questionnaires covered job-related learning transfer factors such as „learning-related self-esteem" (Schyns & Collani, 2014), „fear and uncertainty in learning" (Patzelt & Opitz, 2014) and attitudes to technology (Neyer, Felber, & Gebhardt, 2016).

Cognitive test performance: The z-values shown are standard values. They were determined by looking up the corresponding standard value for the achieved point value of the test persons. A z-value of one, for example, means that a person has achieved such high values that he or she has a standard deviation above the mean value compared to the norm sample. The mean z value for *mental speed* was $M = 0.77$ (*Min* = -1.7, *Max* = 3), *attention performance* was $M = 0.31$ (*Min* = -0.84, *Max* = 1.65) and for *concentration ability* $M = 0.37$ (*Min* = -0.74, *Max* = 1.56). The results of the cognitive tests showed a high heterogeneity of individual performance. This is illustrated by the fact that among the participants, the one with the lowest value at mental speed was 1.7 standard deviations below the norm sample, whereas the one with the highest value was three standard deviations above the mean value of the norm sample. Values of -1.7 can be rated as clearly below average and values of 3 as a particularly high performance. A high degree of heterogeneity was also shown for the attention and concentration ability, which, however, can be rated as lower compared to the processing speed. The mean values show slightly increased but not significant higher mean values compared to the norm sample.

Learning attitudes: The statements of the factor *perceived self-efficacy were* evaluated with a five-point rating scale: refuse completely = 1, partially reject = 2, partially/partially = 3, partially agree = 4 and fully agree = 5. Whereas a five-point rating scale with the following scale points was chosen for the second factor „*feeling of fear and uncertainty of learning*": never = 1, rarely = 2, sometimes = 3, mostly = 4, always = 5. For both scales a value of three can be interpreted as the mean value of the scale and rather as a neutral assessment. In terms of learning attitudes, the *perceived self-efficacy* was rather positive with a mean of $M = 3.76$ (*Min* = 2.57, *Max* = 4.29), while the *feeling of fear and uncertainty of learning* was less pronounced with a mean of $M = 2.53$ (*Min* = 1.67, *Max* = 3.5).

Attitude towards technology: The attitude towards technology contained three factors: *technology acceptance (1), technical competence conviction (2)* and *technology control conviction (3)*. All three factors were assessed using the same five-point rating scale, however different statements which had to be evaluated. This scale contained the following scale points: refuse completely = 1, partially reject = 2, partially/partially = 3, partially agree = 4 and fully agree = 5. First, factor (1) has an average of $M = 3.36$ (*Min* = 1, *Max* = 5) and measures the general interest in and use of new technologies. Second, factor (2) has a mean of $M = 4.00$ (*Min* = 2, *Max* = 4.75) and reflects the self-perception of competence in dealing with (new) technology. Third, factor (3) has a mean of $M = 3.56$ (*Min* = 2.50, *Max* = 5) and reflects the perception of one's own control over technology (Does the machine do what I want or am I helplessly exposed to technology?). Although there was also a high degree of heterogeneity in the sample for these attitude factors, we did not find completely negative attitudes towards technology. This can be seen from the fact that for all three factors the mean values were above three and in the case of *technical competence conviction* four. Therefore, a neutral to partially positive attitude towards technology can be assumed, and, we saw a chance for DLS to be accepted in learning processes. As a result, we developed first prototypes.

3.4.3.2 Loop 2: First prototype

In design loop 2, we tested the use of the first DLS-prototype by qualitative methods. These were applied to collect assessments of the participants during the use of the prototype. The results were included to improve the DLS prototype.

Below, we present some statements of the participants to give an impression of their experiences.

In the beginning there were many negative statements concerning hardware problems (e.g., WLAN connection) and unfamiliarity with the user-interface of the DLS, for example:

„Registration takes too long!"; „Infrastructure just doesn't fit!"; „I'm sick and tired of technical difficulties!"; „Where's the back button?"; „That's far too narrow on the tablet!"

In the course of the testing, statements were mainly given to the language used. They were still negative, for example:

„Language of the plasterers is missing!"; „No talking around the language, more depth."

However, after the DLS was used for about 45 minutes, the statements changed to a more positive evaluation, for example:

„Switching between self-learning and plenary can work. But technology is very important.";
„It's the future, very positive"; „You can see right away if you can do this. What is your learning status, direct feedback and have info where I should get better."

In sum, the first prototype was quite successful, and we thought that learners would be able to manage DLS. However, it was necessary to adapt the proto-type. Consequently, for loop 3, we tweaked the technical language towards domain-specific terms and used laptops instead of tablets to gain a better usa-bility, especially for tasks with tables.

3.4.3.3 Loop 3: Enhanced prototype

In design loop 3, both the LMS and the VR environment were tested and eval-uated ($N = 15$ students in plastering, second year of training). In this contribu-tion, however, we focus on the LMS (for VR see Spilski et al., 2019, 1ff.). We tested the enhanced prototype with standardised questionnaires, including the following aspects:

Different dimensions of the perceived workload were measured with the NASA Task Load Index (NASA-TLX; Hart & Staveland, 1988, 139ff.). It measures the perceived workload in six dimensions, namely mental demands, physical demands, temporal demands, (satisfaction with) performance, effort, and frustration. Self-constructed items were given to evaluate the perceived usability of the DLS and user experience (UX). We also used the same scales as in design loop 1, such as „learning-related self-esteem", and „fear and un-certainty in learning" (see subsection 6.1). In addition, acceptance factors from the Technology Acceptance Model 3 (TAM 3, Venkatesh & Bala, 2008, 273ff.) were assessed, e.g. „Perceived fun while using DLS", „Ease of use", „Perceived usefulness of DLS" as well as the „intention to use DLS".

Perceived workload: The results from the survey with the NASA TLX on a scale of 0 (very low) to 20 (very high) indicate that the average level of phys-ical demands was $M = 5.85$ (*Min* = 1, *Max* = 20), of frustration related de-mands $M = 4.69$ (*Min* = 1, *Max* = 15), effort related demands $M = 8.08$ (*Min* = 2, *Max* = 20), temporal demands $M = 9.38$ (effort related demands); of men-tal demands $M = 10.23$ (*Min* = 1, *Max* = 20) and of performance related (sat-isfaction with) performance $M = 14.54$ (*Min* = 5, *Max* = 20); suggesting that physical-, frustration- and temporal related demands were relatively low, whereas temporal-, performance- and mental-related demands were slightly higher. Figure 5 illustrates the corresponding mean values.

Figure 5: Mean values of the load assessments. Whiskers = 95% confidence intervals of mean values.

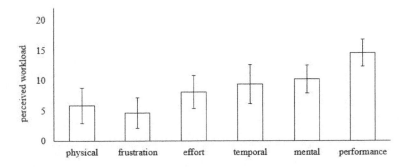

Source: own representation

Fear and uncertainty in learning with the DLS were assessed with six items: The participants rarely felt fear and uncertainty in learning with the DLS, which was reflected by an average of *M* = 1.95 (*Min* = 1, *Max* = 3) on a five-point rating scale never = 1, rarely = 2, sometimes = 3, mostly = 4, always = 5.

Usability Ratings were made on a five-point rating scale: refuse completely = 1, partially reject = 2, partially/partially = 3, partially agree = 4 and fully agree = 5. Table 1 lists the descriptive statistics for eight items. All assessments of the DLS tended to be positive (values greater than three). In contrast, the two items („*At the beginning I would have needed more practice to operate the DLS*", „*I sometimes had the feeling that the DLS no longer reacted*") had lower values (below 3), which also stands for a tendency towards good usability.

Table 1: Descriptive Statistics Usability

	M	**SD**	**Min to Max**
I could see the tasks clearly and distinctly	3.38	0.87	2 to 5
The DLS responded quickly to my input	4.00	0.76	2 to 5
I trusted the information in the DLS, e.g. in the introductory texts	3.62	0.65	3 to 5
I got along well with the way the tasks were presented in the DLS	3.69	1.19	2 to 5
I always knew what to do to get ahead in the DLS	4.00	1.05	2 to 5
At the beginning I would have needed more practice to operate the DLS	2.69	1.38	1 to 5
I could always see the tasks completely	3.85	0.80	2 to 5
I sometimes had the feeling that the DLS no longer reacted	2.62	1.26	1 to 4

Source: own representation *Note. M = Mean, 95% C.I.: 95% confidence interval of the mean*

Acceptance factors: We also measured several constructs from the technology acceptance model, e.g. *fun, ease of use, usefulness and intention to use,* and again we found rather positive results. Factors from TAM 3 were assessed with three items per factor. The results from the survey with the TAM factors on a scale of refuse completely = 1, partially reject = 2, partially/partially = 3, partially agree = 4 and fully agree = 5 indicate that the average level of „*Perceived fun*" were $M = 3.31$ ($SD = 1.28$; $Min = 1$, $Max = 5$), „*Ease of use*" were $M = 3.42$ ($SD = 1.43$, $Min = 1$, $Max = 5$), „*Perceived usefulness*" $M = 3.23$ ($SD = 1.47$, $Min = 1$, $Max = 5$), and „*Intention to use*" were $M = 3.08$ ($SD = 1.38$, $Min = 1$, $Max = 5$). This means that values greater than three were obtained for these acceptance factors, which can be interpreted as neutral to partial agreement. However, this does not mean that, for example, the „Perceived usefulness" is judged completely positive, the same applies to the factor „Ease of use" and the factor „Perceived fun" with the DLS. In order to achieve a higher intention of use, further improvements in the factors mentioned are therefore necessary.

3.4.3.4 Loop 4: Learning performance

In design loop 4, we investigated how the implemented VR environment (cf. subsection 4.2.1) impacts the learning performance in contrast to traditional methods. The learning goal of the VR environment was to train relevant skills and action-oriented knowledge regarding detection and handling of facade damage, e.g. cracks, water damage or mold. In order to have a realistic comparison to other traditional action-oriented learning methods, we compared the virtual site inspection as VR training (experimental condition) with the identical real-world setting as site inspection (control condition). The detected damages (acquisition rate) and a competence test with multiple-choice questions about the damage-handling were used as indicators to evaluate learning performance. Moreover, we used the System Usability Scale (SUS, Brook, 1996, 189) to determine the usability of the VR System.

As mentioned before, the evaluation in design loop 4 involved a total of $N = 35$ students. Since a randomised group allocation was not possible, the students were divided into experiment and control group by class. Therefore, the evaluation was designed as a quasi-experiment based on a between-subject-design. The execution of the study was as follows: The experimental group performed the VR training ($n = 19$) and was able to perform all tasks digitally via VR-Controller. In contrast, the control group had to detect façade damages of the same building on-site ($n = 16$). The participants were given handouts where they marked damages on printed images of the building and answered the multiple-choice questions analogously.

The results of the control group were evaluated paper based whereas the relevant data of each participant of the experimental group was recorded and stored by the VR system in separate log-files.

Figure 6: Traditional on-site inspection (left) vs VR training (right)

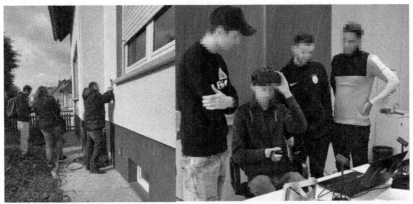

Source: own images

To statistically compare both learning conditions, a *t*-test for independent samples was performed. The results revealed that the acquisition rate of the experimental group (*M* = 19.42, *SD* = 5.54) was significantly higher than the one of the control group (*M* = 12.37, *SD* = 4.37). This results in a statistically significant group difference *t*(33) = 4.12, *p* < .001, *d* = 1.15. The analysis of the multiple-choice questions yielded the following result: The experimental group (*M* = 12.26, *SD* = 5.65) answered more questions correctly compared to the control group (*M* = 7.43, *SD* = 4.63). This difference was also statistically significant *t*(33) = 2.73, *p* = .005, *d* = .85.

Based on the statistical evaluation of the acquisition rates and the multiple-choice questions, the results of the evaluation show that the participants performed better under the experimental conditions. Thus, the VR environment has a positive impact on the learning process. Finally, the SUS questionnaire (based on ten usability-related items) results with SUS-Score M = 72.85, SD = 10.79 represent a good usability of the VR learning environment.

3.5 Conclusion

The research project D-MasterGuide addresses the challenges arising with digitization and the use of new technologies in the context of VET. We use an approach that is suitable for inter-company vocational training centres of the building and renovation trade. Students benefit from increasing different competences like gaining theoretical expert knowledge, solving practical tasks or using new technologies in their working environment.

However, our concept does not only focus on the changed conditions for students but also considers the difficulties of trainers as they are the actual gatekeepers and face a lot of challenges. If they do not accept the technological innovations, the use of the technology will be rare.

One problem is that there is a lack of useful material or solutions are isolated or spread over different platforms and technologies. We develop tailored educational material that is provided by the SGLS. Thus, teachers do not have to search various sources to get fitting digital media for their lessons.

Our evaluation results confirmed another big challenge: the high heterogeneity of individual performance. The different levels of difficulty for each DLS and several types of tasks allow students to work in their individual speed. Finally, trainers are faced with different learning situations that require completely new pedagogical concepts and a positive attitude towards the transformation. However, they are often left alone, do not get time resources to develop expertise with the new methods and feel unsure to use them in front of the class. Some of them even fear that they will be replaced by digital technology and will consequently lose their jobs in near future. Our participative development process helps teachers and students to break down barriers against digitization, to increase acceptance, to trust their own competences and to be open to discover new ways of learning. DLS support trainers to flexibly structure their lessons but cannot replace their knowledge, experience, ability to guide and to encourage their students.

As future work we foresee improvements of the DMG solution and further research questions. The improvements comprise enhancements and refinements of the technical solution. First, in the crafts sector practical work underlies specific working conditions (e.g. dirty hands, little space, and temperature). This demands for easy-to-use solutions to perform small tasks (e.g. document work) and provide results in the SGLS later. Then, we aim to achieve data exchange between our VR App and the LMS. In general, we want to reach interoperability between the LMS and different learning apps and services. Finally, all learning results could be used by the recommender in a consistent way and serve as basis for meaningful prepared statistics (e.g. overall learning progress, competences) to analyse the learning process.

Further research topics could be the questions how the DMG approach has to be modified to reuse our technology, infrastructure or experience for other schools in the crafts sector or even different domains in VET. Moreover, it would be interesting to investigate the effect various SGLS improvements (e.g. recommender, usability, and gamification) on the student's motivation. This could help to increase the students' readiness to use the learning environment voluntarily besides the classroom.

References

Becker, M. (2013). Arbeitsprozessorientierte Didaktik. *Bwpat, 2013*(24). Retrieved from http://www.bwpat.de/ausgabe24/becker_bwpat24.pdf

Bitkom Research; Zentralverband des Deutschen Handwerks (2017). *Digitalisierung des Handwerks*. Presentation material: Rohleder, B. & Schulte K. Berlin. Retrieved March, 2, 2017, from https://www.zdh.de/ fileadmin/ user_upload/Bit-kom-ZDH-Charts-zur-Digitalisierung-des-Handwerks-02-03-2017-final.pdf

Bollen, D., Knijnenburg, B. P., Willemsen, M. C., & Graus, M. (2010). Understanding choice overload in recommender systems. In ACM, *Proceedings of the fourth ACM conference on Recommender systems* (pp. 63-70).

Brolpito, A. (2018). *Digital Skills and Competence, and Digital and Online Learning.* Turin: European Training Foundation. Retrieved January 1, 2020, from https://-www.etf.europa.eu/sites/default/files/2018-10/DSC%20and%20DOL_0.pdf

Brooke, J. (1996). SUS—A quick and dirty usability scale. In P. W. Jordan, B. Thomas, B. A. Weerdmeester, & I. L. McClelland (Eds.), *Usability evaluation in industry* (pp.189-194). London: Taylor and Francis.

DBRC (Design-Based Research Collective). (2003). Design Based Research: An Emerging Paradigm for Educational Inquiry. *Educational Researcher, 32*(1), 5-8. https://doi.org/10.3102/0013189X032001005

Dehnbostel, P. (2008). Shaping learning environments. In F. Rauner & R. Maclean (Eds.), *Handbook of Technical and Vocational Education and Training Research* (pp. 531-536). Dordrecht: Springer.

Dehne, J., Lucke, U., & Schiefner-Rohs, M. (2017). Digitale Medien und forschungs-orientiertes Lehren und Lernen – empirische Einblicke in Projekte und Lehrkon-zepte. In C. Igel (Ed.), *Bildungsräume* (pp. 71-83). Münster: Waxmann.

Gittler, G. (1990). *Dreidimensionaler Würfeltest. 3 DW; ein rasch skalierter Test zur Messung des räumlichen Vorstellungsvermögens*. Weinheim: Beltz.

Hart, S. G. & Staveland, L. E. (1988). Development of NASA TLX (Task Load Index): Results of empirical and theoretical research. In P. A. Hancock & N. Meshkati (Eds.), *Advances in psychology 52* (pp. 139-183). North Holland. https://doi.org/10.1016/S0166-4115(08)62386-9

Heil, M., Fröder, S., & Spilski, J. (2018). *Handwerk Hessen digital. Marktstudie zur Förderung von Digitalisierungsmaßnahmen im hessischen Handwerk*. Wiesbaden: Hessisches Ministerium für Wirtschaft, Energie, Verkehr und Landesentwicklung. Retrieved from https://www.digitalstrategiehessen.de/mm/ Handwerk_Hessen_Digital_WEB.pdf

Howe, F. & Staden, C. (2015). Work Process Oriented and Multimedia-Based Learning in Vocational Education and Training. In M. Gessler & L. Freund (Eds.) *Crossing Boundaries in Vocational Education and Training: Innovative Concepts for the 21st. Century Conference Proceedings*. Evaluate Europe Handbook Series, vol. 6 (pp. 25-32). Bremen.

Koper, R. (2014). Conditions for effective smart learning environments. In *Smart Learning Environments 1, 5*. Berlin, Heidelberg: Springer. https://doi.org/10.-1186/s40561-014-0005-4

McKenney, S. & Reeves, T. C. (2018). *Conducting Educational Design Research* (2nd ed.). London: Routledge. Retrieved from https://ebookcentral.proquest.com-/lib/gbv/det ail.action?docID=5582942. https://doi.org/10.4324/9781315105642

Moosbrugger, H., Oehlschlägel, J., & Steinwascher, M. (2011). *FAIR-2. Frankfurter Aufmerksamkeits Inventar 2 [Frankfurt Attention Inventory 2]*. 2nd revised, amended and newly standardized edition of FAIR of Moosbrugger & Oehlschlägel, 1996. Göttingen: Hogrefe.

Neyer, F. J., Felber, J., & Gebhardt, C. (2016). Kurzskala zur Erfassung von Technikbereitschaft [Short scale for recording technology willingness]. *Zusammenstellung sozialwissenschaftlicher Items und Skalen (ZIS)*. https://doi.org/10.6102/zis244

Nickolaus, R., Abele, S., & Albus, A. (2015). Technisches Vorwissen als Prädiktor für die berufsfachliche Kompetenzentwicklung in gewerblich-technischen Berufen. In L. Windelband & S. Kruse (Eds.), *Technik im Spannungsfeld der Allgemeinen und Beruflichen Bildung* (pp. 9-29). Hamburg: Verlag Dr. Kovac.

Oswald, W. D. (2016). *Zahlen Verbindungs Test [The connecting numbers test]* (3rd revised and newly standardized edition). Göttingen: Hogrefe.

Patzelt, J. & Opitz, I. (2014). Deutsche Version des Academic Procrastination State Inventory (APSId) [German version of the Academic Procrastination State Inventory]. *Zusammenstellung sozialwissenschaftlicher Items und Skalen (ZIS)*. https://doi.org/10.6102/zis139

Rodriguez, F. S., Spilski, J., Schneider, A., Hekele, F., Lachmann, T., Ebert, A., & Rupprecht, F. A. (2019). Relevance of the assessment mode in the digital assessment of processing speed. *Journal of Clinical and Experimental Neuropsychology, 41*(7), 730-739. https://doi.org/10.1080/13803395.2019.1616079

Schmid, U., Goertz, & L., Behrens, J. (2016). *Monitor Digitale Bildung. Berufliche Ausbildung im digitalen Zeitalter*. Gütersloh: Bertelsmann Stiftung.

Schneider, M. & Preckel, F. (2017). Variables Associated with Achievement in Higher Education: A Systematic Review of Meta-Analyses. *Psychological Bulletin*. Advance online publication. http://dx.doi.org/10.1037/bul0000098

Schyns, B. & von Collani, G. (2014). Berufliche Selbstwirksamkeitserwartung [Professional expectation of self esteem]. *Zusammenstellung sozialwissenschaftlicher Items und Skalen (ZIS)*. https://doi.org/10.6102/zis16

Spilski, J., Exner, J.-P., Schmidt, M., Makhkamova, A., Schlittmeier, S., Giehl, C., Lachmann, T., Pietschmann, M., & Werth, D. (2019). *Potential of VR in the vocational education and training of craftsmen. Proceedings of the 19th International Conference on Construction Applications of Virtual Reality*. Bangkok, Thailand.

Spilski, J., Heil, M., Schmidt, M., Schwertel, U., & Mayerl, J. (2017). Herausforderungen, Potenziale und Akzeptanz von eBusiness-Standards im Bauhandwerk. *Wissenschaft trifft Praxis – eBusiness-Standards als Wegbereiter für Industrie 4.0, 7*, 39-46.

Unsworth, N., Heitz, R. P., Schrock, J. C., & Engle, R. W. (2005). An automated version of the operation span task. *Behavior Research Methods, 37*(3), 498-505.

Venkatesh, V. & Bala, H. (2008). Technology Acceptance Model 3 and a Research Agenda on Interventions. *Decision Sciences, 39*(2), 273-315.

4 Tablet PCs in Economics Classes—An Empirical Study on Motivational Experiences and Cognitive Load

Christin Siegfried & Rico Hermkes

4.1 Introduction

Digitalisation and the usage of computers, smartphones, and other digital media are becoming increasingly prevalent in our everyday lives and has in recent years expanded the didactic-methodological options in education (Gros & García-Peñalvo, 2016, 1). Therefore, the use of digital media is linked to the hope of meeting subject-specific needs but also challenges in teaching and learning processes across domains (e.g. Beatty, Merchant, & Albert, 2019; Erbas & Demirer, 2019; Hutchison, Beschorner, & Schmidt-Crawford, 2012). This also applies to economics and business lessons (Schuhen & Froitzheim, 2015; Conrad & Schumann, 2017), whose quality has recently been criticised due to proven economic deficits, both among pupils and among teachers (e.g., Siegfried & Wuttke 2016; Davies, Syed, & Appleyard, 2016). These deficits include systematic deficits in students' prior economic knowledge (Siegfried, 2019; Siegfried & Wuttke, 2016), widespread misconceptions and preconceptions that preclude an understanding of economic terminology (Davies et al., 2016; Meyer & Land, 2006) and difficulties in taking the high complexity of economic interrelations into account—i.e., one must simultaneously consider numerous factors and large amounts of data (Vosough, Kammer, Keck, & Groh, 2019) and handle uncertainty in the context of economic decision-making processes (Altman, 2012).

Lessons in economics should take these points into account, and digital media offer plenty of potential to meet these requirements. For example, deficits in and different levels of learners' prior knowledge require tailor-made instructions, as well as learning support, which can be used individually in situ by the pupils according to their needs. Learning tutorials and digital learning nuggets on basic economic concepts that, for example, have different levels of difficulty can be used for this purpose. Furthermore, to represent complex economic contexts, data visualisation techniques can be used, e.g. by translating economic contexts into diagrammatic representations (Stern & Aprea 2002; Vosough et al., 2019) or by creating models that reduce complexity (see Achtenhagen, 2001). Moreover, lessons should be designed in such a way that multiple solutions and approaches are allowed, and students are not led to a predefined solution, but rather have to justify their own decisions and results. This can be implemented, for example, as problem-based learning scenarios, and virtual enterprises can be created using digital media.

Thus, the question today is (or should) no longer be whether digital media should be used in the classroom, but how it can be meaningfully integrated into educational processes. By investigating digitalisation in educational contexts two aspects seem to be of special interest. First, the learning functions of digital media need to be differentiated systematically. This includes the explication and analysis of learning potential arising from the use of the different functions by digital media. Second, didactic requirements that can be attributed to the learning content should be taken into account. Looking at studies focusing on the field of economics education, not only the role of digital media regarding learning outcomes has been examined (Kim & Frick, 2009), but also students' motivational experiences and information-processing variables (e.g. Beatty et al., 2019; Egloffstein, Kögler, & Kärner, 2012; Conrad & Schumann, 2017). However, the primary emphasis is on analysing the influence of the use of digital devices in general or students' information and communications technology (ICT) skills on these variables. We have yet to see a systematic analysis of teaching and learning processes and their dynamical changes due to different learning functions of digital media; this remains a research desideratum.

In our study, we pursue two research objectives: First, we investigate the influence of the use of digital media on students' motivational experience and cognitive load variables, specifically the question of whether there are significantly different time courses of these variables in „digital classes" and „analogue classes" and which different learning functions are achieved by the use of digital media. Second, based on the temporal patterns of the motivational experience and cognitive load variables, we aim to formulate hypotheses including the interrelationship between learning functions of digital media and the characteristics of learning contents that can subsequently be tested in larger studies. Thus, we are interested in the conditions under which digital learning succeeds or fails.

The following two sections address these two objectives. They include an explication of the learning functions that can be provided by digital media. Subsequently, empirical findings concerning the target variables (motivational experiences and cognitive load) of learners in digital learning scenarios are reported. With respect to the research desiderata, the objectives of our study are formulated and presented, followed by a description of the study design and the present sample. The results and their critical discussion conclude the paper.

4.2 Theoretical background and empirical findings

4.2.1 Process-Mediation-Product paradigm and analysis of digital media usage

In the context of digital transformation processes, opportunities to learn are fundamentally changing. Based on the process-mediation-product paradigm (see Winne, 1987) such changes can refer to (i) teaching activities in situ (process); (ii) learners' state variables like motivational experiences, frustration, boredom, willingness to learn, or enjoyment (mediator variables); or (iii) learning outcomes such as competencies, practical skills, beliefs or value attitudes (product). Thus, investigations of digital media can take place across areas (i) - (iii). Analysis of learning functions of digital media with regard to the target variables 'motivational experience' and 'cognitive load' can be related to the process and mediation components.

4.2.2 Learning functions of digital media

A classification of learning functions can be based on differentiating between external and internal functions. External functions concern the learning environment and the structure of the offered opportunities to learn, while internal functions concern the information processing and knowledge construction of the learner. External functions include immersion, research and communication, whereas internal functions may be differentiated into learning support (facing forwards) and representation of learned content (facing backwards).

Immersion

In fulfilling the immersion function, digital media enable the creation of authentic learning scenarios within teaching-learning situations. This in turn facilitates experiential learning. However, this may also result in undesired side effects, such as increased cognitive effort or even simulator sickness among learners (Meyer, Omdahl, & Makransky, 2019). Nevertheless, immersion is not limited to virtual reality, as it can also exist in the real world (see Mills, 2011). Thus, principles of situated learning, such as mutual engagement, a joint enterprise and a shared repertoire, can be realized (Mills, 2011, 349).

Information searching

With the searching function, digital media offer the potential to use the multitudinous resources available on the Internet for research purposes, leading to increased self-responsibility in learning processes, thereby meeting the autonomy needs of learners (see Deci & Ryan, 2000), as they can choose the sources for themselves. Thus, there is no pre-selection by authorities such as the teacher. Nevertheless, additional skills are required to use the searching function. Learners are challenged to assess the trustworthiness and the credibility of sources and issued information and to negotiate contradictory information. Furthermore, learners must make selections based on the mass of information available. In this respect, ICT skills include not only technical skills but also skills in handling large amounts of data, search strategies and valid judgements (Major et al., 2018; Stadtler et al., 2015).

Communication

The communication function can be used to control the organisation of opportunities and processes by which to learn. Potential arises in particular from measures to provide differentiated and individually adaptive learning opportunities. The communication function not only affects the organisational structure of classes and learning groups, but also their social structure. Thus, the social integration of learners can be increased, including, by means of digital media, over distances (Büchter et al., 2002; Deci & Ryan, 2000). The opposite effect is also conceivable, namely that certain learners are excluded.

Learning support

In terms of support function, digital media enjoy considerable potential because the possibilities offered by artificial intelligence may be exploited. For example, more comprehensive diagnostics can be carried out, whether by the teacher using software or by an artificial tutor on his or her own. On the basis of this diagnosis, individual learning support can be offered, which on the one hand is tailored to the student and on the other hand to the situation (cf. Jordan et al., 2018; Katz et al., 2018).

Representation of content

Using the representation function of digital media, learners can create multimodal external representations of learning content in a variety of ways. Examples include diagrams and graphs as well as animations that enable the representation of dynamics and process features (Vosough et al., 2019). This is of particular didactic relevance when it comes to gaining an understanding of complex economic, biological, physical or chemical processes, among others.

4.2.3 Motivational experiences and cognitive load of learners in digital learning scenarios

Motivational experiences

According to the process-mediation-product paradigm, students' perceptions of educational processes as well as their motivational experiences, feelings of autonomy and responsibility all play an important role regarding learning outcomes. According to Malone and Lepper (1987), students' motivation can be enhanced by at least six factors: (i) challenging tasks, (ii) curiosity or epistemic surprise, (iii) control, (iv) recognition and appreciation of learning results by others, (v) competition and (vi) co-operational learning settings. Learning with digital media may help address these factors (see Ciampi, 2014; Kim & Frick, 2011). Empirical findings confirm the influence of digital media on motivational experiences, but identify two directions.

On the one hand, the use of digital media reduces boredom during teaching and motivates learners (Bastian & Aufenhanger, 2017; Karsenti & Fievez, 2013; Gruner, 2016). This effect can also be seen in quasi-experimental comparison studies (see Furio et al., 2015). In addition, an effect on student motivation can be observed in augmented and virtual learning environments in particular (see e.g. Erbas & Demirer, 2019). These results can be attributed to an increased ownership and responsibility for learning among students (Major et al., 2018).

On the other hand, the use of digital media can also have negative effects and lead to frustration. This seems to depend not only on whether technological and administrative barriers occur in the use of digital devices, but also on whether curricular integration is successful (see Dhir et al., 2013; Hutchison et al., 2012). Among other things, curricular integration implies that digital media do not represent an aim in themselves but should be used in a meaningful way in relation to concrete learning content. The various learning functions by digital media thus need to be taken into account.

Cognitive load

In addition to the variables of motivational experiences presented, variables of cognitive information processing are considered when the mediator variables on learning outcomes are discussed. These especially include measures of cognitive load.

Cognitive load theory focuses on working memory processes in connection with learning activities (e.g. Ayres & Paas, 2012; Paas & Sweller, 2012). Three measures of cognitive load are distinguished: intrinsic load (IL), extrinsic load (EL) and germane load (GL). IL is related to the learning content and is „characterized in terms of element interactivity" (Sweller, 1994, 295). EL emerges through inappropriate instructional design and poor learning materials. The third kind of load, GL, belongs to a different category: it is an endogenous variable and addresses working memory resources *in actu* that are „devoted to dealing with intrinsic cognitive load" (Kirschner et al., 2018, 218). Thus, IL and EL are of particular didactic relevance.

Empirical findings suggest that the use of digital media can have positive as well as negative effects on students' cognitive load measures. Positive effects are assumed if digital media are used to present learning content in multiple forms (e.g. representation of content). As the theory of multimedia learning states, learners learn more easily from text-picture visualisation than from texts alone (see Mayer, 2009). If pictures, animated graphics and so on adequately complement text-based representations (according to criteria such as low redundancy, the relevant features are the salient features), then visualisations and animations through digital media should contribute to reducing EL (see Dindar et al., 2015). On the other hand, digital media can used to create learning environments and scenarios that increase learners' cognitive load. Thus, by introducing authentic problem scenarios to initiate the learning process (e.g. immersion), the „free exploration of a highly complex environment may generate a heavy working memory load that is detrimental to learning" (Kirschner et al., 2006, 80). Especially in virtual reality, EL can arise because additional orientation may be required. In this line, Makransky et al. (2019) refer to the possibility that virtual reality overload and distract the learner.

4.2.4 Research desiderata and aims of the study

In sum, it can be stated that students' motivational experiences and cognitive load are affected in a significant way by the use of digital media. However, existing findings provide an incomplete picture of cause-effect relationships between digital media use on the one hand and motivational experiences and cognitive load on the other. One reason is that the following aspects have yet to be addressed by empirical studies: (i) analysis of teaching processes in high temporal resolution and survey of temporal patterns in experience and load variables (not only retrospective survey), (ii) systematic integration of digital media's different functions in different learning phases, (iii) inclusion of control groups with the same learning content (to control effects related to the learning content).

This study intends to build on this by examining motivational experience and cognitive load both (1) in their development over time and (2) in relation to the usage of digital media and their functions. The investigation is initially explorative and aims to explicate more differentiated hypotheses on the conditions for success of the use of digital media in educational processes. According to these desiderata, our research questions are:

- Are there significant differences in the experience and load variables between 'digital' and 'non-digital' classes in sum and concerning the temporal development (of the target variables)?
- Can such differences be generalised to types of more abstract patterns? Do they coincide with the specific learning functions the students use?

In order to answer the research questions, the following analysis steps were carried out: (i) variance analyses of the global and temporal means of the target variables (motivational experience and cognitive load), (ii) variance analyses of the learners' preconditions to identify whether further effects needed to be controlled in subsequent analyses, (iii) identification of more abstract patterns based on the variance analyses of the target variables, and (iv) coding and analysis of the learning functions of digital media.

The interpretation of the results concerning the interaction of (i) the teaching and learning process, (ii) students' motivational experience and cognitive load, and (iii) different digital learning functions was finally used for the explication of an empirical hypothesis for subsequent studies.

4.3 Method

4.3.1 Design and sample

Design

The study was conducted using a quasi-experimental design with two economic grammar school classes' economics and business lessons over a period of six hours (each lesson being 90 minutes). Whereas one class used tablets during learning (experimental class), the other used conventional analogue media (control group). Assignment to the experimental and control groups was voluntary and did not take into account the particular technological affinities of the learners. The content of the lessons was planned collectively by the teachers of the two classes and took place in both classes simultaneously and in the same form.

All lessons were videotaped using two cameras, one aimed at the teacher and one at the whole class. Moreover, all tablet activities of the experimental class were recorded using the tablet screen.

Learning content

According to the curriculum of an economic grammar school in Hesse, for the first few school weeks of Grade twelve, the subjects of marketing and production were addressed in class. The lessons were designed by the teachers and included at least the requirements listed in the introduction. The central element was a case study about the virtual enterprise 'Fun Factory', which had fallen into financial difficulties. The learners were requested to analyse Fun Factory's situation from different perspectives in order to interpret and justify their decisions. For this purpose, the students of both classes received information about the enterprise and instructions at the beginning of the first lesson. The experimental group was then asked to explicate and refine the actual problem, while the control group started to work directly on the first task after a short introduction by the teacher to the product lifecycle. However, because the learners from the experimental class had difficulties identifying the learning task, the teacher clarified it to them after a while by sending a link to a video explaining the product lifecycle. After that, most of the following lessons were similarly organised in both classes. At the beginning of the lesson, there was a short informational input; specifically, different aspects of market research, such as the Boston Consulting matrix, were presented. After that, students started to work; the learners were always free to work individually or to cooperate with one another by asking other students for advice. During the work phases, the teachers provided occasional support. Differences between the classes mainly owed to the use of digital devices (tablets) by each student: only students in the experimental class had constant access to digital learning aids (e.g. pre-structured data files, tutorials, internet sources, etc.). Students in the experimental group were free to make use of these aids whenever they needed support. The control group—which did not have such permanent access at its disposal and used traditional materials such as paper, pencil, printouts, and (pocket) calculators—was required to develop this content itself or to ask the teacher or other students for help.

In two hours, namely the third and the sixth lesson, the lesson structure just described was interrupted only in the experimental group by an invitation to a 'learning quiz' in the Kahoot application at the beginning of the lessons. After the quiz, the learners continued to work on their problems individually. In the first Kahoot quiz, learners received feedback regarding their learning difficulties. In the second quiz, the teacher asked for feedback on the learning unit course. In order to maintain the similarity of the content over the entire duration of the all lessons, the teachers informed one another after each lesson of the content covered and how to proceed.

Sample

The sample comprised 48 students in the 12th grade (25 male, 19 female) from two classes at an economics grammar school. The high proportion of migrants deserves special mention. Only about 40 percent of the students speak only German at home, with the majority coming from a multilingual home. A total of 54 percent had attended a secondary school before the economics grammar school. Apart from usual entries and exits after each school year, the students in the two classes were already together in grade eleven. The teachers had also taught the class in the 11th grade.

4.3.2 Instrument

Pre-measurement

Self-assessment scales were used to measure ICT skills. The dimensions measured were ICT competence, use of ICT at school and ICT interest (Goldhammer et al., 2016). Computer-related self-efficacy was measured according to the instrument developed by Cassidy and Eachus (2002). The survey of interest in economics was used according to Sparfeldt et al. (2004). Table 1 presents the number of items used in a corresponding example item and the scale consistencies. In addition, sex, age and primary language of the students as well as the professional experience of the teachers were surveyed.

Table 1: Self-assessment scales, items and item consistencies

Scale	Number of items	Cronbach's alpha	Item example
ICT competence	10	.81	When I come across problems with digital devices, I think I can solve them.
Use of ICT at school	9	.84	Browsing the Internet for schoolwork.
ICT interest	13	.72	I forget about time when I'm using digital devices.
Computer-related self-efficacy	30	.92	I find it very easy to work with compute
Interest in economics	8	.93	I enjoy working on tasks in the field of economics

Continuous state sampling

Motivational experience and cognitive load were collected using continuous state sampling. The survey was conducted four times per lesson. Each lesson took 90 minutes. The learning unit was six lessons in total, resulting in 24 measurement points (MP). The survey in the study group was conducted as an online questionnaire using a tablet, whereas in the control group it was administered as a paper and pencil questionnaire.

Motivational experience was determined using three dimensions derived from Schallberger's Circumplex Model (2005) and collected—as in previous studies—in the form of continuous state sampling (cf. e.g. Conrad & Schumann, 2017). The three dimensions were positive activation (two items), negative activation (two items) and valence (one item). The survey was conducted using a ten-point Likert scale from (1 = not at all to 10 = completely).

To assess the cognitive load variables, Leppink et al.'s (2013) instrument, which is oriented to Eysink et al. (2009), was adapted and translated into German. The adaptation concerned the formulation of concrete learning content. Given that repeated measurements were carried out and the learning contents varied from MP to MP, the general formulation „current learning activity" instead of concrete content such as „calculation of the break-even point" was used. The scales of Eysink et al. (2009) and Leppink et al. (2013) also contain an item on germane load. Although this one-item scale was also surveyed in this study, it was not included in the analyses due to a lack of discrimination against the intrinsic load scale (on the interrelations of IL and EL, see also Kirschner et al., 2018). In sum, two items measuring each intrinsic load and extrinsic load (nine point-Likert scale from 1 = very little/very easy to 9 = very much/very difficult) were used.

For the dimensions surveyed, the internal consistencies were calculated for the 24 MP. Table 2 presents the scales and the calculated Cronbach's alpha coefficients.

Table 2: Continuous state sampling of measures of motivational experience and cognitive load, items and item consistencies

Dimension/scale	Number of items	Item example	Cronbach's alpha
Positive activation	2	I feel active right now.	.86-.98
Negative activation	2	I feel stressed right now.	.71-.89
Valence	1	I feel content right now.	---
Intrinsic load	2	The current learning activity is actually ...	.69-.95
Extrinsic load	2	The use of the current materials is for me ...	.69-.89

The survey was conducted anonymously. For later identification and assignment of the tablets or questionnaires, each student received a randomly generated personal code, which he or she entered in the individual surveys over the entire period of the study.

Rating of the learning functions

Video recordings of experimental and control group and tablet screen recordings of the experimental group were used for quantitative data collection. The tablet screen recordings served as the basis for coding learning functions when digital media were used. Coding was time-based (one value per 30-second interval). Each interval saw a coding of the five functions stated in section 2.2. Support function and representation function were mutually exclusive. The other functions could also occur simultaneously. The time intervals in which experience sampling took place were excluded from the coding.

The inter-rater reliability was calculated for each learning function. Tablet streams of two students were coded by two raters across all six lessons. The immersion function was unavailable, as the introduction of the model company, which represented the foundation of all lessons, was paper-based. In addition, the learners did not use the presentation function (all intervals rated zero), hence coefficients were only reported for the communication function, support function and research function. Cohen's kappa was calculated to determine the inter-rater reliability (see Table 3).

Cohen's kappa shows good to excellent results for the coding of the three learning functions.

Table 3: Learning functions of digital media, descriptions of categories and inter-rater reliability coefficients

Learning functions of digital media	Description	Anchor example(s)	Cohen's kappa
Immersion	Creation of authentic learning environment that enables experiential learning	Augmented or Virtual Reality applications; running of business simulations	---
Information research	Navigation in digital informational spaces	Using Internet searching engines, wikis, etc.	$K = .676, p = .000$ $(N = 826)$
Communication	Enabling and controlling participation in learning processes	Chats; invitations to learning quizzes	$K = .816, p = .000$ $(N = 840)$
Support	Concerning knowledge co-construction; tutoring	Formative Feedback; providing structured Excel files	$K = .729, p = .000$ $(N = 850)$
Representation	Knowledge storage and recording results	Digital concept map; creating animations or flow charts for mapping economic cause-effect relationships	---

4.4 Results

4.4.1 Differences between the classes in motivational experience and cognitive load

For the identification of mean differences between the two classes in terms of the target variables cognitive load (EL and IL) and motivational experience (positive activation, negative activation and valence), the global mean (i.e. the mean value across all MP) and MP based mean values were used to calculate t-tests. In addition, the mean differences between classes were reported for the control variables (ICT interest, ICT competence, home language, interest in economics), as they may have affected the target variables (see Table 4).

Table 4: Mean differences of target variables and control variables for the experimental and control group

Variables	Experimental group		Control group		t-Test
	M	*SD*	*M*	*SD*	
Target variable					
Motivational experience					
Positive activation	6.87	1.83	4,05	1.74	$t(46) = -5.45, p < .001$
Negative activation	2.44	1.29	1.83	1.08	$t(46) = -1.75, p = .086$
Valence	7.23	1.57	4.26	2.04	$t(46) = -5.69, p < .001$
Cognitive Load					
Intrinsic Load	3.39	1.25	3.14	1.59	$t(46) = -0.61, p = .548$
Extrinsic Load	2.78	1.07	2.78	1.39	$t(46) = -0.01, p = .996$
Control variables					
Interest in economics	4.49	1.02	3.65	1.03	$t(44) = -2.74, p = .009$
ICT interest	2.87	0.33	2.87	0.33	$t(44) = -1.06, p = .295$
ICT competence	3.37	0.48	3.09	0.43	$t(44) = -2.08, p = .043$
Home language	1.71	0.75	1.85	0.88	$t(44) = 0.58, p = .566$

The means initially referred to the fact that the intensity of negative activation was lower in both classes compared to positive activation and valence. Looking at the differences in means between the classes, significant differences were found for positive activation ($t(46) = -5.449$, $p < .001$) and valence ($t(46) = -5.694, p < .001$). However, for negative activation the descriptive differences of the global means were not significant ($t(46) = -1.753, p < .086$).

The analyses of the cognitive load revealed that there were no significant differences between the two classes in terms of the global means. This was true of both the IL ($t(46) = -0.605, p = .548$) and the EL ($t(46) = -0.006, p = .996$). This result was particularly expected for IL, as both classes were exposed to the same learning content. For the EL, the non-significant differences over the global mean indicated that tablet use does not *per se* seem to lead to a higher EL. At the same time, the need for a more differentiated time-related analysis became clear.

Looking at the individual characteristics, significant differences between the two classes in ICT competence ($t(44) = -2.08$ $p = .043$) and interest in economics ($t(44) = -2.74$, $p = .009$) could be identified. For all other variables there were no significant differences, hence similar student characteristics could be concluded in both classes.

Time-related mean value differences between the classes

In the case of negative activation, significant differences in means between the classes could only be observed at two MP (MP 11: $t(41) = -2.58, p = .014$; MP 12: $t(42) = -2.13, p = .04$). All other non-significant results reflected the previous result of the global mean.

The analyses of the cognitive load variables showed that the IL was only at the first two MP (MP 1: $t(32) = -2.168, p = .038$; MP 2: $t(39) = -3.278, p = .002$) significantly higher in the experimental group. As expected, there were no further significant differences at any other time of measurement. For the EL, the first two lessons should be highlighted. While in the first lesson (MP 2: $t(39) = -2.677, p = .011$) the EL in the experimental group was significantly higher than in the control group, in the second lesson (MP 7: $t(35) = 2.300, p = .029$) the opposite was the case.

Regarding the variables valence and positive activation, for two MP no significant group differences could be identified (positive activation: MP 4 and 12, valence: MP 4 and 11), all other MP indicate significant differences between the experimental and the control group (positive activation: $p < .031$; valence: $p < .026$)

Regression analyses to identify control variables predicting the target variables

In order to exclude the possibility that the group differences found in the global means (positive activation and valence) and in the time course of the target variables (negative activation: MP 11 and 12; El: MP 2 and 7; IL: MP 1 and 2) are exclusively caused by the control variables ICT competence and interest in economics, regression analyses were calculated in a next step. Further, the class variable (dummy) was included as an additional independent variable in the regression models.

Most importantly, the results of the regression analyses showed that in almost all models, variance could be explained by the class variable ($.452 < \beta > .597, .468 < SE > .612, p < .012$). However, this was not the case for EL ($-.197 < \beta > .119, 0.433 < SE > .600, p > .27$) and did not apply to the MP 12 ($\beta = .293, SE = .726, p = .089$) for negative activation. The control variables (ICT competence and interest in economics), which differed significantly between the experimental and the control group, were only significant predictors in two models (positive activation: $\beta = .403, SE = .468, p = .001$; valence: $\beta = .405, SE = .510, p = .001$). Nevertheless, the beta coefficient of the class variable was higher in both models and thus a higher weight could be assigned to them.

These results offered a preliminary indication of the influence of digital media usage on motivational experience and cognitive load. However, in order to explicate more specific hypotheses for the interrelations between different learning functions of the digital media and the selected target variables types of temporal patterns will be analysed.

Temporal pattern

According to the different empirical findings reported in sections two, the use of digital media can have both positive and negative effects. (I) The positive influence of digital media usage could be analysed in our data as 1) increase in motivational experience and cognitive load in the experimental group and 2) higher degree of motivational experience and cognitive load in the experimental group compared to the control group. (II) Respectively, negative influence could be analysed as 1) decrease in motivational experience and cognitive load in the experimental group and 2) lower degree of motivational experience and cognitive load in the experimental group compared to the control group.

In this respect, two salient patterns could be derived. Type one: patterns of positive and negative significant changes between two subsequent MP in the experimental group. However, changes that affected MP between two lessons were excluded due to the lack of interpretation. MP 17 was missing in the tablet class, as organisational questions had to be clarified at the beginning of this lesson and the lesson therefore began late. Type two: patterns that incorporated class differences. Thus, diverging and converging patterns could be distinguished. Divergent patterns meant that similar values in the target variables to one MP were followed by a significant change of at least one class to the next MP. Converging patterns meant that a significant difference in the target variables at one MP was followed by a significant change of at least one class to the next MP, so that the difference between both classes could be reduced.

Depending on whether the patterns refer to the motivational experience variables of positive activation and valence or the variable of negative activation, EL and IL were interpreted differently, as either a positive or a negative pattern. For example, a significant decrease in negative activation was regarded as a positive event, whereas a decrease in positive activation represented a negative event (related to the assumed influence on students' learning outcomes). Figure 1 shows the identified patterns of the present data.

Figure 1: pattern (white line = control group, filled grey line = experimental group, black lines = significant differences between MP, black bars = sign. differences between groups, grey smooth curve = standard deviation of the mean of each MP)

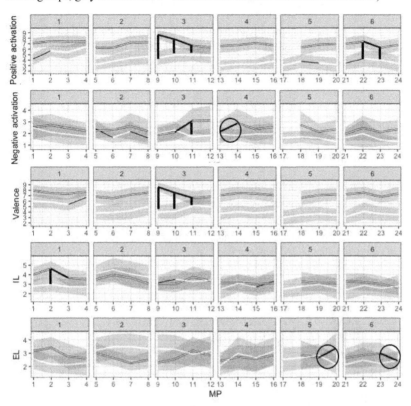

Patterns related to category one (ten patterns in total):

- Significant changes that could be interpreted as negative temporal patterns occurred eight times: for the variable positive activation in three cases between MP 9 and 10, 10 and 11 and 22 and 23; for the variable valence twice between MP 9 and 10 and 10 and 11; for the variable negative activation twice between MP 10 and 11 and between 13 and 14; and for EL between MP 19 and 20.
- Significant changes that could be interpreted as positive temporal patterns occurred twice: for intrinsic load between MP 2 and 3 and for EL between MP 23 and 24.

Patterns related to category two (seven patterns in total):

- Converging patterns occurred six times: for the variable positive activation between MP 9 and 10, between MP 11 and 12 and between MP 22 and 23. The same was true of the variable valence. These five patterns could be interpreted as negative temporal patterns. The sixth pattern concerned intrinsic load (MP 2 and 3) and could be interpreted as a positive pattern.
- Diverging patterns occurred once: with the variable negative activation between MP 10 and 11. This pattern was interpreted as a negative temporal pattern.

4.4.2 Learning functions of digital media

In the following Figure 2, the use of the various digital learning functions throughout the teaching unit is shown.

Figure 2: Lines indicate the proportion of students who used the corresponding function in the time interval. The bars indicate the proportion of time spent using the functions within the 15-minute period between two MP.

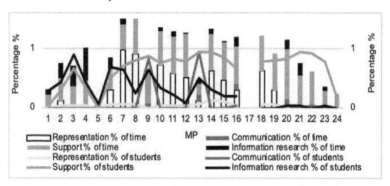

Note: the connecting lines between the individual MP are only drawn for representational reasons and cannot be interpreted as an increase or decrease between subsequent MP.

The results in detail:

- Learning support was permanently offered during the lessons (except in MP 5).
- Tablet PC's were used for information research at the beginning of the learning session (MP2-4).
- They were used to represent learning contents very seldom and by

only some students, especially in the middle phase of the lesson. Moreover, when digital media was used for representational purposes, it was done to temporarily save results or for format transformations (data to graphics).
- Two conspicuous peaks in the use of the communication function—MP 9 and MP 13—emerged.
- Immersion was text-based and therefore not represented here.

4.5 Discussion of results and conclusion of hypothesis

4.5.1 Differences between classes

Our study confirms the findings of other investigations indicating that positive motivational experiences increase with the use of digital media. Thus, the values of the variables *positive activation* and *valence* were significantly higher in the experimental group than in the control group. This applied to both, the global mean and most of the time-related differences in the mean. However, for the variable *negative activation*, there were no significant global differences between the two classes.

With regard to the cognitive load variables, there were hardly any significant differences between the classes. For the IL, this result corresponds to expectations and can be interpreted as a confirmation that the learners actually dealt with the same learning content in both classes across the lessons. Furthermore, in EL no global differences were found between the two classes. Nevertheless, the low level of EL in the experimental group suggests that tablet use did not require any additional cognitive resources from the learners.

4.5.2 Temporal patterns in connection with learning functions of digital media: derivation of hypotheses

In order to explicate hypotheses regarding the conditions for success when digital media are used in teaching, temporal patterns are related to the learning functions of digital media.

(A) Communication and the class as a social entity

According to the communication function, negative temporal patterns occurred at two different MP. The patterns revealed that negative activation increases following communication via tablets. There are two possible explanations for this. On the one hand, this finding may be due to the fact that after the whole class was invited to a „learning event" (in this case a Kahoot quiz), the joint learning situation dissolved again and the learners continued to work on their problems individually. Here one might conclude that learning is to be understood not only as a cognitive process but also as a social process and that involvement and learners' integration into the social entity „class" would constitute an important factor for positive motivational experiences. Another explanation might be that it was less about the communication function itself and more about the characteristics of the learning event to which the learners were invited. The first quiz round (at MP 9) was conducted for diagnostic purposes and learners received feedback on where their current learning difficulties lay. This feedback mainly referred to still existing knowledge deficits and could therefore be interpreted as negative for the learners. In contrast, the second quiz round was implemented by the teacher in order to ask the learners for feedback regarding the teacher and the course of the learning unit. Thus, as a result of the first Kahoot round, in addition to the patterns showing an increase in negative activation in the experimental group, four more negative convergent patterns (concerning positive activation and valence) and one negative divergent pattern (negative activation) could be observed. This might suggest an additional effect for the first quiz round. Regarding positive activation, it must be noted that the degree of positive activation was at MP 9 the highest in the experimental class and decreased after the quiz to the former level. Negative activation, which was identical in both classes before MP 9, subsequently increased in the experimental group. Interestingly, a similar agglomeration of negative patterns did not occur as a result of the second quiz. As mentioned above, the first passage seemed to require a further explanation in addition to the effect of the dissolution of the class as a social entity. Both explanations should be pursued with regard to the question of the conditions for successful digital media use.

Conclusions:

- The class as a social entity is a decisive factor in the development and maintenance of motivational experiences in the classroom. The dissolution of social structures and the increasing personalisation of learning processes may lead to negative motivational experiences among learners. This is especially true for transitions between collective and individual learning phases. However, this does not have to do with a lack of learning support, but can be understood as a social effect.
- If feedback that serves as formative feedback turns out to be negative, it has immediate consequences for learners' motivational experiences.

Hypotheses:

- H1a) Transitions from collective learning to an individual digital learning setting may lead to negative effects in students' experiences if students do not have the opportunity to communicate with each other.
- H1b) Negative feedback in the context of formative assessment leads to a decrease in positive activation and an increase in negative activation when the assessment step is immediately followed by an individual learning phase.

(B) Problem induction, web-based information searching and cognitive load

Convergence in IL corresponds with the research activity that the students begin and intensifies in MP 3 and 4. What is salient here is not that IL converges to this MP (again) between both classes, but rather that at MP 2 such a large difference in IL between the two classes occurs at all (note that both classes had the same teaching content). One explanation could be that the learners in the experimental class at MP 2 were unaware of what the learning task actually involved, this information only being clarified to them during the research activity.

Conclusions:

- To avoid an increase in intrinsic load (because for instance the learning content is already complex), problem induction must take place before the research phase starts. If the learners know in advance for what exact purpose they are carrying out the research, then no additional intrinsic load will arise.
- If, on the other hand, the intention is that the explication and sharpening of the problem is to be carried out by the learners, then this can be done via web-based research, although this then implies at least a short-term increase in IL.

Hypotheses:

- H2a) If a combination of three factors takes place, namely that the problem is unclear, that the research serves to explicate the problem and that the research is web-based without any pre-selected sources, then this leads to an increase in IL.
- H2b) As soon as the problem is clear to students and web-based work-

ing on the solution of the problem commences, the intrinsic load decreases.

(C) Learning support and motivational experience

As Figure 2 shows, students in the experimental class made ongoing use of the support offered via digital media. Even though there was no specific pattern available and it could not be disentangled in our data whether the higher expression in positive activation and valence (in comparison to the control group) owed to the support provided, the global course exhibited at least one coincidence in both variables. It is of particular interest to emphasise that the use of the support offer also requires learners' own initiative (e.g. to recognise for themselves if learning difficulties are emerging and to look for corresponding explanatory videos). This makes it possible to derive two explanatory approaches for the potential connection between positive activation, valence and the anticipated permanent use of support by learners. On the one hand, the permanent support offer ensures access to support during the problem-solving process without waiting times (but an increase in time on-task), while on the other hand, the use of the support offer (especially autonomy support) is self-determined. These are two aspects that were usually not given in the control group.

Conclusion:

- To increase positive motivational experience, learning support should be permanently available to learners. However, this does not mean that the more learning support provided by the teacher the higher the positive motivational experience. Rather, the degree of self-determination in the use of learning support and the availability of support according to individual needs in order to reduce waiting times seems crucial.

Hypothesis:

- H3) Permanent support has a positive effect on learners' motivational experience if delays (waiting time) in task processing are reduced (and hence time on-task is increased) and the use of support can be self-determined.

Limitations

The analyses of significant group differences in relation to the control variables examined showed systematic differences between the classes for the variables economic interest and ICT competence. Although the regression analyses revealed that the mean value differences between the two classes could not be explained exclusively by these varied characteristics of the learners, they must be taken into account when interpreting differences between experimental and control groups concerning the use of digital media. Moreover, teaching content—but not instructional formats—was controlled. The video analyses revealed comparable format in both classes: learners mostly worked alone, cooperation was allowed, as required by the learners themselves. In addition, due to the small sample of only two classes, no effects of teacher variables can be examined statistically.

4.5.3 Conclusion

The results of our study show significant differences in learner's motivational experience and cognitive load between the „digital" and the „non-digital" class. The identification of more abstract temporal patterns allows the explication of more specific hypotheses concerning the conditions for the successful use of digital media. These are hypotheses on how
- communication and social involvement in digital classrooms can affect motivational experiences,
- problem-based learning steps affect students' cognitive load when they are integrated in web-based information searching activities,
- self-determination for the usage of (permanently offered) learning support affects—or does not affect—the positive motivational experience of learners.

Literature

Achtenhagen, F. (2001). Criteria for the development of complex teaching-learning environments. *Instructional Science. Special Issue: Epistemology, Psychology of Learning and Instructional Design, 29*(4/5), 361-380.

Altman, M. (2012). Implications of behavioural economics for financial literacy and public policy. *The Journal of Socio-Economics, 41*(5), 677-690.

Ayres, P. & Paas, F. (2012). Cognitive load theory: New directions and challenges. *Applied Cognitive Psychology 26*(6), 827–832.

Bastian, J. & Aufenanger, S. (2017). *Tablets in Schule und Unterricht. Forschungsmethoden und -perspektiven zum Einsatz digitaler Medien.* Wiesbaden: Springer.

Beatty, B., Merchant, Z., & Albert, M. (2019). Analysis of student use of video in a flipped classroom. *TechTrends 63*(4), 376–385.

Büchter, A., Dalmer, R., & Schulz-Zander, R. (2002). Innovative schulische Unterrichtspraxis mit neuen Medien. Nationale Ergebnisse der internationalen IEA-Studie SITES-M2. In H.-G. Rolff, G. Holtappels, K. Klemm, H. Pfeiffer, & R. Schulz-Zander (Eds.), *Jahrbuch für Schulentwicklung. Bd. 12* (pp 163-197). Weinheim/-München: Juventa.

Cassidy, S. & Eachus, P. (2002). Developing the computer user self-efficacy (CUSE) scale: investigating the relationship between computer self-efficacy, gender and experience with computers. *Journal of Educational Computing Research, 26*, 133–153.

Ciampa, K. (2014). Learning in a mobile age: an investigation of student motivation. *Journal of Computer Assisted Learning, 30*, 82-96.

Conrad, M. & Schumann, S. (2017). Lust und Frust im Tablet-PC-basierten Wirtschaftsunterricht. Befunde einer Interventionsstudie zur Erfassung des affektiven Unterrichtserlebens mittels Continuous-State-Sampling. *Zeitschrift für Berufs- und Wirtschaftspädagogik, 113*(1), 33-55.

Davies, P., Syed, F., & Appleyard, L. (2016). Secondary school students' understanding of the financial system. In E. Wuttke, J. Seifried, & S. Schumann (Eds.), *Economic Competence and Financial Literacy of Young Adults. Status and Challenges* (pp. 41-62). Opladen, Berlin, Toronto: Barbara Budrich.

Deci, E. L. & Ryan, R. M. (2000). Self-determination theory and the facilitation of intrinsic motivation, social development, and well-being. *American Psychologist, 55*, 68-78.

Dhir, A., Gahwaji, N. M., & Nyman, G. (2013). The Role of the iPad in the Hands of the Learner. *Journal of Universal Computer Science, 19*(5), 706-727.

Dindar, M., Yurdakul, K., & Dönmez, F. I. (2015). Measuring cognitive load in test items: static graphics versus animated graphics. *Journal of Computer Assisted Learning, 31*, 148-161.

Egloffstein, M., Kögler, K., & Kärner T. (2012). Unterrichtserleben in Notebook-Klassen. Eine explorative Studie im kaufmännischen Unterricht. In R. Schulz-Zander, B. Eickelmann, H. Moser, H. Niesyto, & P. Grell (Eds.), *Jahrbuch Medienpädagogik 9* (pp. 223-245). Wiesbaden: VS Verlag für Sozialwissenschaften.

Erbas, C. & Demirer, V. (2019). The effects of augmented reality on students' academic achievement and motivation in a biology course. *Journal of Computer Assisted Learning, 35*, 450-458.

Eysink, T. H. S., Jong, T., Berthold, K., Kolloffel, B., Opfermann, M., & Wouters, P. (2009). Learner performance in multimedia learning arrangements: An analysis across instructional approaches. *American Educational Research Journal, 46*, 1107-1149.

Goldhammer, F., Gniewosz, G., & Zylka, J. (2016). ICT engagment in learning environments. In S. Kuger, E. Klieme, N. Jude, & D. Kaplan (eds.), *Assessing Contexts of Learning—An International Perspective* (pp. 331-351). Cham: Springer.

Gros, B. & García-Peñalvo, F. J. (2016). Future Trends in the Design Strategies and Technological Affordances of E-earning. In M. Spector, B. B. Lockee, M. D. Childress (eds.), *Learning, Design, and Technology*. Cham: Springer. https://doi.org/10.1007

Gruner, D. T. (2016). New digital media and flow: A study of experience. *Creativity, 3*, 343-362.

Hutchison, A., Beschorner, B., & Schmidt-Crawford, D. (2012). Exploring the Use of the iPad for Literacy Learning. *The Reading Teacher, 66*(1), 15-23.

Jordan, P., Albacete, P. L., & Katz, S. (2018). A comparison of tutoring strategies for recovering from a failed attempt during faded support. In C. Penstein Rosé, R. Martínez-Maldonado, H. U. Hoppe, R. Luckin, M. Mavrikis, K. Porayska-Pomsta, B. McLaren, & B. du Boulay (eds.), *Artificial Intelligence in Education. AIED 2018. Lecture Notes in Computer Science, Vol. 10947* (pp. 212-224). Cham: Springer.

Karsenti, T. & Fievez, A. (2013). *The iPad in education: uses, benefits, and challenges—A survey of 6,057 students and 302 teachers in Quebec, Canada.* Montreal, QC: CRIFPE.

Katz, S., Albacete, P., Jordan, P., Lusetich, D., Chounta, I.-A., & McLaren, B. M. (2018). Operationalizing the contingent scaffolding of human tutors in an intelligent tutoring system. In S. D. Craig (Ed.), *Tutoring and Intelligent Tutoring Systems* (pp. 187-219). NY: Nova Science Publishers.

Kim, B., Park, H., & Baek, Y. (2009). Not just fun, but serious strategies: Using metacognitive strategies in game-based learning. *Computers & Education, 52*, 800-810. doi: 10.1016/j.compedu.2008.12.004.

Kim, K.-J. & Frick, T. W. (2011). Changes in student motivation during online learning. *Journal of Educational Computing research, 44*, 1-23.

Kirschner, P. A., Sweller, J., & Clark, R. E. (2006). Why minimal guidance during instruction does not work: An analysis of the failure of constructivist, discovery, problem-based, experiential, and inquiry-based teaching. *Educational Psychologist, 41*, 75-86.

Kirschner, P. A., Sweller, J., Kirschner, F., & Zambrano, J. (2018). From cognitive load theory to collaborative cognitive load theory. *International Journal of Computer-Supported Collaborative Learning, 13*, 213-233.

Leppink, J., Paas, F., Van der Vleuten, C. P. M., Van Gog, T., & Van Merriënboer, J. J. G. (2013). Development of an instrument for measuring different types of cognitive load. *Behavior Research Methods, 45*(4), 1058-1072.

Major, L., Warwick, P., Rasmussen, I., Ludvigsen, S., & Cook, V. (2018). Correction to: Classroom dialogue and digital technologies: a scoping review. *Education and Information Technologies, 23*(5), 1995-2028.

Makransky, G., Terkildsen, T. S., & Mayer, R. E. (2019). Adding immersive virtual Reality to a science lab simulation causes more presence but less learning. *Learning and Instruction, 60*, 225-236.

Malone, T. W. & Lepper, M. R. (1987). Making learning fun: A taxonomy of intrinsic motivations for learning. In R. E. Snow & M. J. Farr (eds.), *Aptitude, Learning, and Instruction: III. Conative and Affective Process Analyses* (pp. 223-253). Hillsdale, NJ: Erlbaum.

Mayer, R. E. (2009). *Multimedia Learning* (Second Edition). New York: Cambridge.

Meyer, J. H. F. & Land, R. (2006). Threshold concepts and troublesome knowledge: Issues of liminality. In J. H. F. Meyer & R. Land (eds.), *Overcoming Barriers to Student Understanding: threshold concepts and troublesome knowledge* (pp. 19-32). London and New York: Routledge.

Meyer, O. A., Omdahl, M. K., & Makransky, G. (2019). Investigating the effect of pre-training when learning through immersive virtual reality and video: A media and methods experiment. *Computers & Education, 140*. doi:103603.

Mills, N. (2011). Situated learning through social networking communities: The development of joint enterprise, mutual engagement, and a shared repertoire. *CALICO Journal, 28*(2), 345-368.

Paas, F. G. & Sweller, J. (2012). An evolutionary upgrade of cognitive load theory: Using the human motor system and collaboration to support the learning of complex cognitive tasks. *Educational Psychology Review, 24*, 27-45.

Schallberger, U. (2005). *Kurzskalen zur Erfassung der Positiven Aktivierung, Negativen Aktivierung und Valenz in Experience Sampling Studien (PANAVA-KS).* Forschungsberichte aus dem Projekt „Qualität des Erlebens in Arbeit und Freizeit", Nr. 6. Zürich: Fachrichtung Angewandte Psychologie des Psychologischen Instituts der Universität.

Schuhen, M. & Froitzheim, M. (2015). Konzeption des ECON EBooks mit dem Fokus „Gute Aufgaben". In M. Schuhen & M. Froitzheim (Eds.), *Das Elektronische Schulbuch. Fachdidaktische Anforderungen und Ideen treffen auf Lösungsvorschläge der Informatik* (pp. 139-156). Münster: LIT Verlag.

Siegfried, C. (2019). Wirtschaftswissenschaftliche Lerngelegenheiten als notwendiger Bestandteil der universitären Ausbildung von allgemeinbildenden Lehramtsstudierenden in der Domäne Wirtschaft. *Zeitschrift für Erziehungswissenschaft, 22*, 593-616.

Siegfried, C. & Wuttke, E. (2016). How can Prospective Teachers Improve their Economic Competence? *Zeitschrift für ökonomische Bildung, 4/2016.* doi: 10.7808/-8087.7.

Stadtler, M., Paul, J. M., Globoschütz, S., & Bromme, R. (2015). Watch out!—An instruction raising students' epistemic vigilance augments their sourcing activities. In D. C. Noelle, R. Dale, A.S. Warlaumont, J. Yoshimi, T. Matlock, C. D. Jennings, & P. P. Maglio (Eds.), Proceedings of the 37th Annual Meeting of the Cognitive Science Society (pp. 2278-2283). Austin, TX: Cognitive Science Society.

Stern, E. & Aprea, C. (2002). Effects of active graphical representation on cross content transfer in business education. In K. Beck (Ed.), *Teaching-learning Processes in Vocational Education: Foundations of Modern Training Programmes* (pp. 319-326). Frankfurt am Main: Lang.

Sweller, J. (1994). Cognitive load theory, learning difficulty, and instructional design. *Learning and Instruction, 4*, pp 295-312.

Vosough, Z., Kammer, D., Keck, M., & Groh, R. (2019). Visualization approaches for understanding uncertainty in flow diagrams. *Computer Languages, 52*, 44-54.

Winne, P. H. (1987). Why process-product research cannot explain process-product findings and a proposed remedy: The cognitive mediational paradigm. *Teaching and Teacher Education, 3*, 333-356.

Yorganci, S. (2017). Investigating students´ self-efficacy and attitudes towards the use of mobile learning. *Journal of Education and Practice, 8*, 181-185.

5 Gamification. A Novel Didactical Approach for 21st Century Learning

Silke Fischer & Antje Barabasch

5.1 Introduction

The main task of vocational education and training (VET) is to provide young people with a vocational competence that enables them to act competently in today's digitally transformed labour market. For this reason, e-learning elements, e.g. digital media and web-based communication and cooperation media, have been implemented into the curricula of all apprenticeships over the last decades. In most cases, the e-learning elements themselves are not the object of learning (education for technology), but act only as a tool to convey learning content (education through technology; cf. Cattaneo, 2018). One such tool is gamification, which has been used in the field of mainly higher education so far to convey learning content and objectives on the basis of playful experiences and, moreover, to promote the fun of learning as a whole.

Gamification can be a vessel to convey 21st century skills such as communication, cooperation, creativity and critical thinking at all places of learning (Qian & Clark, 2016). Studies have shown that, for example, the problem-solving skills (Eseryel, Law, Ifenthaler, Ge, & Miller 2014) as well as the critical thinking skills (Yang & Chang, 2013) of learners can be significantly improved by the use of gamification. At the core, most games are social games that demand communication and cooperation between players. Teachers can convert individual learning activities into gamified teamwork quests, tasks, in order to evoke communication and cooperation between players. Since gamification often involves digital technology and connectivity, learners can also enlarge their 21st century information, media and technology literacy skills. In VET, 21st century skills are classified as interdisciplinary competences, which must be taught transversally, i.e. at all places of learning (Scharnhorst & Kaiser, 2018).

However, it must be noted that 21st century skills are also viewed critically. It is often argued that 21st century skills are not new, but can be traced back to the writings of Socrates, Plato and Aristotle (Paul, Elder, & Bartell, 1997). Beyond that, Rose (2009), for example, criticises that the educational philosophy of 21st century skills is purely economic, with the primary goal of training particularly efficient workers. Education, however, has the task of promoting different human abilities equally. According to Rose (2009) important aspects of a good education like *"aesthetics, intellectual play, imagination"* etc. are missing. Another point of criticism is that 21st century skills are partly contextual or content-dependent. For example, creative and critical thinking in mathematics does not automatically lead to the same in English (Lamb, Maire, & Doecke, 2017).

Gamification corresponds to the currently highly relevant principles of action- and competence-oriented learning, too. The individual competence levels of the learners can be taken into account by designing quests with different degrees of difficulty as well as various options within the storyline that enable individual learning paces (Bartel, Figas, & Hagel, 2015; cf. Ifenthaler, Gibson, & Zheng, 2018). Using points, badges, leader boards and individual forms of feedback, it can provide feedback about the competence development of the single learner. As such, gamification represents a new teaching approach that counteracts the recurring critique of existing teaching practice, e.g. short-term and less networked knowledge processes (Stern, 2006). The question therefore arises as to whether and how gamification could find its way into VET and how it could meet the didactic demands of current teaching approaches.

This paper addresses the didactic application of gamification in VET, taking into account the didactic peculiarities of VET. For this purpose, the relevance of the topic in relation to VET is first pointed out (chapter one). Then, in the second chapter, the concepts of gamification and game-based learning are distinguished from each other and examples of how gamification meets the didactic demands of current didactic principles are outlined briefly. In the following, chapter three covers the didactic implementation of gamification in VET, especially considering 21st century skills and action- and competence-oriented learning. The didactic guideline *Gamification in Four Steps* is presented in chapter four, which is specifically adjusted to the context of VET. Here didactic principles of VET are combined with conditions for successful gamified applications and, in particular, with the promotion of intrinsic motivation. Finally, in chapter five challenges of gamification are explored and a conclusion is drawn.

5.2 Gamification in VET

As literature analyses in prominent scientific journals, such as *Journal of Vocational Education and Training (JVET), International Journal for Research in Vocational Education and Training (IJRVET)* and *Vocations and Learning* have shown, little attention has been paid to the topic of gamification with reference to VET so far. Many studies in other educational contexts, e.g. in higher education and partly also in lower secondary education, have shown that gamification can improve student performance and, thus, promote learning (de-Marcos, Garcia-Cabot, & Garcia-Lopez, 2017) as well as increase motivation and engagement (Stansbury & Earnest, 2016) among other things. Nevertheless, the use of gamification in VET is still very unusual and even considered to be an *"avant-garde innovation"* (Drager, 2015).

In principle, multitudes of definitions exist for gamification. In most scientific publications, however, the definition of Deterding, Khaled, Nacke and Dixon (2011a) has been established, which defines gamification as "the use of game design elements in non-game contexts". Since this definition, is not self-explanatory, we will briefly distinguish the terms *"game"*, *"game design elements"* and *"non-game contexts"*.

"Firstly, 'gamification' relates to game, not play (or playfulness), [...]" (Deterding, Khaled, Nacke, & Dixon, 2011b, 11). Gamification is often traced back to the two opposite poles of gaming activity—ludus (game) and paida (play)—established by Caillois (1960). Whereas ludus is characterized by structured, rule-based and objective-oriented gaming activities, paida comprises free-form, improvisational and unstructured gaming behaviours. Gamification focuses primarily on gaming activities in the sense of the ludus component (Deterding et al. 2011b).

"Game design elements" determine the character of a game. As countless game design elements exist, Deterding et al. (2011b) suggest the following definition knowing that this heuristic definition leaves much room for interpretation (12):

> *"Elements that are characteristic to games—elements that are found in most (but not necessarily all) games, readily associated with games, and found to play a significant role in gameplay."*

Characteristic game design elements are badges, progress bars, points, leader boards etc. (cf. Kapp, 2012).

"Non-game contexts" refers to the fact that gamification uses game design elements or games outside their original purpose of entertainment, assigning that entertainment is the primary reason for gaming. Deterding et al. (2011a) recommend not to limit the concept of gamification to special objectives as such limitations are not advantageous.

Other concepts like game-based learning or serious games use complete games instead of game design elements only to convey knowledge content (Jacob & Teuteberg, 2017). To this day, there is no clear distinction between these concepts (Fromme, Biermann, & Unger, 2010). The common basis of these game offers is that not only the game fun is in the foreground, but also is played with serious intentions. In this way, knowledge content can also be conveyed or learners can be sensitized to certain topics. The distinction between gamification and game-based learning is often ambiguous. Whether an application is gamification or game-based learning depends on the assessment and use of the evaluator (Deterding et al. 2011a).

If one bases the fundamental mission of VET on the fact that action- and competence-oriented education should take place, which on the one hand is oriented towards basic technical content and on the other hand towards 21st century skills, it is obvious to use tools that can support these developments in a variety of ways. Following Bonaiuti, Calvani, Menichetti, and Vivanet (2017), Cattaneo (2018) classified technologies according to the way they support learning. Gamification belongs to the third classification of technologies

"that support us in performing demanding cognitive activities, such as acquiring new knowledge and integrating it into existing knowledge structures" (19).

This group is characterized by technologies that contribute to cognitive expansion of the learner, e.g. collecting and processing information. As such gamification can support learning processes in a meaningful way. Therefore, a suitable didactic design needs to be implemented as the mere use of gamification alone does not lead to better learning. This is realized by the following three didactic principles that are common for VET.

First of all, action- and competence-oriented teaching is guided by the principle of self-activity of the learners. Generally, the teacher's need to encourage the learners to actively approach the subject matter of the lesson. Through the use of gamification, individual tasks or even learning paths can be created which demand a high form of self-activity of learners that may lead to intrinsic motivation. Plus, a lack of intrinsic motivation can be overcome by promoting the fun of learning through the fun of playing. In videogames, fun results from mastery, e.g. to master the next level, and from the feeling of control (Simões, Redondo, Vilas, & Aguiar, 2015). With an *"optimal level of difficulty"* of the learning tasks to be solved (cf. Kramer, 2002, 33), intrinsically motivated learners can experience *flow* even with less motivating topics and activities. *Flow* as a state of happiness is described as a condition between anxiety and boredom (Csikszentmihalyi, 1990). Facilitating intrinsic motivation, a good gamified application should promote the experience of competence and autonomy as well as the experience of social integration in the game (cf. Deci & Ryan, 1993). In sum, one can say that gamification can contribute to a more positive connotation of learning due to the experience of fun, intrinsic motivation or even flow which contributes to the development of deeper knowledge structures, too.

The dichotomy of reality and virtual reality in gamified learning environments takes into account the teaching principles of authenticity and security. According to Jantke (2014) real actions are important for learning, as what is not done cannot be practiced and learned. Hence, it is important that contents to be learned are integrated into the game. The virtual acts as an attractive means of transport for the real learning content. Gamification, thus, helps learners to practice real-life situations and challenges in a safe environment in which they can fail without fear of consequences. It encourages experimentation and permits trial and error. As such, it can function as a *safety net* for players enabling them to practice *to get it right* and re-start, if necessary, at a certain point before their performance is evaluated in exams und real-life situations. Hence, gamification can provide *"learners with the opportunity to succeed through multiple attempts, resulting in experimental learning [...]"* (Wood, Teräs, Reiners, & Gregory, 2013, 519). This is also in contrast to traditional exams, where learners have only one chance to succeed in class (cf. Wood et al., 2013). Further, gamification may be useful to support students to integrate what is learned in the company and at school in dual VET by connecting practice and theory. The opportunities of students to use their knowledge from school at work and to transfer their work experiences to school are often limited. Gamification can help to narrow this *"skills gap"* (Dillenbourg, 2017, 1). Researchers of the *Leading House Dual-T* (Technologies for VET)[1] try to better connect the two learning locations by applying a principle referred to as *Erfahrraum* (Dillenbourg & Jermann, 2010, 541f.) which could be translated as *giving room to experience*. For example, in logistics or in carpentry the students use augmented-reality tools at school to simulate flows of goods or forces affecting a roof-structure. The possibility to repeat, intentionally vary and discuss these virtual experiences helps them to induce and better understand theoretical concepts, e.g. related to warehouse management or to statics, which are part of their school curriculum but which they often cannot directly experience at their workplace.

5.3 Didactic Implementation of Gamification in VET

In principle, gamification can be used in all subject areas for all kinds of teaching contents at all places of learning. Each learning content of any subject or place of learning can be gamified—partially or completely. Gamification can be used digital, non-digital or in mixed forms, e.g. with a non-digital storyline. As playing is part of our nature and, thus, motivates us, gamification is particularly suitable for teaching contents and units that are characterised by a low degree of intrinsic motivation on the part of the learner (Fischer & Reichmuth, 2020). Such teaching contents are often characterised by complex and rather abstract learning contents, with which the learners are not faced with in their daily living environment. Aprea, Schultheis, & Stolle, (2018), for example, use gamification to make the topic of financial literacy more effective and attractive.

---

[1]   https://www.epfl.ch/labs/chili/dualt/

The implementation of gamification in educational contexts should always involve the creation of a *"systematic motivation design"* which also includes cooperative game design elements (Seufert, Preisig, Krapf, & Meier, 2017). In VET, such a systematic motivation design should be based on the requirements of the curriculum and the overall objective, the development of vocational competence. Purpose-free gamification in which mere playing is in the foreground are not feasible in VET due to relatively short teaching time and high substance density (Fischer & Reichmuth, 2020). The mere use of single game design elements is therefore not effective. Some tools like *Socrative, Kahoot!, FlipQuiz* or *Duolingo* only allow the short-term use of game design elements, but not the implementation of an effective motivation design. Therefore, such tools should be used only in conjunction with an online platform that allows interaction between the players. An online platform can be used, for example, to discuss strategy between players or to provide mutual feedback.

5.3.1 Didactic Implementation of 21st Century Skills in Gamification

Communication and Cooperation

Gamification should always include cooperative game design elements to promote social competences and to increase intrinsic motivation of leaners by experiencing social inclusion. (Fischer & Reichmuth, 2020). Thus, it is not surprising that the most successful games are social games, such as *Bridge, Domino* or *Poker* (cf. Zichermann & Cunningham, 2011), which contain elements of communication and cooperation. Teachers should include teamwork quests, team leader boards and challenges that can only be solved in a team or together with other teams into gamified applications to promote communication and cooperation between players. According to Kramer (2002), the respectful and appreciative interaction between players and within the social group is of particular importance. The teacher could check this, for example, by reading chat histories or by analysing communication in the classroom. In order to promote language, different text forms such as blogs, social networks and magazines should be integrated into quests. By integrating such media, a connection to the real world and events can be established (Seufert et al., 2017), which increases the credibility of the game. An advantage of classroom gamification is that players might not realize they are cooperating as they are so engaged in the quests or challenges.

Creativity

There is a lack of empirical studies *"that would consider gamification as one of the facilitators in raising creativity"* (Kalinauskas, 2014, 63). However, several studies show that gamification can increase creative thinking (Dennis, Minas, & Bhagwatwar, 2013). Sternberg and Williams (1996), for example, compiled a list of 25 ways to promote creativity in the classroom. The development of self-efficacy is mentioned here as a prerequisite for creativity. Learners should first be helped to believe in their own capacity for creativity. As basic techniques to be used in class questioning assumptions, defining and redefining problems as well as encouraging idea generation are mentioned. Accordingly, the teacher should implement such activities into the gamified learning environment and allow a variety of different approaches and procedures in the processing of tasks (free spaces). Kingsley and Grabner-Hagen (2015), for example, describe a quest called *Act it Out* where players had to create a video to demonstrate a change in matter. Learners had to write a script, act it out and record their video with an informative description of the process. In order to succeed, players had to think creatively and use certain techniques that have been proved successful in fostering creativity, like mind-mapping or brainstorming. Beyond that, quests should be cross-disciplinary, as creative ideas and insights of learners often result from learning to integrate material across subject areas. Another essential aspect that encourages creative thinking is to broaden one's own perspective by seeing the world from the perspective of others (Sternberg & Williams, 1996). Therefore, the various tasks should be reflected and justified in the viewpoints of other people. The teaching of creativity also means to teach learners to take responsibility for success and failure (self-responsibility). This means that learners *"(1) understand their creative process, (2) criticise themselves and (3) take pride in their best creative work"* (Sternberg & Williams, 1998).

Critical Thinking

In VET, real, authentic task situations, which contain complex problems, are particularly important for building competences. In the context of gamification, it offers itself to gamify case studies that are characterized by a high degree of application and problem orientation (Fischer & Reichmuth, 2020). Besides, most games involve critical thinking and problem solving at the core. McGonigal (2007), for instance, invented a game named *World Without Oil,* where players had to cope with a situation where the world runs out of oil. The players had to think about how their lives would change living without oil. Similar alternative reality games, where the players act as themselves in a changing environment, are conceivable in accordance with the curriculum, especially in the field of ecology. In *World Without Oil* and other gamified learning experiences players should be encouraged to conceptualize, apply, analyse, synthesize, and evaluate information of an issue in order to form a judgement. Players need to think systematic, reflective and reasonable for critical thinking and problem solving (cf. Ennis, 1985). Jahn (2013) recommends also to enable *real* experiences beyond the classroom as an opportunity for critical thinking. Gamification enables learning on a large scale by solving real problems that exist outside an educational institution (Ifenthaler, Eseryel, & Ge, 2012). The game should be designed in such a way that doubts, amazement and borderline experiences are made possible, so that the learners are challenged to embark on unknown paths of thought (Jahn, 2013). Even in offline phases, learners should be given sufficient time for contemplation and discussion, as critical thinking only unfolds after longer reflection and discussion of a subject (cf. Jahn, 2013).

5.3.2 Didactic Implementation of Action- and Competence-Oriented Learning in Gamification

Learning Objectives

For experiencing competence, an *"optimum degree of difficulty"* (Kramer, 2002, 33), which does not over- or underchallenge the learners, is important. Therefore, the cognitive learning objectives of the gamified teaching unit should be challenging but achievable. To ensure that the chosen cognitive learning objectives are perceived as challenging, higher taxonomy levels in the range of levels three to six according to Bloom (1956) should be taken into account (Fischer & Reichmuth, 2020). By choosing higher levels of taxonomy, the learners are able to show their competence not only their knowledge. In order to promote social competences, affective learning objectives, i.e. learning objectives in the area of feelings, values and attitudes (Meyer & Stocker, 2011), should also be integrated into teaching. They can be promoted through the use of cooperative game design elements, e.g. quests and team leader boards, by practicing reflection and exchange and, thus, give players the feeling of fighting for the same goal (Seufert et al., 2017). Besides, cooperative game design elements can support social competencies, e.g. the ability to communicate, the ability to work in a team, empathy etc. (Bartel et al., 2015). Finally, some learning objectives could be integrated which must be achieved through the use of cooperative game design elements.

Narrative of Game

As said before, in VET, for competence building authentic task situations, which contain complex problems are important. Hence, case studies could serve as the basis of a narrative. In terms of content, competence-oriented learning environments can promote the autonomy experience of the learners. Therefore, individual learning paths that consider heterogeneous competence levels and interests among learners should be integrated within the narrative (Fischer & Reichmuth, 2020). According to Bartel et al. (2015) the narrative *"can help to illustrate a kind of holistic learning map with transparent learning objectives"* where the learners can see the individual learning paths respectively choices the players have (460). In order to prevent a pure point hunt of the learners (Seufert et al., 2017), the narrative should be well connected with the learning progress made by learners illustrated by points, levels etc. Therefore, the narrative should be closely linked to the competence levels of a competence model, e.g. Meyer (2012). It should further be motivating for the players, as their motivation determines their commitment during gameplay (Eseryel et al., 2014). A third condition is that the narrative needs to relate to the world in which the players live and to the curriculum. Narratives are particularly motivating for the learners when surprising twists occur within the storyline or at different levels that influence the course of the game and, furthermore, trigger emotions. Emotions are important for the learning processes as they can lead to intrinsic motivation (Hascher, 2011). An example of such a surprising twist could be that the leaners can rewrite the end of the game. Vos, van der Meijden and Denessen (2011) showed that learners who designed their own game have a significantly higher interest and a significantly higher perception of competence.

Levels of Difficulty

A reasonable but demanding level of difficulty of tasks is central to the experience of competence and at the same time positively linked to learning performance (Ifenthaler et al., 2018). To do justice to the heterogeneous competence levels of learners, game mechanism and elements with different levels of difficulty must be integrated into the learning game environment. Such game design mechanism and elements can be quests, levels, challenges, constraints and competitions. The learner, for instance, has to finish a quest in a certain time (Bartel et al., 2015). In competence-oriented gamification,

"metrics like required time, achieved goals or quality of the results need to be defined in the design, (...). The definition does not only include what units are measured in a certain activity. In addition, it is important how and when the values are collected and reflected and how these rules (in a learner/player view) are made transparent" (Bartel et al., 2015, 460).

Generally, performance levels that take into account all taxonomy levels of Bloom (1956) should be integrated into a gamified lesson. As a result, the following levels of difficulty result for competence-oriented tasks.

Table 1: Competence-oriented tasks

Operator	Taxonomy level (according to Bloom, 1956)	Marking	Level of grade (Equivalent to American grades)
Reproduction	1-2	Beginner	C-D
Transfer of knowledge	3-4	Advanced	B
Reflection and problem solving	5-6	Expert	A

Source: Own depiction based on Fischer and Reichmuth (2020, 42)

Feedback

In competence-oriented learning settings, feedback should be immediate and criteria-oriented about the individual competence progress. Individual feedback can have a positive influence on the experience of competence if it supports the autonomy of the learner (Kramer, 2002), e.g. by using the principle of minimum assistance. Consequently, the teacher should take an individual reference norm orientation in gamified lessons, which focuses on the increase in learning and, thus, the development of a learner's competence in comparable tasks. Performance graphs, for example, are subject to individual reference norm orientation. Furthermore, reflection phases could be integrated into the learning process, in which the learners, for example, keep a learning journal and reflect the achievement of self-imposed learning goals. In these phases the teacher could also give individual feedback on learning tasks, e.g. via the online platform. Above that, in gamified learning environments there should be a clear separation of play phases with formative feedback, where making mistakes is explicitly allowed, and play phases with summative feedback where the teacher assesses the acquired competences (Fischer & Reichmuth, 2020).

Each gamified lesson should contain game design elements of competition, e.g. (team) leader boards, points, badges and levels etc., because they can lead to competence experience, an increase in self-efficacy and intrinsic motivation (cf. Sailer, 2016). Such game design elements can also serve as feedback tools in which learners can assess their current learning state. Most of these tools are based on a social reference norm orientation which measures one's own performance in comparison to others. In addition to the positive motivational factor that these game design elements have, they can also demotivate lower performing learners (Sailer, Hense, Mayr, & Mandl, 2017). This problem can be partially solved by displaying only certain elements to learners at a given level in order to reduce the performance heterogeneity of learning groups (Fischer & Reichmuth, 2020).

5.4 Gamification in Four Steps—A Didactical Approach for VET Teachers

Since gamification comes from marketing, most guides to implementing gamification relate to the business context (cf. Heilbrunn & Sammet, 2015). In the field of education, gamification has so far mainly been used in higher education, which is why the few existing guidelines or recommendations mostly refer to it (cf. O'Donovan, Gain, & Marais, 2013). In case of other educational guidelines for implementing gamification, such as the HEXA-GBL (Romero, 2015), the target group is not defined. However, since the framework conditions between higher education and upper-secondary education, e.g. vocational education, differ considerably, the following short guide was developed explicitly for the implementation of gamification in vocational schools. Therefore, on the one hand, the particularities of VET with regard to good teaching, competence-oriented learning and 21st century skills were taken into account, as well as on the other hand, with regard to an efficient gamified design, e.g. have special meaning for players, motivate players, give players freedom of choice (cf. Deterding, 2011c). Furthermore, it is assumed that the teachers already know their learners well, which is why a learner-centred need analysis as in HEXA-GBL (Romero, 2015) is omitted. It is also assumed that the learning game environment is continuously evaluated and developed after its implementation. Consequently, the integration of such steps into the following didactical approach *Gamification in Four Steps* was waived. The didactical approach *Gamification in Four Steps* consists of the following four phases which are shown in figure 1, and Table 1 introduces the contents of each step of the four phases of "Gamification in Four Steps".

Figure 1: Gamification in Four Steps

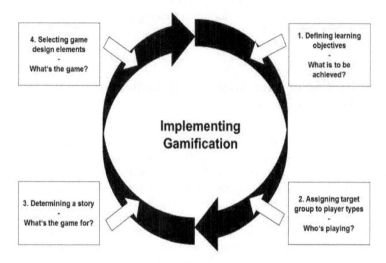

Source: Own depiction based on Fischer and Reichmuth (2020)

Table 2: Gamification in Four Steps

Step	Contents

1. What is to be achieved? —Defining Learning Objectives	• Defining all objectives
	  ○ What are the reasons for implementing gamification in class?
	  ○ Which behaviour and/or which learning objectives are to be achieved by the gamified application?
	  ○ Which competences (professional expertise, methodological, social and personal competences) should be promoted through the use of gamification?
	• Importance of fun in the application (learning vs. fun)
	• Verifiability of learning objectives (description of final behaviour)
	• Importance of learning objectives for learners
	• Consideration of higher taxonomy levels, e.g. levels three to six according to Bloom (1956), to demonstrate competences
	• Integration of affective learning objectives that are particularly important when it comes to teaching social competences
	• Selection of compulsory and optional learning objectives
	  ○ Which learning objectives have to be achieved alone or through the use of cooperative game design elements in a team?

Table 2: Gamification in Four Steps (cont.)

Step	Contents
2. Who's playing? —Assigning Target Group to Player Types	• Assigning of target group to player types, i.e. achiever, explorer, socializer, killer, according to Bartle (1996) based on their preferences to maximize the game enjoyment and learning actions ○ 1. Option: Filling out the *Bartle-Test* which is freely accessible on the Internet to determine the so-called *Bartle-Quotient.*[2] ○ 2. Option: Acquisition of study results from Zichermann and Cunningham (2011). Accordingly 75% of all people are mostly socializers, 10 % are achievers, another 10% are explorers and 5% are killers.
3. What's the game for? —Determining a Story	• Determining the meaning of the game by selecting a suitable narrative ○ Is the narrative motivating for the learners? ○ Can the learners identify themselves with the narrative? ○ Is the topic of the narrative for the learners important, i.e. related to the curriculum and life of the learners? ○ Does the narrative give the players the feeling that they are doing the right thing, i.e. not violating ethical standards? • Integration of individual learning paths that consider heterogeneous competence levels and interests among learners • Connection of narrative and learning progress • Integration of illustrations that motivate the learners, i.e. to which learners have a personal connection
4. What's the game? —Selecting Game Design Elements	• Selection of game design elements according to player types (cf. step two) ○ Socializers: Leader boards, points, virtual goods, cooperation, transaction etc. ○ Achievers: Badges, leader boards, levels, feedback, challenges, rewards etc. ○ Explorers: Badges, points, virtual goods, secrets, rewards etc. ○ Killers: Leader boards, points, levels, feedback, competition, win states etc.

Source: Own depiction based on Fischer and Reichmuth (2020)

---

[2] The *Bartle-Quotient* determines the assignment to the four player types according to Bartle (1996). Hence, you are always a mix of all four player types.

5.5 Conclusion

The didactic model presented in this paper should help to establish gamification in VET. The use of gamification can increase learning performance, motivation and engagement of learners in the short term. In VET, gamification as both – an academic study topic and didactic implementation area – is relatively young. Hence, empirical research is needed first of all that confirms the positive effects of gamification in the short term and, desirably, in the long term, too (Seelhammer & Niegemann, 2009). Further, it should be noted that the use of gamification can also result in some disadvantages:

Firstly, online platforms, social networks or websites that are integrated into a gamified application often collect a variety of sensitive data from their users, e.g. log data, visited places etc. In this way, usage and behaviour profiles of players can be created. Each gamified application must provide ways to protect this data from access by unauthorized third parties. In this regard, gamified applications should have privacy policies that inform the player about data collection and usage exactly (Giannakes, Kambourakis, Papasalouros, & Gritzalis, 2018).

Secondly, video games can be addictive. These are mainly the *MMORPG (massive multiplayer online role-playing game)* online games like *World of Warkraft*. According to Jantke (2018) games that strike a balance between self-determination and indeterminacy often have addictive potential, which is not a problem of the game, but of the living environment of people. In principle, this usually only affects a small proportion of adolescents who are mentally or family-inflicted and who thus try to avoid difficult situations (Quinche, 2013).[3]

Thirdly, creating a suitable systematic motivation design for a gamified application is a very complex and time-consuming task. Plus, the learners' motivation, engagement and problem-solving performance are strongly influenced by design of the game tasks (Eseryel et al., 2014). Often there are also limitations with regard to use of technology and interdisciplinary know-how on part of the teaching staff (Le, Weber, & Ebner, 2013).

Overall, a theoretical-didactic discourse on gamified learning environments, in which implementation attempts are critically reflected, would be extremely important for a profound professionalization. To sum up, one can say that gamification can offer a cognitively stimulating and socially integrated learning experience, which can be used at least partially to promote 21st century skills and competence development by enabling learner-centred, didactic settings that promote individualized learning (cf. Ifenthaler et al., 2018).

---

[3]   The proportion of the German population with problematic gambling behaviour is 0.42% (241,000 persons; cf. https://www.automatisch-verloren.de/de/gluecksspiel/zahlen-und-fakten-zu-gluecksspiel.html (2019-16-19)).

References

Aprea, C., Schultheis, J., & Stolle, K. (2018). Instructional integration of digital learning games in financial literacy education. In T. Lucey (Ed.), *Financial literacy for children and youth* (pp. 69-88). Frankfurt a. M.: Lang.

Bartel, A., Figas, P., & Hagel, G. (2015). Towards a Competency-based Education with Gamification Design Elements. In ACM, *CHI PLAY '15, Proceedings of the 2015 Annual Symposium on Computer-Human Interaction Play* (pp. 457-462). London, United Kingdom.

Bartle, R. (1996). Hearts, Clubs, Diamonds, Spades. Players who Suit MUDs. *Journal of MUD research, 1*(1). Retrieved October 29, from http://www.arise.mae.usp.-br/wp-content/uploads/2018/03/Bartle-player-types.pdf

Bloom, B. S. (1956). *Taxonomy of Educational Objectives. Handbook—the Cognitive Domain.* New York: David McKay.

Bonaiuti, G., Calvani, A., Menichetti, L., & Vivanet, G. (2017). *Le tecnologie educative [Educational technologies].* Roma: Carocci.

Caillois, R. (1960). *Die Spiele und die Menschen – Maske und Rausch.* Stuttgart: Schwab.

Cattaneo, A. (2018). Wie können digitale Technologien im Unterricht effektiv umgesetzt werden? In J. Schweri, I. Trede, & I. Dauner (Eds.), *Digitalisierung und Berufsbildung. Herausforderungen und Wege in die Zukunft. OBS EHB Trendbericht 3* (pp. 18-21). Zollikofen: Eidgenössisches Hochschulinstitut für Berufsbildung EHB.

Csikszentmihalyi, M. (1990). *Flow—The Psychology of Optimal Experience.* New York: Harpers Perennial.

Deci, E. L. & Ryan, R. M. (1993). Die Selbstbestimmungstheorie der Motivation und ihre Bedeutung für die Pädagogik. *Zeitschrift für Pädagogik, 39*, 223-238.

De-Marcos, L., Garcia-Cabot, A., & Garcia-Lopez, E. (2017). Towards the Social Gamification of e-Learning. A Practical Experiment. *International Journal of Engineering Education, 33*(1), 1-14.

Dennis, A. R., Minas, R. K., & Bhagwatwar, A. P. (2013). Sparking Creativity. Improving Electronic Brainstorming with Individual Cognitive Priming. *Journal of Management Information Systems, 29*(4), 195-215.

Deterding, S., Khaled, R., Nacke, L. E., & Dixon, D. (2011a). Gamification—Toward a Definition. In ACM, *CHI 2011 Gamification Workshop Proceedings* (pp. 1-4). Vancouver.

Deterding, S., Khaled, R., Nacke, L. E., & Dixon, D. (2011b). From Game Design Elements to Gamefulness: Defining "Gamification". In ACM, *Proceedings of the 15th International Academic MindTrek Conference—Envisioning Future Media Environments* (pp. 9-15). Tampere, Finland.

Deterding, S. (2011c). *Meaningful Play. Getting Gamification Right.* [Online video]. Retrieved July 27, 2019, from http://www.youtube.com/watch?v=7ZGCPap7GkY

Dillenbourg, P. (2017). Digitale Möglichkeiten in der Berufsbildung. *SGAB Newsletter, 6*, 1-4.

Dillenbourg, P. & Jermann, P. (2010). Technology for Classroom Orchestration. In M. S. Khine & I. M. Saleh (Eds.), *New Science of Learning* (pp. 525-552). New York: Springer Science+Business Media.

Drager, Y. (2015). VET Trade Training: Prepare to Be Stimulated. Charles Sturt University. Retrieved April 5, 2018 from http://thinkspace.csu.edu.au/gblcompendium/part-3-invitation/vet-trade-training-prepare-to-be-simulated/

Ennis, R. H. (1985). A logical bias for measuring critical thinking skills. *Educational Leardership, 43*(2), 44-48.

Eseryel, D., Law, V., Ifenthaler, D., Ge, X., & Miller, R. (2014). An Investigation of the Interrelationships between Motivation, Engagement, and Complex Problem Solving in Game-based Learning. *Educational Technology & Society, 17*(1), 42-53.

Fischer, S. & Reichmuth, A. (2020). *Gamification. Spielend lernen.* Bern: hep.

Fromme, J., Biermann, R., & Unger, A. (2010). „Serious Games" oder „taking games seriously"? In K. U. Hugger & M. Walber (Eds.), *Digitale Lernwelten – Konzepte, Beispiele und Perspektiven* (pp. 40-57). Wiesbaden: VS Verlag für Sozialwissenschaften.

Giannakas, F., Kambourakis, G., Papasalouros, A., & Gritzalis, S. (2018). A critical review of 13 years of mobile game-based learning. *Educational Technology Research and Development, 66(*2), 341-384.

Hascher, T. (2011). Learning and emotion. Perspectives for theory and research. *European Educational Research Journal, 9*(1), 13-28.

Heilbrunn, B. & Sammet, I. (2015). G-Learning – Gamification im Kontext von betrieblichem eLearning. *HMD Praxis der Wirtschaftsinformatik, 52*(6), 866-877.

Ifenthaler, D., Eseryel, D., & Ge, X. (2012). Assessment for game-based learning. In D. Ifenthaler, D. Eseryel, X. Ge (Eds.), *Assessment in game-based learning. Foundations, innovations, and perspectives* (pp. 3-10). New York: Springer.

Ifenthaler, D., Gibson, D., & Zheng, L. (2018). Attributes of engagement in challenge-based digital learning environments. *CELDA 2018* (pp. 225-232). Lisbon: International Association for Development of the Information Society (IADIS).

Jacob, A. & Teuteberg, F. (2017). Game-Based Learning, Serious Games, Business Games und Gamification – Lernförderliche Anwendungsszenarien, gewonnene Erkenntnisse und Handlungsempfehlungen. In S. Strahringer & C. Leyh (Eds.), *Gamification und Serious Games.* Edition HMD (pp. 97-112). Wiesbaden: Springer Vieweg.

Jahn, D. (2013). Was es heißt, kritisches Denken zu fördern – Ein pragmatischer Beitrag zur Theorie und Didaktik kritischen Nachdenkens. *Mediamanual, 28*, 1-17.

Jantke, K. P. (2014). *Serious Games.* Leipzig: Streifband.

Jantke, K. P. (2018). *No Thrill—No Skill. Ein systematischer Zugang zum Konzept Gamification.* Retrieved October 16, 2019 from https://www.researchgate.net/profile/Klaus_Jantke/publication/329239792_No_Thrill_No_Skill_Ein_systematischer_Zugang_zum_Konzept_Gamification/links/5bfe746992851c63-caae567e/No-Thrill-No-Skill-Ein-systematischer-Zugang-zum-Konzept-Gamification.pdf

Kalinauskas, M. (2014). Gamification in Fostering Creativity. *Social technologies, 4*(1), 62-75.

Kapp, K. M. (2012). *The Gamification of Learning and instruction—Game-based methods and strategies for training and education.* San Francisco: Pfeiffer.

Kingsley, T. L. & Grabner-Hagen, M. M. (2015). Gamification. Questing to integrate content knowledge, literacy, and 21st-century learning. *Journal of Adolescent & Adult Literacy, 9*(1), 51-56.

Knautz, K. (2015). *Gamification in der Hochschuldidaktik. Konzeption, Implementierung und Evaluation einer spielbasierten Lernumgebung.* Düsseldorf: Heinrich-Heine-Universität.

Kramer, K. (2002). *Die Förderung von motivationsunterstützendem Unterricht. Ansatzpunkt und Barrieren.* Ph.D. thesis. Kiel: Christian-Albrechts-Universität.

Lamb, S., Maire, Q., & Doecke, E. (2017). *Key skills for the 21st century. An evidence-based review.* Sydney: NSW Department of Education.

Le, S., Weber, P. & Ebner, M. (2013). Game-based Learning – Spielend lernen? In S. Schön & M. Ebner (Eds.), *Lehrbuch für Lernen und Lehren mit Technologien (L3T).* 2. Edition. Berlin: epubli.

McGonigal, J. (2007). *Welcome to a world without oil.* [Online video]. Retrieved July 27, 2019, from http://worldwithoutoil.org/metavideo.htm

Meyer, H. (2012). *Kompetenzorientierung allein macht noch keinen guten Unterricht! Skripts.* Oldenburg: Carl von Ossietzky Universität.

Meyer, R. & Stocker, F. (2011). *Lehren kompakt I.* 4. Edition. Bern: hep.

O'Donovan, S., Gain, J., & Marais, P. (2013). A Case Study in the Gamification of a University-level Games Development Course. In J. McNeill (Ed.), *Proceedings of the South African Institute for Computer Scientists and Information Technologists Conference* (pp. 242-251). New York: ACM.

Paul, R., Elder, L. & Bartell, T. (1997). *A brief history of critical thinking.* Retrieved January 14, 2020, from http://www.criticalthinking.org/pages/a-brief-history-of-the-idea-of-critical-thinking/408

Qian, M. & Clark, K. R. (2016). Game-based Learning and 21st century skills—A review of recent research. *Computers in Human Behavior, 63,* 50-58.

Quinche, F. (2013). *Game-based Learning – Lernen mit Videospielen.* Bern: Educa.

Romero, M. (2015). Work, games and lifelong learning in the 21st century. *Procedia – Social and Behavioral Sciences, 174,* 115-121.

Rose, Mike (2009). *21st Century Skills: Education's New Cliché.* Retrieved January 1, 2020, from https://www.truthdig.com/articles/21st-century-skills-educations-new-cliche/

Sailer, M. (2016). *Die Wirkung von Gamification auf Motivation und Leistung.* Wiesbaden: Springer.

Sailer, M., Hense, J. U., Mayr, S. K., & Mandl, H. (2017). How gamification Motivates—An experimental study of the effects of specific game design elements on psychological need satisfaction. *Computers in Human Behavior, 69,* 371-380.

Scharnhorst, U. & Kaiser, H. (2018). Transversale Kompetenzen für eine ungewisse digitale Zukunft? In J. Schweri, I. Trede, & I. Dauner (Hrsg.), *Digitalisierung und Berufsbildung. Herausforderungen und Wege in die Zukunft. OBS EHB Trendbericht 3* (pp. 18-21). Zollikofen: Eidgenössisches Hochschulinstitut für Berufsbildung EHB.

Seelhammer, C. & Niegemann, H. (2009). Playing to learn. Does it actually work? *ICCE 2009.* Hong Kong: Asia-Pacific Society for Computers in Education.

Seufert, S., Preisig, L., Krapf, J. & Meier, C. (2017). *Von Gamification zum systematischen Motivationsdesign mit kollaborativen und spielerischen Gestaltungselementen*. St. Gallen: scil.

Simões, J., Redondo, R., Vilas, A., & Aguiar, A. (2015). *Using Gamification to Improve Participation in a Social Learning Environment*. Retrieved October 29, 2019, from https://www.researchgate.net/publication/281273484_USING_GAMIFICATIONTO_IMPROVE_PARTICIPATION_IN_A_SOCIAL_LEARNING_ ENVIRONMENT

Stansbury, J. A. & Earnest, D. (2016). Meaningful Gamification in an Industrial/Organizational Psychology Course. *Teaching of Psychology, 44*(1), 38-45.

Stern, E. (2006). Was wissen wir über erfolgreiches Lernen in der Schule? *Pädagogik, 58*(1), 45-49.

Sternberg, R. J. & Williams, W. M. (1996). *How to develop student creativity*. Alexandria, VA: Association for Supervision and Curriculum Development.

Sternberg, R. J. & Williams, W. M. (1998). *Teaching for creativity. Two dozen tips*. Retrieved January 20, 2020 from http://www.cdl.org/resource-library/articles/-teaching_creativity.php

Stöcklin, N., Steinbach, N., & Spannagel, C., (2014). QuesTanja: Konzeption einer Online-Plattform zur computerunterstützten Gamification von Unterrichtseinheiten. In S. Trahasch, R. Plötzner, G. Schneider, D. Sassiat, C. Gayer, & N. Wöhrle (Hrsg.), *DeLFI 2014 – Die 12. e-Learning Fachtagung Informatik* (pp. 151-156). Bonn: Gesellschaft für Informatik e.V.

Vos, N., van der Meijden, H., & Denessen, E. (2011). Effects of constructing versus playing an educational game on student motivation and deep learning strategy use. *Computers & Education, 56*(1), 127-137.

Wood, L. C., Teräs, H., Reiners, T., & Gregory, S. (2013). The role of gamification and game-based learning in authentic assessment within virtual environments. In S. Frielick, N. Buissink-Smith, P. Wyse, J. Billot, J. Hallas, & E. Whitehead (Eds.), *Research and Development in Higher Education. The Place of Learning and Teaching, 36* (pp. 514-523). Auckland, New Zealand.

Yang, Y. T.C. & Chang, C. H. (2013). Empowering students through digital game Authorship—Enhancing concentration, critical thinking, and academic achievement. *Computers & Education, 68*, 334-344.

Zichermann, G. & Cunningham, C. (2011). *Gamification by Design. Implementing Game Mechanics in Web and Mobile Apps*. Sebastopol: O'Reilly Media.

Section II:
Teacher Education and
Professional Competence of Teachers
in the Age of Digitization

6 Development of a Video-based Test Instrument for the Assessment of Professional Competence in the Vocational Teacher Training Course

Andrea Faath-Becker & Felix Walker

6.1 Initial Situation

The university education for the teaching profession at vocational schools in Germany is intended not only to enable students to work scientifically but also, among other things, to create the conditions for a successful transition to professional practice (Saas, Kuhn, & Zlatkin-Troitschanskaia, 2020). The aim is to develop the professional competence of future teachers. A frequent focus of empirical work is on professional knowledge as part of professional action or professional competence. However, the reduction of professional competence to the knowledge facet (based on Shulman (1986) pedagogical knowledge (PK), technical knowledge (CK) and didactic knowledge (PCK)) seems to fall short, as university graduates do not feel adequately prepared for the complex requirements of teaching (Böhner, 2009). To solve practical problems in real teaching situations, prospective teachers feel unable to translate the content knowledge (CK) and pedagogical content knowledge (PCK) they acquired during their studies into effective action (Gruber, Mandl, & Renkl, 1999).

A characteristic feature of the expertise of teachers is their ability to act flexibly and appropriately in everyday teaching situations. Current research largely agrees that the competence of teachers that are the basis of their teaching activities are so complex that their differentiated description requires correspondingly highly developed approaches (Blömeke, Gustafsson, & Shavelson, 2015; Saas et al., 2020). Even if knowledge components alone do not seem sufficient to shape effective teaching, a solid basis of knowledge facets (propositional, case and strategic knowledge, Shulman, 1986) is nevertheless indispensable for the development of teachers' ability to work in the classroom. The complexity of these competences requires that their development should start at an early stage.

Therefore, national standards for teacher training at vocational schools demand an early orientation of the studies towards professional requirements with the aim of continuous competence development. In order to promote problem-solving thinking and action, students should be systematically confronted with problems of their future professional practice (Saas et al., 2020).

In this context, Hatch, Shuttleworth, Taylor Jaffee and Marri (2016) point to a long-standing problem in the preparation for many professions: the gap between abstract bodies of professional knowledge and the „craft knowledge" of practitioners.

According to Darling-Hammond (2010), the key to effective teaching and thus to the quality of public education and presumably also vocational education is the competence of teachers. Although there are different international findings on the existence of corresponding training standards, many training systems share the lack of a suitable instrument for measuring the effectiveness of teachers and, in consequence, their professional competence.

There is evidence that teachers can have large effects on student achievement (Darling-Hammond, 2010). However, it appears problematic there, for example, that the associated factors („teachers` initial preparation for teaching, licensing in the field taught, strength of academic background, level of experience") are not systematically controlled by corresponding standards in training and during employment. Instead, the assessment of teachers is often based on subjective observations of school administrators in the classroom or refer to knowledge tests documented in advance by academic qualifications (see above). The ability to teach, this includes the assessment of experienced teachers, is thus not sufficiently considered (Darling-Hammond, 2010).

At the end of teacher training, two comprehensive exams are taken before the degree is awarded: the first at the end of the first phase of university training with typical written and oral knowledge tests and the second at the end of the second phase of pre-service teacher training in schools an in teacher training institutions, in which prospective teachers have to demonstrate their (subject) didactic and pedagogical (PC) skills in authentic teaching application and its theoretical foundation (Blömeke et al., 2015, 10).

An analysis of the nationwide curricula of, e.g., the German Business Education degree programme makes it clear that a systematic examination of the competences required for everyday teaching is often neglected in didactic courses (Kuhn, Zlatkin-Troitschanskaia, Brückner, & Saas, 2018), despite all locations providing for practical school studies, which usually include a preparatory and follow-up event to accompany a school internship. This is an indication of the explicit promotion of reflective competences that are necessary for planning and reflecting lessons. However, the promotion of action-oriented competences is usually implicitly carried out within the framework of individual teaching attempts at schools and not explicitly considered in the context of higher education (Saas et al., 2020).

The situation in the study programmes for the industrial-technical, vocational disciplines of teacher training is very similar: To date, university tutorials on teaching methodology (PC) for the vocational teaching profession have been focused almost exclusively on the planning of lessons (e.g., in the form of written elaborations on a fictitious teaching sequence). Until now, the students' competence to carry out lessons or to reflect has been largely disregarded.

This contribution presents a video-based tool to capture action-related elements as part of the professional competence of prospective teachers in university teacher training. Essential aspects here are, on the one hand, the presentation of models of professional competence and, on the other, the understanding of competence-enhancing or quality teaching. Both aspects are combined to form an action-oriented model that takes into account both knowledge and (action-oriented) competence components. The extent to which the model generated in this way is suitable for identifying video vignettes (video sequences), which contain action-related components of competence-enhancing teaching, how objectively these features can be identified in the video sequences and how these can be integrated into an online-based environment are additional goals of this article.

6.2 State of Research and Theoretical Framework

The fields of action described and the resulting requirements give rise to three starting points for examination: the professional competence of teachers, the quality of teaching and, on the technical part, video-based instruments to assess both aspects. The complexity of teaching is due, among other things, to the fact that personal, individual dispositions (PID model by Blömeke et al. (2015) and model by Zlatkin-Troitschanskaia, Kuhn, Brückner and Leighton (2019) of both teachers and learners influence its course and, in particular, its effectiveness. A possible approach also consists in the professional perception (Seidel, Blomberg, & Stürmer, 2010) of teaching. The focus of this work is first to create an objective basis for the assessment of professional competence and then deduce from its effects on the quality of teaching at a later stage. Therefore, the quality characteristics of teaching must be taken into account when designing an instrument for assessing professional competence. Due to the sometimes highly spontaneous character of teaching, an instrument is needed that comes close to the reality of teaching and enables observers to look at the situation as if they were actually present in class. Video-based instruments are also suitable for this purpose, as they offer both visual and acoustic dimensions, can be recorded and viewed from different perspectives, and can be repeated as often as required.

6.2.1 Professional Competence

The comments on the professional competence of student teachers and their outlined problems of transferring the knowledge acquired during their studies to real teaching situations in preparatory service (section 6.1) clarify that the gathering of action-related competences is relevant. Accordingly, a model of professional competence must include both knowledge and action-related competence facets.

Model by Lindmeier (2011)

Lindmeier (2011) proposes a model that meets these requirements. In addition to knowledge components, competence components are represented in this model (Figure 1) (ibid.).

The professional knowledge of teachers with the components specialist knowledge, subject-related didactic knowledge and pedagogical knowledge, based on Shulman (1986), stands alongside action-oriented professional skills. Competences are thereby understood in the sense of Klieme and Hartig (2007) as requirement-specific achievement dispositions and thus understood more broadly than the knowledge components (Lindmeier, 2013). Lindmeier`s examinations of these teacher cognitions are also reflected in the analytical part of the PID model from Blömeke et al. (2015).

Figure 1: Competence structure model according to Lindmeier (2011)

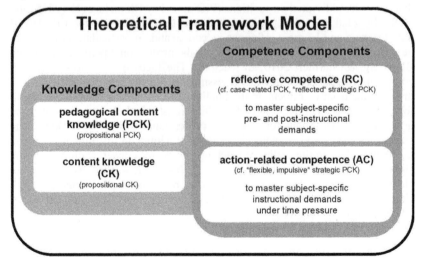

The knowledge components (Figure 1, left) comprise the basic pedagogical content knowledge (PCK) and the content knowledge (CK), which form the basis of professional action. The competence components (Figure 1, right) are again divided into a component of reflective competence (RC) and a component of action-related competence (AC). In this model, action-related competence components are thus formulated as a component of professional competence (Lindmeier et al., 2013).

Reflective competence (Figure 1, right, above) is „a term used here to describe domain-specific professional skills that are required in the preparation and follow-up of lessons (reflective competences, RC). The requirements include, for example, tasks to be performed in the planning of lessons". „Reflective competence therefore includes skills that teachers need on the basis of their basic knowledge in order to master the professional demands outside the actual teaching process. In this context, the reflective handling of the respective knowledge is characteristic" (c.f. Schön, 2002, reflection-on-action; Lindmeier et al., 2013, 105).

Further professional requirements arise from the superordinate „core business" of teaching. Ideas or mistakes made by learners can create challenging situations which can lead to learning opportunities or require a special reaction from the teacher, e.g. to prevent the development of misconceptions. Teaching situations are generally characterised by the fact that they require a spontaneous but also technically adequate reaction of the teacher. Time pressure does not allow the teacher to activate reflective processes outside the action (cf. Schön 2002, reflection-in-action). The action-related competence (AC) (Figure 1, right, below) „is determined above all by this spontaneous and immediate requirement character" (Lindmeier et al., 2013, 106).

Model by Zlatkin-Troitschanskaia et al. (2019)

Zlatkin-Troitschanskaia et al. (2019) draw on the Lindmeier model (2011) and distinguish between action-related and reflective competences. This holistic approach comprises two levels: a latent one with two areas (Figure 2, left: dispositions; centre: situation specific skills) and a manifest one (Figure 2, right: performance).

According to Zlatkin-Troitschanskaia et al. (2019), dispositions of teachers (Figure 2, left, dispositions) include knowledge components (cf. Figure 1, left) as well as generic characteristics and motivational factors as a basis for all teaching. According to this model, the quality of this teaching action is manifested in the reflective or action-based performance (Figure 2, right, performance) of the teachers. This requires situation-specific skills (Figure 2, centre, situation-specific skills): on the one hand, the (direct) reaction of prospective and experienced teachers to real instruction (i.e., AS) (Figure 2, action-related skills) and, on the other, the ability to prepare and follow-up instruction (i.e., RS) (Figure 2, reflective skills) in the specific discipline (ibid.). This model thus focuses on those situation-specific skills in which university graduates themselves do not feel adequately prepared (Böhner, 2009).

Figure 2: Competence structure model according to Zlatkin-Troitschanskaia et al. (2019)

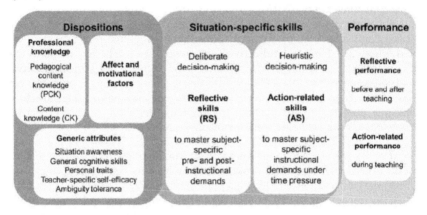

6.2.2 Quality of Teaching

Teaching action always raises the question of the quality of these actions regardless of a distinction between reflective (RC) and action-related (AC) competences. The consideration of the understanding of competence-enhancing or quality teaching can create a possible approach here.

Quality Teaching

Following Berliner (2005), quality teaching represents the synergy of good and effective teaching. According to ibid. (2005) good teaching is characterised by the fact that it follows normative principles and current standards of the field. A second evaluation criterion for teaching is its effectiveness (ibid., 2005). Teaching is considered effective when it achieves the desired goals. The goals of teaching can be manifold, such as individual learning success or collective, short or long-term goals (Kunter & Ewald, 2016). In addition, a distinction can be made between the acquisition of subject-related knowledge and the development of interdisciplinary competences as learning objectives, as well as between objectives at the cognitive (knowledge, skills) or the emotional-motivational level (e.g., development of interests, promotion of self-esteem) (ibid.). The extent to which teachers actually achieve these goals in their teaching can be described, for example, by the three fundamental dimensions of teaching quality (Klieme & Rakoczy, 2003; Praetorius, Klieme, Herbert, & Pinger, 2018), which are described in the next section.

Berliner (2005) considers with this distinction the empirical findings on the low effectiveness of teaching subjectively perceived as „good" as well as on the higher effectiveness of strongly directive forms of teaching and combines them to an idea of „quality teaching". In this context, Kunter and Ewald (2016) emphasise the central role of scaffolding (type of support and structure) in open teaching settings.

Visible and Depth Structures

According to Kunter and Ewald (2016), it does not make sense to view and evaluate lessons superficially, but always to include interactions that are not easy to evaluate at first glance as well as the role of learners and teachers. A meaningful conceptual distinction in this context dating back to Oser and Patry (1990) is that between the visual and depth structures of teaching (Kunter & Trautwein, 2013; Oser & Baeriswyl, 2001; Seidel, 2003; Kunter & Ewald, 2016).

The visual structures of teaching are the easily accessible features of teaching that refer to superordinate structures and settings (Kunter & Ewald, 2016, 13). The depth structures represent the levels of interaction between teachers and learners and their quality. The quality of the interaction between the learners and the way in which the learners deal with the subject matter is therefore at stake (ibid., 14), irrespective of the overarching organisation of the learning situation.

Characteristics of Quality Teaching

In empirical studies on the quality of teaching, the depth structures of teaching in particular have proven to be significant (Hattie, 2009; Seidel & Shavelson, 2007; Kunter & Ewald, 2016, 13). Important depth structures (Helmke, 2007; Lipowsky, 2015; Mayer, 2004; Seidel & Shavelson, 2007) mentioned are characteristics such as structuring, clarity of objectives, support, pupil orientation or individual support (Kunter & Ewald, 2016, 14). Compared to the depth structures of teaching, the visual structures have proven to be less relevant for the effect of teaching (ibid.).

Indicators of teaching quality include the three dimensions of class management, (constructive) learner support and cognitive activation (Praetorius et al., 2018). These are regarded as conditions and indicators for learning-enhancing pupil-specific processes in the classroom. Theoretically, the dimensions are conceived as generic and thus applicable across subjects, class levels and possibly even countries and cultures (Kunter & Ewald, 2016).

Lipowsky (2015) also categorises the subject by citing as quality characteristics the structured nature of teaching, clarity and coherence of content, feedback, cooperative learning, practice, cognitive activation, supportive learning climate and inner differentiation. In addition, the characteristics individualisation and scaffolding as forms of adaptive teaching (ibid.) differ in their complexity and degree of inference (ibid., 96).

6.2.3 Video-based Tools for Measuring Professional Competence

Basically, there are various conceivable ways of capturing action-related competences as part of the professionalisation of prospective teachers during their studies, like through practical phases (effectiveness discussed controversially; e.g. König, Rothland, & Schaper, 2018) or forms of teaching simulation, such as microteaching or role plays (effectiveness proven; e.g., Hattie, 2009, 112, d=0.88).

Video vignettes (didactically integrated video segments/sequences) are a diagnostic approach that can be easily integrated into studies due to technological progress or digitalisation. They are suitable for acquiring professional competence through an authentic depiction of the teaching reality especially in the area of university teacher training (Riegel, 2013, 14–15). The fact that the use of video vignettes can promote the skills of (prospective) teachers is well documented (at a glance, e.g., Hatch, Shuttleworth, Taylor Jaffee, & Marri, 2016). Video vignettes are suitable as a form of examination, as they can, for example, be attributed to the character of an invitation to actively continue the teaching activity instead of the teacher shown in the video (Seifried & Wuttke, 2017). Beyond that, focussing on the execution of the instruction is also possible. The decisive factor is that this can be put additionally on the planning and reflection of lessons. This means that video vignettes, as the only solution option to date, can cover all three areas of the requirement of the national standards: planning, implementation and reflection. Hence, in the following this approach will be presented in more detail.

Due to the lack of connection between theoretical education at university and later practical work at school, as described, for example, by Hatch et al. (2016), the multimedia representation of teaching (e.g. videos or animations) is already referred to. This is seen as a way of observing and analysing lessons involved in the training process, with the aim of helping prospective teachers transfer theoretical knowledge to authentic application in the teaching practice (ibid.).

Occurrence and Existence of Video Vignettes

In recent years, increasing numbers of video vignettes have been produced for the continuation or reflection of teaching in general education (Seidel & Thiel, 2017). An exception in the vocational field is the domain of business education, in which more and more video vignettes have been developed recently (Seifried & Wuttke, 2017; Saas et al., 2020). No video vignettes are currently available for the industrial-technical part of vocational (teacher) education (Riegel, 2013; Walker & Faath-Becker, 2019).

According to Zlatkin-Troitschanskaia et al. (2019), in order to assess the ability of teachers to act in complex teaching situations realistic and situation demanding action formats like classroom and learning observations or videos are required. Competence modelling must be based on a detailed analysis of real vocational teaching requirements (Oser, Salzmann, & Heinzer, 2009; Zlatkin-Troitschanskaia et al., 2019).

At national level, Seifried and Wuttke (2017), for example, report on the assessment of the quality of actions in authentic teaching situations using video vignettes in business education. There, video vignettes are used as a test instrument. Further work on the use of videos in general education at national level is available, for example, from Seidel, Blomberg and Stürmer (2010). Riegel and Macha (2013) provide an overview of video-based competence research in the subject didactics.

Internationally, worth mentioning is the approach of Darling-Hammond (2010), who, for example, has students of the teaching profession or trainees analyse the videography of their teaching attempt in order to reflect on their lesson planning as part of the „Performance Assessment for California Teachers (PACT)". The focus in this context is on effective teaching and includes the development of students` competences (ibid., 44).

Definition of Video Vignettes

Teacher training and further training should also include instruction videos and video vignettes that enable students to deal with realistic situations (Blomberg, Renkl, Sherin, Borko, & Seidel, 2013; Keuffer, 2010; Pauli & Reusser, 2006). It is often difficult for students to put into practice the knowledge acquired during their studies (Cochran-Smith & Zeichner, 2005). Videos and video vignettes play a supporting role in this transfer (Santagata, Gallimore, & Stigler, 2005; Seifried & Wuttke, 2017).

Videos are usually used to show learners` sequences from their own or other people`s lessons, to reflect or evaluate the teaching action. „(Video) vignettes, on the other hand, usually depict real, condensed instructional videography or fictional, realistic scenarios and invite the observer to act on behalf of the protagonists of the vignette action based on knowledge and experience" (Seifried & Wuttke, 2017, 306).

Videography and Technical Aspects

The use of videography is determined by the amount of recording technology required, the possibilities of knowledge (reduced authenticity and wholeness) limited by the camera detail and the camera perspective, and the invasiveness of the camera (influence on the actors) (Riegel & Macha, 2013, 13–14). These limits seem to at least influence or complicate the creation of videos.

Standards such as those summarised by Seidel, Dalehefte and Meyer (2003) in their technical report on the IPN video study are helpful for the implementation of videography. Compliance with these standards is intended to ensure the scientific use of video recordings through an appropriate methodology for recording and to provide as comprehensive a view as possible of the complex classroom teaching environment (ibid.).

Extensive preparations have to be made for videography lessons in such a way that different perspectives (teacher, learner, and observer) are covered and the technical quality (image, light, sound) is also implemented in an acceptable way. These requirements in particular concern the technical equipment (cameras, microphones) and the staffing of the undertaking. In addition, access to teaching must first be opened up, including formal written approval processes and the willingness of school management and teachers to open their lessons. Last but not least, data protection regulations are decisive for the later use of the videos, such as in online environments.

Video material for the production of video vignettes can be obtained as a possibility by filming scripts (specific situation descriptions). An alternative is teaching videography, which is described as more time-consuming and random (Oser, Salzmann, & Heinzer, 2009; Seifried & Wuttke, 2017). Ultimately, in this case the occurrence of certain situations is hardly predictable even desired typical teaching situations cannot be planned in advance (ibid.). The video should show typical and even faulty situations (ibid.). In the case of scripted teaching scenes, however, there may be a risk or temptation to want to show „ideal" teaching (= good and effective teaching?). In this respect, this can also be seen as an argument for choosing real lessons.

Video recordings are based on two cameras and two microphones (one fixed and one moving camera as well as a teacher`s and a pupil`s microphone) (cf. Seidel et al., 2003; Riegel & Macha, 2013, 16–17).

6.2.4 An Action-oriented Model of Professional Competence

If one takes up the critical feedback mentioned at the beginning, particularly with regard to the action-related competences required in the preparatory service but subjectively perceived as inadequate student preparation (Böhner, 2009), this must be manifested in a model of professional competence as the basis for the development of video vignettes. Here, both the idea and understanding of professional competence (Zlatkin-Troitschanskaia et al., 2019; Blömeke et al., 2015; Lindmeier, 2011) of future teachers and the central aspect of teaching quality (Berliner, 2005; Oser & Patry, 1990; Kunter & Ewald, 2016; Lipowsky, 2015) must be taken into account.

On the basis of the above considerations, the approach of Lindmeier (2011) on subject-specific competences (competence structure model, Figure 1) required for the preparation and follow-up of teaching (Lindmeier et al., 2013, 105) is an essential part of this theoretical framework.

Accordingly, in line with the first objective (section 6.1 or 6.2.1), the question was which idea or understanding is the basis of the professional competence of future teachers. On the basis of presented the models, a model of teachers' professional competence was to be selected whose components reflect both the above-mentioned arguments regarding the training situation and the practical situation, as well as the requirements of the national standards. The action-oriented model shown in Figure 3 is based on the work of Zlatkin-Troitschanskaia et al. (2019), Blömeke et al. (2015) and Lindmeier (2011).

Figure 3: Action-oriented model of professional competence of Walker/Faath-Becker (2019) based on Zlatkin-Troitschanskaia et al. (2019), Blömeke/Gustafsson/Shavelson (2015), and Lindmeier (2011)

The elements of the PCK and CK (Figure 3, top centre) are summarised according to Lindmeier (2011) under basic knowledge (section 6.2.1, Figure 1, left), while below they can be distinguished between two fields of competence. In the model by Zlatkin-Troitschanskaia et al. (2019) (section 6.2.1), these competence components can be found under situation-specific skills.

The ability to act under time pressure and make teaching decisions can be related to the delivery of instruction under the concept of action-based competence (Figure 3, right). For our model, action-based competence is defined as follows: Action-based competence refers to the ability of a teacher to react spontaneously and adequately based on professional knowledge (Lindmeier, 2013) and taking into account the dimensions of teaching (Holzberger & Kunter, 2016, 43-45; Lipowsky, 2015, 77-94) in teaching situations under time pressure. Spontaneous means that an activation of reflective processes is not possible (cf. Schön, 2002, reflection-in-action) (section 6.2.1).

With the other two phases, planning and reflection (Figure 3, left), the competence facet of reflective competence is linked. This is understood to mean coping with pre-instructional (planning) and post-instructional (reflection) teaching requirements (Lindmeier, 2011).

Reflective competence is the ability to cope with pre- and post-instructional situations (Lindmeier, 2011) on the basis of subject-specific basic knowledge (Lindmeier et al., 2013, 106) and taking into account the dimensions of teaching quality (Holzberger & Kunter, 2016, 43-45; Lipowsky, 2015, 77-94). These are complex skills that are needed to draw conclusions from the reflection of lessons held and to plan lessons (Lindmeier, 2011, 106-107).

Pre-instructional reflective competence refers to the ability to reflect the didactic design of instruction based on subject-specific basic knowledge and the characteristics of teaching quality. Post-instructional reflective competence is defined as the ability to reflect on learners' learning processes and products, the quality of interaction between teachers and learners and their (re-)actions, and the methodological and organisational design of teaching based on the characteristics of teaching quality through class observation (section 6.2.1).

The second goal of the work what is meant by competence-enhancing or quality instruction (section 6.1 or 6.2.2) is covered by the presentation of Berliner (2005). Following this idea, instruction is of high quality if it is good (by adhering to normative principles) and effective (by achieving the required competence goals). The distinction between visual and depth structure in class observation is important here (Oser & Baeriswyl, 2001). Above all, the characteristics of the depth structure proved to be characteristics of effective teaching and are operationalised by corresponding quality characteristics (section 6.2.2).

In addition to class leadership, cognitive activation and constructive support (Kunter & Ewald 2016; Praetorius et al., 2018), Lipowsky (2015) emphasises, among other things, structured teaching, clarity and coherence of content, cognitive activation and informative feedback as quality characteristics (ibid., 95; Fauth, Decristan, Rieser, Klieme, & Büttner, 2014; Kunter & Baumert, 2006; Praetorius et al., 2014; Kunter & Ewald, 2016) (section 6.2.2).

Based on the models mentioned above and the idea of quality teaching, the action-oriented competence facets are now combined with the quality criteria of teaching (Figure 4). The characteristics of the depth structure in particular are seen as indicators of quality teaching, which can be related to the expression of the reflective and action-based competence facets as part of the professional competence of the (prospective) teachers.

Figure 4: Action-oriented model of professional competence (Figure 3), combined with characteristics of teaching quality (Walker & Faath-Becker, 2019; translated from German into English)

These exemplarily listed characteristics of the depth structure (Figure 4 below, in the middle, c.f. section 6.2.2) are operationalised for a more detailed examination of the assessment of action-related professional competences in interaction with teaching quality in video vignettes. For this purpose, the respective feature definitions are related to real teaching situations in which actions can be observed and reflected upon or which can provide occasions for the active continuation of a teaching action.

As an example of the characteristics of teaching quality, the feedback characteristic is considered in more detail here. First, a definition of feedback/constructive support is given on the basis of the above-mentioned literature: This dimension focuses on supporting learners with comprehension problems and creating a learning environment in which the interaction between teachers and learners is characterised by respect and appreciation (Kunter & Ewald, 2016, 16).

6.2.5 Development of a Video-based Instrument for the Assessment of Professional Competence: Video Vignettes

The video vignettes should serve to capture the professional competence of future teachers at vocational schools and can also be used for examination purposes in the future. The question to be answered here is what access to teaching (teachers, school managements) is possible and how video material can be obtained. This means both—formal preparatory work such as approval steps or the basic decision for real or scripted instruction, but also technological conditions such as multimedia equipment and questions of recording technology (section 6.2.3). A further prerequisite is that the video vignettes meet scientific quality criteria.

Data protection regulations must also be observed. In fact, data protection can only be satisfactorily regulated by a responsible regulation of access to the videos. Legal security can be achieved by obtaining the written consent of the videographers (Riegel & Macha, 2013, 13–14), which was provided during the preparation of the videography.

Moreover, not every teacher is willing to open their lessons to video observations (Keuffer, 2010).

Video Vignette Creation Process

In a first step, real lessons in the industrial-technical field of vocational training are recorded by means of standardised videography (Asbrand & Martens, 2018; Seidel & Thiel, 2017). For this purpose, student and teacher perspectives are each captured with a fixed camera as well as selectively interesting scenes with a moving camera, and separate microphones are used for teacher and learner. Three cameras, a teacher microphone and three table microphones for the learners are available for the videography on which this work is based. The recorded video material is then divided into sections. The evaluation objectivity of the criteria for capturing professional competence in this context is determined after the next step: The video recordings are then divided by trained observers into sections in which specific characteristics of teaching quality and the requirements of the RC and AC can be identified (Figure 5, centre) (Walker & Faath-Becker, 2019). From these video sequences video vignettes can be produced in the last step.

Figure 5: Overview of the creation process of video vignettes (Walker & Faath-Becker, 2019; translated from German into English)

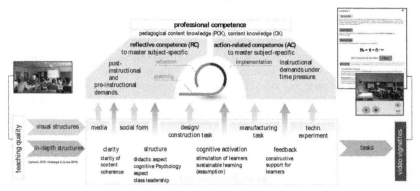

Vignettes Identified

So far, 21 vignettes have been identified from the recorded lessons and assigned to the two competence areas RC (13) and AC (8). For the above-mentioned characteristic „feedback" (see also section 6.2.4), the corresponding definition was used as a basis and a targeted search was made in the video material for passages in which the designated actions could be observed either in terms of reflective or action-based competence. Thus, for example, the support of learners with comprehension problems is expressed in the fact that the teacher shows a corresponding reaction (AC) to a pupil`s question by either answering directly, reflecting the question back to the class, putting the answer to the question back and referring to another process, or leaving the question as is without clarifying it. So it is not yet a question of checking the quality of feedback given or evaluating it as positive or negative. Rather, sequences in the video material were selected for the mere occurrence of the feature and thus only perception whether positive or negative played a role. This characteristic is thus assessed purely from an observational and not a judgmental attitude. A suitable sequence can thus be selected both by the occurrence of the feature and the absence of an expected feature. The assessment and allocation of the observed actions to the features is carried out by two independent observers, in order to secure each of them against each other in a first step. The observations of both are examined with respect to the agreement in the assignment of the vignettes to the same characteristic of teaching quality regarding the associated competence area (AC or RC). Initial analyses of the objectivity of the evaluation show sufficient quality (K_{RC} = .64; K_{AC} = .47) with a simultaneous large variance between the vignettes (Walker & Faath-Becker, 2019, 18).

Implementation in the Online Environment

Finally, the vignettes are integrated into an online environment and enriched with additional materials. The following example shows the video vignette implemented on the online platform for action-based competence and the feedback feature. The introduction to the online environment is a brief description of the teaching situation (Figure 6, „Situation" above). In addition, it is possible to view further planning documents for the lessons, such as essential information on the learning group, the classification in the curriculum and a reference to the subject content (Figure 6, left). Once the required information on the lessons has been obtained, the processing of the assignment can begin. In this example, a technically correct feedback on a pupil`s answer is to be provided (Figure 6, above). Before the video is started, the editors of this action-based competence video vignette are informed that the editing must take place with an audio recording/voice output within a predefined period of time. After confirmation of the message, the video starts automatically and the editing time runs (Figure 6, right). Now it is possible to document one`s own reaction orally, thereby providing technically correct feedback on the student`s response within the given time. The recording is automatically saved (Walker & Faath-Becker, 2019, 18).

Figure 6: Start view of a video vignette in the online environment (Walker & Faath-Becker, 2019; translated from German into English)

Assignment 1

SITUATION

You are teaching tool mechanics in the first year of training at the vocational school. In the field of learning 4 "Maintenance of technical systems" you are going to address the topics of corrosion and corrosion protection. After a learner-centered elaboration phase, a pupil gives a statement regarding hot-dip galvanizing during the discussion.

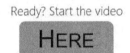

Ready? Start the video
HERE

TASK 📹 🎤 ⏱ 3 min

Give **feedback** to the pupil. Focus on the **technical correctness** of the pupil's statement.

AID

6.3 Discussion and Limitations

A video-based instrument for measuring „action-oriented" facets of professional competence was presented in the context of the article (section 6.2.5). This development took place on the theoretical basis of the models of Zlatkin-Troitschanskaia et al. (2019) and Lindmeier (2011), whereby the action-based competence facets focus in particular on the characteristics of competence-enhancing and quality teaching action (section 6.2.4). The generated video vignettes are based on real teaching (section 6.2.5). The video vignettes developed in this way (21 pieces) and the characteristics of quality teaching contained therein could be identified with satisfactory objectivity (section 6.2.5). The integration of the video vignettes into an online environment in which further information on the teaching situation (lesson plans, worksheets, specialist information, etc.) can be viewed completes the instrument.

To the authors' knowledge, the instrument presented here represents the first instrument in the industrial-technical field of teacher training in Germany and Europe. The use of the instrument is not limited to diagnostic purposes: the identified video vignettes can be used to build up action-oriented competences within the framework of the studies or the second phase of teacher training.

The focus on the characteristics of quality teaching obviously limits the significance of the instrument developed here, as only a part of the characteristics of quality teaching is depicted. The same applies to the construct of professional competence. Although, in comparison to other models of professional competence, „action-oriented" competence facets were integrated into the model, knowledge aspects (section 6.2.4; dispositions) remained only implicit in the instrument, that is, as a basis for teaching action.

The video vignettes integrated into the instrument show real lessons, which have both negative and positive consequences. It should be positively emphasised that the teaching situations represented in the video vignettes depict authentic teaching in all its complexity. However, this is also connected with the negative aspect. It is precisely this multidimensional nature of teaching that can lead to the fact that several characteristics of quality teaching of varying intensity occur in the video sequences and thus the construct to be captured is not exactly depicted (construct irrelevant variance (Downing & Haladyna, 2006; Haladyna & Rodriguez, 2013)).

The video-based instrument presented in this context for the assessment of „action-oriented" facets of professional competence forms a central component of a more comprehensive development process. In a first step, the video vignettes developed so far are checked for their acceptance, suitability and objectivity through their use by actors along the teacher training chain (student teachers, pre-service teachers and in-service teachers) and, if necessary, the vignettes are adapted according to the target group. The aim is to determine the evaluation objectivity of the focused quality features of teaching against the background of different work experience and to determine the acceptance in these target groups with regard to the use of the instrument in the online environment as well as the content aspects.

According to the theoretical model of professional competence on which this instrument is based, the instrument or online environment is systematically supplemented by further cognitive aspects of professional competence. Following on from the model of Zlatkin-Troitschanskaia et al. (2019), steps are also being taken to develop instruments for the elements of teacher cognition (dispositions: professional knowledge, affective and motivational factors, generic attributes) that have not yet been considered and to integrate them into the online environment.

Although the diagnosis of professional competence is of fundamental importance, it is unsatisfactory from a (subject-) didactic (CK/PCK) perspective without supporting or intervention approaches. Accordingly, it is not sufficient to provide only an instrument for assessing professional competence. Rather, suitable didactic approaches are needed to develop competence on the part of the students. To this end, the support approaches must be suitable for integration into the course of study.

The video vignettes developed in this article are used in a current research project in the subject didactic courses of the studies. Following the example of Arya, Christ and Chiu (2015) and Christ, Arya and Chiu (2017), the students are invited a) to view, discuss and reflect on the video vignettes with „peers" in addition to the lecturer-centred presentation of them, or b) to create the video vignettes themselves.[1]

With regard to the scientific output, these follow-up projects make a contribution to open national and international questions regarding the „video-supported" development of professional competence among prospective teachers at vocational schools. The results allow for the first-time statements about the actual effect of digital media (in this case video vignettes) on the acquisition of professional competence by future teachers at vocational schools. In addition, a „teaching concept" for the promotion of professional competence is promised for vocational teacher training studies.

With the help of these online-based video vignettes, both the assessment and prospectively the development of professional competence can be authentically integrated into the teacher training course for vocational schools. The

---

[1]   The sub-project ProKom LAB (promotion of professional competence with the help of video vignettes for students studying to become teachers at vocational schools) is being promoted as part of the German quality offensive for teacher training.

approach presented here thus offers potential for the second (preparatory service) and third phase (e.g., in the form of further training) of teacher training beyond the industrial-technical field (Walker & Faath-Becker, 2019).

References

Arya, P., Christ, T., & Chiu, M. (2015). Links between Characteristics of Collaborative Peer Video Analysis Events and Literacy Teachers' Outcomes. *Journal of Technology and Teacher Education, 23*, 2, 159-183.

Asbrand, B. & Martens, M. (2018). Analyse von Unterrichtsvideografien. In *Dokumentarische Unterrichtsforschung*. Wiesbaden: Springer VS

Berliner, D. C. (2005). The Near Impossibility of Testing for Teacher Quality. *Journal of Teacher Education, 56*, 3, 205-213.

Blömeke, S., Gustafsson, J.-E., & Shavelson, R. J. (2015). Beyond dichotomies. Competence viewed as a continuum. *Zeitschrift für Psychologie, 223*(1), 3-13.

Blomberg, G., Renkl, A., Sherin, M., Borko, H., & Seidel, T. (2013). Five research-based heuristics for using video in pre-service teacher education. *Journal für Bildungsforschung Online, 5*(1), 90-114.

Böhner, M. M. (2009). Wirkungen des Vorbereitungsdienstes auf die Professionalität von Lehrkräften. In O. Zlatkin-Troitschanskaia, K. Beck, D. Sembill, R. Nickolaus, & R. Mulder (Eds.), *Lehrprofessionalität. Bedingungen, Genese, Wirkungen und ihre Messung* (pp. 439-450). Weinheim: Beltz.

Christ, T., Arya, P., & Chiu, M. M. (2017). Video use in teacher education: An international survey of practices. *Teaching and Teacher Education, 63*, 22-35.

Cochran-Smith, M. & Zeichner, K. M. (Eds.) (2005). *Studying teacher education. The report of the AERA Panel on Research and Teacher Education*. New York, London: Routledge Taylor & Francis Group.

Darling-Hammond, L. (2010). *Evaluating Teacher Effectiveness. How Teacher Performance Assessments Can Measure and Improve Teaching*. Washington: Center for American Progress.

Downing, S. M. & Haladyna, T. M. (Eds.) (2006). *Handbook of test development*. Mahwah, NJ: Erlbaum.

Fauth, B., Decristan, J., Rieser, S., Klieme, E., & Büttner, G. (2014). Grundschulunterricht aus Schüler-, Lehrer- und Beobachterperspektive. Zusammenhänge und Vorhersage von Lernerfolg. *Zeitschrift für Pädagogische Psychologie, 28*(3), 127-137.

Gruber, H., Mandl, H., & Renkl, A. (1999). Was lernen wir in Schule und Hochschule: Träges Wissen? Forschungsbericht Nr. 101. München: LMU.

Haladyna, T. M. & Rodriguez, M. (2013). *Developing and validating test items*. New York: Routledge.

Hatch, T., Shuttleworth, J., Taylor Jaffee, A., & Marri, A. (2016). Videos, pairs, and peers: What connects theory and practice in teacher education? *Teaching and Teacher Education, 59*, 274-284.

Hattie, J. (2009). *Visible learning: A synthesis of over 800 meta-analyses relating to achievement.* London, New York: Routledge.

Helmke, A. (2007). *Was wissen wir über guten Unterricht? Wissenschaftliche Erkenntnisse zur Unterrichtsforschung und Konsequenzen für die Unterrichtsentwicklung.* Retrieved from https://www.bildung.koeln.de/imperia/md/content/selbst_schule/ downloads/andreas_helmke_.pdf

Holzberger, D. & Kunter, M. (2016). Unterricht aus der Perspektive der Pädagogischen Psychologie und der empirischen Unterrichtsforschung. Schule und Unterricht – Lehren und Lernen. In J. Möller, M. Köller, & T. Riecke-Baulecke (Eds.), *Basiswissen Lehrerbildung: Schule und Unterricht – Lehren und Lernen* (pp. 39-52). Seelze: Klett-Kallmeyer.

Keuffer, J. (2010). Videofeedback-Ein Konzept für die Lehrerbildung mit Zukunft. In M. Trautmann & J. Sacher (Eds.), *Unterrichtsentwicklung durch Videofeedback. Besser kommunizieren lernen* (pp. 187-200). Göttingen: Vandenhoeck & Ruprecht.

Klieme, E. & Hartig, J. (2007). Kompetenzkonzepte in den Sozialwissenschaften und im erziehungswissenschaftlichen Diskurs. In M. Prenzel, I. Gogolin, & H.-H. Krüger (Eds.), *Kompetenzdiagnostik* (pp. 11-29). Zeitschrift für Erziehungswissenschaft. Sonderheft. 8. Wiesbaden: VS Verlag für Sozialwissenschaften.

Klieme E. & Rakoczy, K. (2003). Unterrichtsqualität aus Schülerperspektive: Kulturspezifische Profile, regionale Unterschiede und Zusammenhänge mit Effekten von Unterricht. In Deutsches PISA-Konsortium (Eds.), *PISA 2000 – Ein differenzierter Blick auf die Länder der Bundesrepublik Deutschland* (pp. 333-359). Wiesbaden: VS Verlag für Sozialwissenschaften.

König, J., Rothland, M., & Schaper, N. (Eds.) (2018). *Learning to Practice, Learning to Reflect?* Wiesbaden: Springer Fachmedien.

Kuhn, C., Zlatkin-Troitschanskaia, O., Brückner, S., & Saas, H. (2018). A new video-based tool to enhance teaching economics. *International Review of Economics Education, 27,* 24-33.

Kunter, M. & Baumert, J. (2006). Who is the expert? Construct and criteria validity of student and teacher ratings of instruction. *Learning Environments Research, 9*(3), 231-251.

Kunter, M. & Ewald, S. (2016). Bedingungen und Effekte von Unterricht: Aktuelle Forschungsperspektiven aus der pädagogischen Psychologie. In N. McElvany, W. Bos, H. G. Holtappels, M. M. Gebauer, & F. Schwabe (Eds.). *Bedingungen und Effekte guten Unterrichts. Dortmunder Symposium der Empirischen Bildungsforschung, Band 1 (pp. 9-31).* Münster: Waxmann.

Kunter, M. & Trautwein, U. (2013). *Psychologie des Unterrichts.* Paderborn: Ferdinand Schöningh.

Lindmeier, A. (2011). *Modeling and measuring knowledge and competencies of teachers: A threefold domain-specific structure model for mathematics.* Zugl.: München, Techn. Univ., Diss., 2010. *Empirische Studien zur Didaktik der Mathematik: Vol. 7.* Waxmann.

Lindmeier, A. (2013). Video-vignettenbasierte standardisierte Erhebung von Lehrerkognitionen. In U. Riegel & K. Macha (Eds.). *Video-vignettenbasierte standardisierte Erhebung von Lehrerkognitionen. Videobasierte Kompetenzforschung in den Fachdidaktiken, Band 4* (pp. 45-62). Münster: Waxmann.

Lindmeier, A. M., Heinze, A., & Reiss, K. (2013). Eine Machbarkeitsstudie zur Operationalisierung aktionsbezogener Kompetenz von Mathematiklehrkräften mit videobasierten Maßen. *Journal für Mathematik-Didaktik, 34*(1), 99-119.

Lipowsky F. (2015). Unterricht. In E. Wild & J. Möller (Eds.), *Pädagogische Psychologie* (pp. 69-105). Berlin, Heidelberg: Springer-Lehrbuch.

Mayer, R. E. (2004). Should there be a three-strikes rule against pure discovery learning? The case for guided methods of instruction. *The American psychologist 59*(1), 14-19.

Oser, F. K. & Baeriswyl, F. J. (2001). Choreographies of Teaching: Bridging Instruction to Learning. In V. Richardson (Ed.), *Handbook of Research in Teaching* (pp. 1031-1065). Washington, D.C.: American Educational Research Association.

Oser, F. & Patry, J.-L. (1990). *Choreographien unterrichtlichen Lernens: Basismodelle des Unterrichts*. Berichte zur Erziehungswissenschaft: Pädagogisches Institut der Universität Freiburg.

Oser, F., Salzmann, P., & Heinzer, S. (2009). Measuring the competence-quality of vocational teachers: An advocatory approach. *Empirical Research in Vocational Education and Training, 1*(1), 65-83.

Pauli, C. & Reusser, K. (2006). Von international vergleichenden Video Surveys zur videobasierten Unterrichtsforschung und -entwicklung. *Zeitschrift für Pädagogik, 52*(6), 774-798.

Praetorius, A.-K, Klieme, E., Herbert, B., & Pinger, P. (2018). Generic dimensions of teaching quality. The German framework of Three Basic Dimensions. *ZDM, 50*(3), 407-426.

Praetorius, A.-K., Pauli, C., Reusser, K., Rakoczy, K., & Klieme, E. (2014). One lesson is all you need? Stability of instructional quality across lessons. *Learning and Instruction, 31*, 2-12.

Riegel, U. (2013). Videobasierte Kompetenzforschung in den Fachdidaktiken. In U. Riegel & K. Macha (Eds.), *Video-vignettenbasierte standardisierte Erhebung von Lehrerkognitionen. Videobasierte Kompetenzforschung in den Fachdidaktiken, Band 4* (pp. 9–24). Münster: Waxmann.

Riegel, U. & Macha, K. (Eds.) (2013). *Video-vignettenbasierte standardisierte Erhebung von Lehrerkognitionen. Videobasierte Kompetenzforschung in den Fachdidaktiken, Band 4*. Münster: Waxmann.

Saas, H., Kuhn, C., & Zlatkin-Troitschanskaia, O. (2020). Ein videobasiertes Lehr-Lernformat als innovativer hochschuldidaktischer Ansatz in der wirtschaftspädagogischen Lehramtsausbildung. In I. Gogolin, B. Hannover, & A. Scheunpflug (Eds.), *Evidenzbasierung in der Lehrkräftebildung, Band 4* (pp. 315-340). Wiesbaden: Springer.

Schön, D. A. (2002). *The reflective practitioner: how professionals think in action.* Ashgate: Aldershot.

Seidel, T. (2003). *Lehr-Lernskripts im Unterricht: Freiräume und Einschränkungen für kognitive und motivationale Lernprozesse; eine Videostudie im Physikunterricht.* Zugl.: Kiel, Univ., Diss., 2002. *Pädagogische Psychologie und Entwicklungspsychologie: Vol. 35.* Waxmann.

Seidel, T., Blomberg, G., & Stürmer, K. (2010). Projekt OBSERVE „OBSERVER" – Validierung eines videobasierten Instruments zur Erfassung der professionellen Wahrnehmung von Unterricht. In E. Klieme, D. Leutner, & M. Kenk (Eds.), *Kompetenzmodellierung. Zwischenbilanz des DFG-Schwerpunktprogramms und Perspektiven des Forschungsansatzes. 56. Beiheft* (pp. 296-306.). Weinheim: Beltz.

Seidel, T., Dalehefte, I. M., & Meyer, L. (2003). Aufzeichnen von Physikunterricht. In T. Seidel, M. Prenzel, R. Duit, & M. Lehrke (Eds.), *Technischer Bericht zur Videostudie „Lehr-Lern-Prozesse im Physikunterricht"; BIQUA. IPN-Materialien* (pp. 47–76). Kiel: IPN.

Seidel, T., Prenzel, M., Duit, R., & Lehrke, M. (Hrsg.) (2003). *Technischer Bericht zur Videostudie „Lehr-Lern-Prozesse im Physikunterricht"; BIQUA.* IPN-Materialien. Kiel: IPN.

Seidel, T. & Shavelson, R. J. (2007). Teaching Effectiveness Research in the Past Decade: The Role of Theory and Research Design in Disentangling Meta-Analysis Results. *Review of Educational Research, 77*(4), 454-499.

Seidel, T. & Thiel, F. (2017). Standards und Trends der videobasierten Lehr-Lernforschung. *Zeitschrift für Erziehungswissenschaft, 20*(1), 1-21.

Seifried, J. & Wuttke, E. (2017). Der Einsatz von Videovignetten in der wirtschaftspädagogischen Forschung. Messung und Förderung von fachwissenschaftlichen und fachdidaktischen Kompetenzen angehender Lehrpersonen. In C. Gräsel & K. Trempler (Eds.), *Entwicklung von Professionalität pädagogischen Personals: Interdisziplinäre Betrachtungen, Befunde und Perspektiven* (pp. 303-322). Wiesbaden: Springer Fachmedien.

Sektion Berufs- und Wirtschaftspädagogik der Deutschen Gesellschaft für Erziehungswissenschaft (BWP). (2014). Basiscurriculum für das universitäre Studienfach Berufs- und Wirtschaftspädagogik. Beschluss der Mitgliederversammlung am 25.09.2014. *Zeitschrift für Berufs- und Wirtschaftspädagogik, 100.*

Shulman, L. S. (1986). Those Who Understand: Knowledge Growth in Teaching. *Educational Researcher, 15*(2), 4-14.

Walker, F. & Faath-Becker, A. (2019). Videovignetten. Ein Ansatz zur Einlösung der Anforderungen an die professionelle Kompetenz zukünftiger Lehrkräfte für berufsbildende Schulen? *Berufsbildung, 73*(177), 16-19.

Zlatkin-Troitschanskaia, O., Kuhn, C., Brückner, S., & Leighton, J. P. (2019). Evaluating a Technology-Based Assessment (TBA) to Measure Teachers' Action-Related and Reflective Skills. *International Journal of Testing, 19*(2), 148-171.

7 Assessing Professional Knowledge of Teachers at Vocational Schools—Using the Example of a Professional Development for Automation and Digitized Production

Pia Schäfer, Nico Link und Felix Walker

7.1 Introduction

The use of digital technologies in professional learning arrangements is currently experiencing a boost in the scientific and educational policy debate. This is influenced and accelerated, among other things, by technological changes (e.g. Digitization, Industry 4.0). Due to the increasing complexity of systems, the fault diagnoses ability of employees is and will remain of great importance (cf. Spath et al., 2013, 124; Gronau, 2015, 19). Walker et al. (2016) tested the fault diagnosis ability among trainees of electronics technicians for automation technology. The results indicate that the trainees have difficulties in diagnosing and correcting faults in automated systems.

The implementation of content from Industry 4.0 and fault diagnosis in vocational training poses a challenge. Not only pre- but also in-service teachers have to be prepared in their content, pedagogical and pedagogical content knowledge. For this reason, appropriate professional developments are necessary.[1] This represents a long-term transformation (Tenberg & Pittich, 2017, 27).

The extent to which such training courses are offered has been investigated in own analyses (Schäfer, Huber, & Walker, 2019). For the topics Industry 4.0 and fault diagnosis on automated systems, all professional developments offered by the state institutes[2] were recorded throughout Germany. For both content areas, professional developments with a content focus were identified almost exclusively. Training courses with a focus on pedagogical content or technological content knowledge are rarely offered (Schäfer et al., 2019).

---

[1] In this publication, the following terms are used synonymously to describe teacher training for in-service teachers: professional development, training course, training programme.

[2] The educational state institutes are partners and central service providers of and for schools, teachers, students and parents as well as all other parties involved in school. The state institutes offer professional developments, advice, and materials for teachers.

131

Since there is evidence for the influence of pedagogical content knowledge of teachers on student performance (Kunter, Klusmann, Baumert, & Richter, 2013; Köller et al., 2016), the results of the analysis are surprising. For this reason, two training courses were developed and evaluated (EELBA & EELBI).[3] One teacher training has been developed to promote fault diagnosis. Fault diagnosis is practiced on a computer simulation of an automation system. In the second training, different aspects and technical implementation possibilities of Industry 4.0 will be covered. With the help of an Industry 4.0 training plant, the use of smart devices (like tablets and smartphones) in production will be shown.

The evaluation of these two teacher training courses is measured by questionnaires based on the TPACK-model by Mishra and Koehler (2006). The questionnaire will be used to determine the correlations between the TPACK-dimensions. In addition, the development in the TPACK-dimensions between pre- and posttest will be examined.

The Sections 7.2 and 7.3 deal with the theoretical framework of the article. First, aspects (offer-and-use model) and the current state of research on the effectiveness of teacher training are listed. This is followed by the presentation of the TPACK-model and current research results on correlations within the TPACK-dimensions. In addition, the authors show how they developed the teacher trainings based on the offer-and use model in Section 7.4. Section 7.5 and 7.6 explain the research aims and the methods (random sample, research design, measuring instrument). In the last two Sections 7.7 and 7.8, the results of the two projects are presented and discussed. The article concludes with a discussion and consideration of the limitations.

[3] EELBA is a sub-project of "U.EDU: Unified Education – Medienbildung entlang der Lehrerbildungskette" (funding code: 01JA1616). It is part of the "Qualitätsoffensive Lehrerbildung", a joint initiative of the Federal Government and the Länder. The programme is funded by the Federal Ministry of Education and Research. EELBI is a sub-project of "Mittelstand 4.0-Kompetenzzentrums Kaiserslautern". The programme is funded by the Federal Ministry of Economics and Energy.

7.2 The Effectiveness of Professional Development

7.2.1 Modelling the Effectiveness of Professional Development

The effectiveness of training programs depends on various factors, which Lipowsky summarises in the offer-and-use model (Lipowsky, 2014, 515; Lipowsky & Rzejak, 2015, 30). The influencing factors relate both to the quality of the event and the facilitator as well as to the characteristics of the participants and the school context (Vigerske, 2017). "The success of professional development programs for teachers can depend on this spectrum of factors" (Lipowsky & Rzejak, 2015, 29). In addition to the influencing factors (cf. Figure 1 upper and middle section), the model also contains levels for the evaluation of teacher training (cf. Figure 1 lower section). These four levels in the offer-and-use model are based on Kirkpatrick and Kirkpatrick (2006).

Figure 1: Offer-and-use model for research on teachers' professional development (Lipowsky, 2014, 515; Lipowsky & Rzejak, 2015, 30)

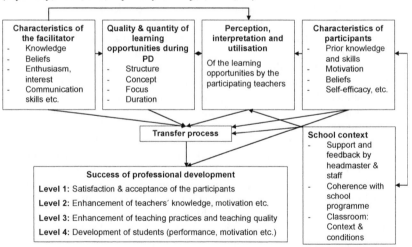

The characteristics of the trainers include their knowledge, beliefs, interests, etc. which influence the quality of the learning opportunities during professional development. The quality of the training involves the structure, the concept, the content focus, and the duration. The quality and quantity of learning opportunities during the professional development interact with the perception, interpretation and utilization of the learning opportunities by the participating teachers. The perception and use of professional development are in turn influenced by the characteristics of the facilitator and the characteristics of the participants. The requirements of the participants include their knowledge and skills, motivation, beliefs, etc. These characteristics are influenced by the school context. The school context includes, among other things, the support of the school management and colleagues. All factors mentioned have an influence on the transfer process of the participants. This transfer process, in turn, determines the success of professional development (see Figure 1). Further details can be found in Lipowsky & Rzejak (2015).

In order to be able to evaluate a training program, it must first be decided at which level the effectiveness should be considered. The authors Kirkpatrick and Kirkpatrick (2006) developed an inter-professional model for the evaluation of further training. This model contains four different levels: reaction, learning, behaviour, and results (Kirkpatrick & Kirkpatrick 2006, 21). Based on this model, Lipowsky (2014) established four levels for teacher training. These are part of the offer-and-use model (Lipowsky & Rzejak, 2015, 30). The names of the levels are similar to the original labels of Kirkpatrick and Kirkpatrick (2006). The difference is that they are specifically designed for the profession of teachers and the learning of students. Lipowsky & Rzejak (2015, 30) call the four levels: satisfaction and acceptance, enhancement of teachers' knowledge and motivation, enhancement of teaching practices and quality, development of students (see the lower section in Figure 1).

The lowest level is the satisfaction and acceptance of the teachers for professional development (Level 1). "The effectiveness of teacher training can only be deduced from participants' acceptance and satisfaction data to a limited extent" (Lipowsky & Rzejak 2015, 28). The information gained in this way can essentially be used for the evaluation and further development of the teacher training concept (cf. Kirkpatrick & Kirkpatrick, 2006, 27). At the next higher level, teacher training is recorded on the basis of teacher cognition (Level 2). This includes changes in the knowledge, skills, beliefs and motivation of the participants. "These teacher characteristics are important predictors for teaching quality and student learning" (Lipowsky & Rzejak, 2015, 28). The third level comprises the practical teaching activities of the teachers (Level 3). Changes in the "participants' in-class behaviour" (Lipowsky & Rzejak, 2015, 28) are observed. Capturing changes on level three is more challenging than on the first two levels (cf. Kirkpatrick & Kirkpatrick, 2006, 52). Finally, the effectiveness of teacher training can be assessed at the student level (Level 4). This includes changes in learning achievement and student motivation. "The first three levels of evaluation attempt to determine the degree to which these three things have been accomplished" (Kirkpatrick & Kirkpatrick, 2006, 65).

7.2.2 State of Research of Effectiveness of Professional Development

As already mentioned, the effectiveness of teacher training can be measured at four levels (see Figure 1). In the following, different findings from international studies on the effectiveness of professional developments are listed. A distinction is made between the four levels of teacher training. Although initial findings exist in the field of economic education (e.g. Seifried & Wuttke, 2017; Krille, Salge, Wuttke, & Seifried, 2017; Krille, 2019), the following findings refer to the field of general education.

Various studies assessed the influence of different factors on these levels. On the international scene, the metastudies by Kennedy (1998), Yoon, Duncan, Lee, Scarloss, and Shapley (2007), Timperley, Wilson, Barrar, and Fung (2007) and Darling-Hammond, Hyler, and Gardner (2017) are frequently cited. These studies consider the effectiveness of teacher training at the student level (Level 4). Furthermore, the influence of different factors of teacher training on student performance is considered in quantitative studies. Results of such studies can be found, for example, in the publications of Ingvarson, Meiers, and Beavis (2003, 2005), Thiel, Ophardt, and Piwowar (2013), Kiemer, Gröschner, Pehmer, and Seidel (2015), Pehmer, Gröschner, and Seidel (2015) and Kleickmann, Tröbst, Jonen, Vehmeyer, and Möller (2016). While the quantitative studies focus primarily on the type of event (e.g. blended learning, class time and private study) and the content focus, the metastudies also consider active learning, duration and time span.

Other studies have examined the influence or relationship between factors influencing teacher training and teaching quality (Level 3). For level 3, the international studies by Garet, Porter, Desimone, Birman, and Yoon (2001, 2002), Ingvarson, Meiers, and Beavis (2003, 2005) and Penuel, Fishman, Yamaguchi, and Gallagher (2007) should be highlighted. In the national (German-speaking) area, research results are also available in the publications of Thiel et al. (2013), Pehmer et al. (2015), Kiemer et al. (2015), Kleickmann, Tröbst, Jonen, Vehmeyer, and Möller (2016), and Vigerske (2017).

In the following, the main results on the influence of different factors on changes in teacher cognition (Level 2) are presented. Some of the studies that considered the influence of different factors on the level of teacher cognition also evaluated the level of teaching quality (e.g. Garet et al., 2001; Penuel et al., 2007; Ingvarson et al., 2003, 2005). Studies that have exclusively assessed the effectiveness at level 2 are Thiel et al. (2013), Besser, Leiss, and Eckhard (2015), Kleickmann et al. (2016), Tröbst, Kleickmann, Depaepe, Heinze, and Kunter (2019) and Akiba, Murata, Howard, and Wilkinson (2019).

Factors most influencing changes in teachers' cognition are follow-up support from the trainer, coherence,[4] content focus, professional learning community and active learning (Garet et al., 2001; Ingvarson et al., 2003; Ingvarson et al., 2005, Penuel et al., 2007; Besser et al., 2015). The results of other influencing factors mentioned by Lipowsky (2014) in the offer-and-use model are not considered in detail for two reasons. Either studies show ambiguous results on the influence of the factors on teacher cognition. Or these factors are poorly studied on level 2. These include the type of event, feedback, time span, duration and collaboration. Nevertheless, this does not mean that these factors have no influence on the effectiveness of teacher training. There are studies (e.g. Kennedy, 1998; Yoon et al., 2007; Timperley et al., 2007; Watson & Manning, 2008; Darling-Hammond et al., 2017) that demonstrate the effectiveness of these factors at level 3 and 4. However, the influence at the level of teacher cognition is not confirmed. The three influencing factors active learning, content focus and coherence were considered in the design of the two teacher training courses. For this reason, the influences of these factors on the knowledge of teachers are listed in Table 1.

The studies by Garet et al. (2001) and Ingvarson et al. (2003, 2005) report a significant influence of active learning on teacher knowledge. Even higher standardized regression coefficients are reported for the coherence and content knowledge of teacher training (see Table 1, lines 2 and 3). The regression coefficients for the content focus show highly significant values between .19** and .33** across the analysed studies (Garet et al., 2001; Ingvarson et al., 2003, 2005). In addition to these studies, reference is made to the results of Besser et al. (2015). In their study training courses with pedagogical content knowledge and a pedagogical focus were compared. Besser et al. (2015) concluded that professional developments with a focus on pedagogical content knowledge are more effective than professional developments with a pedagogical focus ($d = 1.63**$, $\eta_p^2 = .412**$). There is evidence that the influence of coherence on teachers' knowledge is even greater than the influence of content focus. The results of Garet et al. (2001) show an influence on the knowledge of teachers, whereas Penuel et al. (2007) examined an influence on the pedagogical knowledge of teachers (see Table 1, line 3).

---

[4] Coherence describes a meaningful linking of structures, contents and phases of teacher training. Coherent learning opportunities establish systematic relationships that enable learners to experience these structures, contents and phases as coherent and meaningful (cf. Hellmann 2019; Garet et al., 2001).

Table 1: Results of the active learning, content focus and coherence on the knowledge of in-service teachers

Influencing factor	Publication	Research results
Active learning	Garet et al. (2001)	K: $\beta = .14$**
	Ingvarson et al. (2003)	K: $\beta = .09$*
	Ingvarson et al. (2005)	K: $\beta = .08$-.27**
Content focus	Garet et al. (2001)	K: $\beta = .33$**
	Ingvarson et al. (2003)	K: $\beta = .35$*
	Ingvarson et al. (2005)	K: $\beta = .19$**-.39**
	Besser et al. (2015)	PCK vs. PK: $d = 1.63$**, $\eta_p^2 =$ .412**
Coherence	Garet et al. (2001)	K: $\beta = .42$**
	Penuel et al. (2007)	PK: $\beta = .59$**

Note. This table only lists factors for which there is evidence of influence from in-service teacher training on changes in teacher knowledge. Ingvarson et al. (2005) examined a total of four training programs. The results, therefore, represent the lowest and highest of the four values.

K = teachers' knowledge, PK = teachers' pedagogical knowledge, PCK = teachers' pedagogical content knowledge

β = standardized regression coefficient, d = effect size, η_p^2 = effect size

Significance values: *$p < 0.05$; **$p < 0.01$

The results from Table 1 illustrate the relevance of the three influencing factors listed for the design and effectiveness of professional developments for changes in teacher knowledge. The training courses were developed based on these results. The two professional developments focused on changes in cognitive aspects and, more specifically, on the knowledge of teachers. The evaluation will be carried out on the second level according to Lipowsky and Rzejak (2015) as well as Kirkpatrick and Kirkpatrick (2006). For this reason, a model of teacher cognition is presented below.

7.3 Model of Professional Knowledge of Teachers

7.3.1 Professional Knowledge of Teachers

The professional knowledge of teachers can be operationalized in different ways. In Germany, the PCK-model of Shulman (1986) dominates in studies (e.g. Hohenstein, Köller, & Möller, 2015). However, this model lacks the knowledge to integrate technologies into teaching (cf. Walker et al., 2017). Today, digital media and smart devices are at the heart of the integration of technologies into the classroom. Comparative studies such as ICILS (cf. Bos, Eickelmann, & Gerick, 2014) illustrate the importance of this technological knowledge. Wang, Schmidt-Crawford, and Jin (2018) state that "technology can no longer be treated as a separate body of knowledge that is isolated from the pedagogical and content knowledge that teachers require" (Wang et al., 2018, 235). The TPACK-model by Mishra and Koehler (2006) takes technological knowledge into account (see Figure 2). Therefore, Wang et al. (2018) support the TPACK-model to describe the professional knowledge of teachers. TPACK is the abbreviation for technological pedagogical content knowledge. Content, pedagogical and technological knowledge are regarded as basic dimensions. These three knowledge dimensions cannot be completely separated from each other. There are overlaps, which form a total of four knowledge dimensions. In addition to the knowledge dimensions, the model also contains a context (see the frame in Figure 2).

Figure 2: The TPACK-model according to Mishra and Koehler (2006)

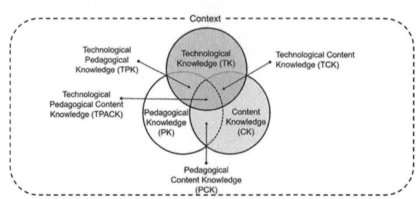

- **Technological knowledge (TK):**[5] Technological knowledge includes knowledge about all technologies, from low-tech (e.g. chalkboard, worksheet, book) to high-tech (e.g. computer software, smart devices) (Mishra & Koehler, 2006, 1027).
- **Technological content knowledge (TCK):** Technological content knowledge is knowledge about the selection of technologies for teaching specific content. "The teachers need to know [...] the manner in which the subject matter can be changed by the application of technology" (Mishra & Koehler 2006, 1028).
- **Technological pedagogical knowledge (TPK):** Technological pedagogical knowledge is the knowledge about the fit of teaching methods and content (Mishra & Koehler, 2006, 1028).
- **Technological pedagogical content knowledge (TPACK):** Technological pedagogical content knowledge is the knowledge of the flexible use of pedagogical and technological components to teach specific content (Mishra & Koehler, 2006, 1029).
- **Context:** The various dimensions of knowledge are integrated into a context (see Figure 2). The context is "dependent on subject matter, grade level, student background" (Mishra & Koehler, 2006, 1032), type of school and type of available technologies.

7.3.2 State of Research of Interrelations in the Professional Knowledge of Teachers

The seven TPACK-dimensions are initially theoretical assumed dimensions. Voogt, Fisser, Roblin, Tondeur, and van Braak (2013) list studies in their article that confirm empirical separability. Although there is evidence for empirical independence, there are medium to high correlations between the knowledge dimensions. According to the theoretical model, the correlations between knowledge dimensions that are closer together in terms of content or definition are higher in natural science education (cf. Walker et al., 2017). Table 2 lists the findings of various studies in general education on the relationships between the TPACK-dimensions. The studies by Schmidt et al. (2009) and Sahin (2011) exclusively interviewed pre-service teachers and those by Koh, Chai, and Tsai (2013) and Walker et al. (2017) exclusively interviewed in-service teachers. In the study by Dong et al. (2015), both pre-service and in-service teachers were interviewed. Lin et al. (2013) made no distinction.

---

[5] For reasons of limited space, a definition of the knowledge dimensions known from the PCK model is not given (PK, CK and PCK). Shulman (1989) as well as Mishra and Koehler (2006) should be mentioned here.

Table 2: Correlations between the dimensions of the technological pedagogical content knowledge

	$r_{TPK/PK}$ & $r_{TPK/TK}$ > $r_{TK/PK}$	$r_{TCK/TK}$ & $r_{TCK/CK}$ > $r_{TK/CK}$	$r_{PCK/PK}$ & $r_{PCK/CK}$ > $r_{PK/CK}$
Schmidt et al. 2009	.51** & .40** > .21*	.54** & .21*/.36** > .07/.41**	.56** & .25**/.33** > .14/.42**
Sahin 2011	.67** & .46** > .28**	.53** & .59** > .36**	.80** & .63** > .61**
Lin et al. 2013	.59 & .72 > .42	.65 & .56 > .31	.40 & .51 > .52
Koh et al. 2013	.49** & .72** > .42**	.63** & .47** > .35**	.40** & .42** > .61**
Dong et al. 2015	.55** & .69*** > .58**	.72** & .50** > .55**	.57** & .58** > .69**
	.56** & .64** > .49**	.70** & .45** > .46**	.62** & .49** > .59**
Walker et al. 2017	.11 & .58** > .03	-.26/.46 & .76**/.82* > -.42/.57**	.12/.13 & .81**/.86** > -.08 /.07

Note. The study by Schmidt et al. (2009) examined four, the study by Walker et al. (2017) two different content areas. Therefore, the smallest (before the slash) and largest values (behind the slash) were given for the content knowledge (row 1). In the study by Lin, Tsai, Chai, and Lee (2013) are no significance values reported (row 3). The study by Dong, Chai, Sang, Koh and Tsai (2015) lists the findings of pre-service (upper line) and in-service (lower line) teachers (row 5).

TK = Technological knowledge; PK = Pedagogical knowledge; CK = Content knowledge; TPK = Technological-pedagogical knowledge; TCK = Technological content knowledge; PCK = Pedagogical content knowledge.

Significance values: * $p < 0.05$; ** $p < 0.01$

The correlations between knowledge dimensions close to each other, e.g. TPK/TK and TPK/PK, are compared to the correlations between TK/PK. As expected, for the knowledge dimensions TPK, PK and TK the correlations between the closer dimensions are higher than between the two basic dimensions (see Table 2, left column). The relationships between TCK, TK and CK are similar (see Table 2, middle column). However, three of the studies reported only partially results corresponding to the theory. In the studies by Schmidt et al. (2009) and Dong et al. (2015), the correlations between the basic knowledge dimensions TK/CK are similar or higher than the correlations between TCK/CK. In addition, the correlations between TK/CK in Walker et al. (2017) are higher than those between TCK/CK. The correlations between the PCK and the adjacent dimensions are less clear (see Table 2, right column). Only two studies (Sahin, 2011; Walker et al., 2017) show higher or at least equal correlations between the PCK and the basic knowledge dimensions than between the PK/CK. The studies by Lin et al. (2013), Koh et al. (2013) and Dong et al. (2015) each report higher correlations to at least one of the two PCK/PK and PCK/CK correlations for these knowledge areas. The findings of Lin et al. (2013) could be attributed to the very small number of items in PCK and CK. While the PK was queried by six items, only three items were used for the CK and two items for the PCK (Lin et al., 2013, 331). In the study by Koh et al. (2013), the PK was also queried with more items (5) than the PCK (3 items) and the CK (3 items) (Koh et al., 2013, 800). It seems questionable whether with two to three items per content area the PCK and the CK can be comprehensively mapped. In addition, the items are not formulated in terms of concrete content, but only in terms of a general subject, e.g. science. In summary, the closer knowledge dimensions tend to correlate more closely with each other than with more distant knowledge dimensions (see Table 2, Figure 2).

7.4 Introduction of the Professional Developments

The offer-and-use model, as well as the TPACK-model, presented in Section 7.2 and 7.3 form the theoretical framework for the development of the two training courses. In terms of content, one training course focused on pedagogical content knowledge in the field of automation technology. The other professional development focused on technological content knowledge in the field of digitized production.

- **Automation technology:** Pedagogical components of the teacher training are the cognitive apprenticeship (CA)-approach (Brown, Collins, & Duguid, 1989) as well as the informative tutorial feedback (ITF) according to Narciss (2008). The participating teachers will be shown how to teach fault diagnosis using the CA-approach and the ITF. Rowold et al. (2008) were able to demonstrate the effectiveness of the CA-approach for training the fault diagnosis capability of trainees in automation systems. There is evidence that feedback from teachers has an impact on students' learning (Kulhavy, 1977). For this reason, the ITF is used in training and its benefits are identified. The feedback is integrated into the coaching, scaffolding and fading phases of the CA-approach. On the one hand, in the form of individual feedback for the participants and on the other hand via stepped learning aids. Strategies for fault diagnosis based on Rasmussen (1981) and Konradt (1992) form the content component. These are practiced on authentic computer simulation (Walker et al., 2015). This computer simulation is the technological and thus also the digital component of teacher training in automation technology. A more detailed description of the professional development in automation technology can be found in Schäfer and Walker (2018) as well as Schäfer and Walker (in press).

- **Digitized production:** In order for teachers to be able to prepare their trainees well for everyday work in Industry 4.0, they must possess the appropriate qualifications (acatech, 2016; bayme vbm study, 2016). These include topics such as identification systems (RFID: radio-frequency identification, QR-code: quick response code) in smart production, the basics of network technology as well as a strong focus on modern open-loop technology and information technology. These are the content components of teacher training. These contents will be demonstrated using an Industry 4.0 training plant. The plant is the technological and digital component of the training. Various smart devices (tablets, smartphones) are used on it. The CA-approach is also used as a pedagogical component in this teacher training course. The training on digitized production is described in the articles Walker et al. (2018) and Link, Schäfer, and Walker (2020).

The influencing factors content focus, coherence, and active learning, from the offer-and-use model (Lipowsky & Rzejak, 2015), were considered. In Table 3, the formal framework of both advanced training courses is listed.

Table 3: Introduction of the professional development concepts

Automation technology	Digitized production
Content Focus	
Pedagogical content knowledge in the field of fault diagnoses in automation technology	Technological content knowledge for the Introduction of technologies for Industry 4.0
Coherence	
Fault diagnosis in the field of automation technology is an integral part of the curricula of various training occupations in Germany. e.g. EAT: LF13; INME: LF13, MECH: LF11	The following topics are an integral part of the curricula: Identification systems: INME: LF13, MECH: LF11, EAT: LF11; networking technology: MECH: LF9, EAT: LF9; modern control technology EAT: LF7+11, MECH: LF7

Table 3: Introduction of the professional development concepts (cont.)

Automation technology	Digitized production
Concept/ active learning	
1) Theoretical input on fault diagnosis in automation technology 2) Presentation and testing of the functionality of the software simulation 3) Training of the fault diagnosis a) Independent fault diagnosis of the teachers in the simulation b) Run through the CA-approach (modelling, coaching, scaffolding/ fading) c) Feedback depending on the CA-approach phase (given by the trainer or by staged learning aids) 4) Discussion of the design and the functionality of the learning aids 5) Provision of handouts and worksheets	1) Theoretical input on Industry 4.0 2) Presentation of the Industry 4.0-training plant 3) Training for Industry 4.0 a) Action oriented learning with identification systems (RFID, QR-code) b) Enhancement of modern control technology based on the CA-approach phases (modelling, coaching, scaffolding /fading), basics of network technology 4) Provision of handouts and worksheets 5) Discussion of actual problems at vocational education and training schools in the context of Industry 4.0

Note: EAT = electronics technicians for automation technology, INME = industrial mechanics, MECH = mechatronics technicians, LF = learning field

7.5 Research Aims and Research Questions

The evaluation of professional developments is an essential goal of this article. As already described in Section 7.3.1 the TPACK-model of Mishra and Koehler (2006) was chosen as the theoretical basis for the evaluation of the two professional developments. Accordingly, the first research question is related to the relationships between individual TPACK-dimensions. Section 7.3.2 lists various studies that have investigated the relationships between the TPACK dimensions (see Table 2). However, all of these studies were conducted in general education, some of them only surveyed pre-service teachers. Whether the results can be transferred to the vocational education and training in the technology sector is still open. The second research question considers the changes in the self-assessments of the teachers in the individual TPACK-dimensions.

Research Question 1: What are the Relationships Between the More Closely Related Knowledge Dimensions of the TPACK-Model?

In Section 7.3.2, various research results on the relationships between the TPACK-dimensions were reported. The extent to which these also apply to vocational education and training in the technology sector is still unclear. In

143

the literature (e.g. Sahin, 2011; Lin et al., 2013) it is assumed that closer related knowledge dimensions (e.g. PCK and PK) are correlating stronger with each other than more distant knowledge dimensions (e.g. PK and CK). Accordingly, the following assumptions on the interrelationships of the fields of knowledge are examined:

1) $r_{TPK/PK}$ & $r_{TPK/TK} > r_{TK/PK}$
2) $r_{TCK/TK}$ & $r_{TCK/CK} > r_{TK/CK}$
3) $r_{PCK/PK}$ & $r_{PCK/CK} > r_{PK/CK}$

Research Question 2: What Development can be Observed in the Individual TPACK-Dimensions?

According to the different focus of the teacher training courses (see Table 3), the self-assessed teacher knowledge is expected to develop in different TPACK-dimensions. The professional development in automation technology focuses on PCK. In this knowledge dimension, the highest change is expected. For further training in digitized production, changes are expected, specifically in TK, CK and TCK.

7.6 Methods

7.6.1 Random Sample

In the following, the characteristics of the participants of both professional developments are presented in tabular form (see Table 4).

Table 4: Characteristics of the participants

	Automation technology ($n = 57$)	Digitized production ($n = 40$)
Teaching subject	64% electrical engineering 29% mechanical engineering 5% information technology 2% mechatronics	44% electrical engineering, 38 % mechanical engineering 18 % automation or information technology
Gender	9% female, 91% male	3% female, 97% male
Age	M: 44 years ($min = 27$; $max = 61$)	M: 48 years ($min = 32$; $max = 66$)
Working experience	M: 12 years ($min = 0$; $max = 38$)	M: 15 years ($min = 1$; $max = 26$)

Note. Participants with a working experience of 0 years are student teachers ("Referendare")

7.6.2 Research Design

The teacher training on automation technology took place as a one-shot training with a duration of six hours. The advanced training on digitized production was carried out on two separate dates with six hours each. In both professional developments, the data collection was carried out in pre-post-test design. A questionnaire was used to collect demographic data and a self-assessment of the teachers in the seven TPACK-dimensions. After a short welcome and an introduction, the teachers completed the questionnaire for the first time. Afterward they went through further training. At the end of the event, the participants were asked to complete the questionnaire again.

Control variables were only recorded during further training in automation technology.[6] The implementation of further surveys was not desired by the external cooperation partners (state institutes). The reason for this was the short duration of the training courses. The fact that data collection is limited to the self-assessment questionnaire also applies to further training in digitized production. No control group was used in further training on digital production. In Rhineland-Palatinate, for example, there were no comparable events at the time of the development of teacher training. Since no standard for teacher training for digital production had yet been developed, the research design was conceived without a control group.

7.6.3 Measuring Instrument

For the testing of in-service teachers in a one-shot professional development, a knowledge test could lead to teachers not participating in the study. Therefore, self-assessment questionnaires were developed for both professional developments. These are based on the English instrument by Schmidt et al. (2009) and the German translation by Walker et al. (2017). Accordingly, the assessment of the effectiveness of the two teacher training courses is based on level 2 of the offer-and-use model of Lipowsky and Rzejak (2015) (see Figure 1, Section 7.2.1). The survey instruments were developed to record the seven TPACK-dimensions of the participants (see Section 7.3.1). For each knowledge area, five to nine items were identified. All items of the questionnaire were to be answered with a five-level Likert scale (1 = applies; 4 = does not apply at all; 5 = I do not know).

---

[6] The evaluation of this training is part of a dissertation project. The transmissive and constructivist beliefs of the teachers (cf. Kunter et al., 2013) were collected as control variables in addition to the self-assessment questionnaire. Furthermore, a distinction was made between experimental and control group. The examination of the results of experimental and control group as well as the beliefs of the teachers are main components of the dissertation project.

The questionnaire for automation technology was tested in a pilot phase and subsequently optimized. A high internal consistency from .81 to .94 could be achieved for the sub-scales. The questionnaire for digitized production has also a satisfying internal consistency. Cronbach's alpha coefficients range from .77 to .93 for the seven TPACK-dimensions. Example items can be found in Schäfer and Walker (2018) as well as Schäfer and Walker (in press) for the professional development in automation technology. The corresponding information for teacher training in digitized production can be found in the publication of Link et al. (2020).

7.7 Results

7.7.1 Correlations between the TPACK-Dimensions

If the correlations between TPK/PK and TPK/TK are considered, they are higher for both professional developments than for PK/TK (cf. Table 5, line 1). This is in line with the results reported in Section 7.3.2. The same applies to the results of TCK/CK and TCK/TK compared to CK/TK. Nevertheless, the correlations between TCK and CK in both training courses are significantly higher than between TCK and TK (cf. Table 5, line 2). Also, for the comparison between PCK/PK and PCK/CK with PK/CK, the results agree with those from the theoretical Section (cf. Table 5, line 3).

Table 5: Correlations according to Pearson of individual TPACK-dimensions

			&		>	
1) $r_{TPK/PK}$ & $r_{TPK/TK}$ > $r_{TK/PK}$	Automation technology	.45**/.71*	&	.39**/.33*	>	.18/.15
	Digitized production	-.13/.17	&	.31/.23	>	.04/.09
2) $r_{TCK/TK}$ & $r_{TCK/CK}$ > $r_{TK/CK}$	Automation technology	.16/.16	&	.79**/.89**	>	.07/.10
	Digitized production	.10/.42**	&	.78**/.87**	>	.30/.40*
3) $r_{PCK/PK}$ & $r_{PCK/CK}$ > $r_{PK/CK}$	Automation technology	.56**/.61**	&	.43**/.56**	>	.20/.29*
	Digitized production	.28/.26	&	.71**/.68**	>	.27/.32*

Note. The values of the pre-test are before those of the post-test after the slash.

TK = Technological knowledge; PK = Pedagogical knowledge; CK = Content knowledge; TPK = Technological-pedagogical knowledge; TCK = Technological content knowledge; PCK = Pedagogical content knowledge; TPACK = Technological-pedagogical content knowledge. Significance values: * $p < 0.05$; ** $p < 0.01$

What is noticeable, however, is that the correlation between the PK/CK is higher than between PK/TK. In addition, PK/CK is higher than CK/TK in the professional development for automation technology. In contrast, the relationship between TK/CK in digitized production is the highest relationship between more distant areas of knowledge recorded in these studies. In digitized production the focus was on expanding the CK and TK of teachers.

7.7.2 Changes in the Mean Values of TPACK-Dimensions

To assess the changes in the mean values of the TPACK-dimensions, standardized sum scores were formed. Based on these sum scores, t-tests for dependent samples were calculated for both professional developments. Table 6 contains the t-values, the number of degrees of freedom, the significance levels and the effect size Cohen's d per knowledge dimension.

Table 6: Results of the t-test (paired samples) and the effect size

TPACK-dimensions	Digitized production		
	t-value	p-value	effect size d
TK (pre-post)	$t(37) = 3.14$	.003	0.51
PK (pre-post)	$t(38) = 3.96$	.000	0.63
CK (pre-post)	$t(37) = 6.28$	.000	1.02
PCK (pre-post)	$t(37) = 6.02$	.000	0.98
TPK (pre-post)	$t(39) = 1.72$	.094	0.27
TCK (pre-post)	$t(39) = 5.70$	.000	0.90
TPACK (pre-post)	$t(38) = 6.76$	.000	1.08
TPACK-dimensions	Automation technology		
	t-value	p-value	effect size d
TK (pre-post)	$t(50) = 2.80$	.007	0.39
PK (pre-post)	$t(46) = 5.41$	.000	0.79
CK (pre-post)	$t(48) = 5.80$	.000	0.83
PCK (pre-post)	$t(47) = 12.09$	.000	1.75
TPK (pre-post)	$t(53) = 5.09$	.000	0.97
TCK (pre-post)	$t(53) = 7.11$	.000	0.69
TPACK (pre-post)	$t(43) = 5.90$	.000	0.89

Note. When interpreting the effect sizes, it must be noted that the comparison between the pre- and post-test was made without a control group.

For both professional developments, positive changes in the self-assessment of all knowledge dimensions can be recorded. As was already made clear in Section 7.4 (cf. Table 3), the focus in both training courses was on building up different dimensions of knowledge. While the professional development on digitized production focuses on the development of the CK, TK and TCK, the training on automation technology focuses on the development of the PCK.

The self-assessments in the knowledge dimensions have also changed in line with these objectives (cf. Table 6).

- **Digitized production:** Six of the seven dimensions of knowledge achieve significant changes in digitized production. The biggest changes in digitized production have taken place in TPACK (t (38) = 6.76, $p < .001$) and CK (t (37) = 6.28, $p < .001$). But the PCK and TCK also have similarly high values. Both the t-values and the effect size are highest in these four knowledge dimensions. The TPK is not significant and at the same time achieves the lowest value (t (39) = 1.72, $p = .094$). All knowledge dimensions that contain aspects of CK have large effects according to Cohen's d, e.g. $d_{CK} = 1.02$, $d_{PCK} = .98$, $d_{TCK} = .90$ and $d_{TPACK} = 1.08$.
- **Automation technology:** In the professional development of automation technology, the changes are significant in all knowledge dimensions. The largest change took place in the PCK (t (47) = 12.09, $p < .001$), the smallest in the TK (t (50) = 2.80, $p < .01$). The effect size of TK is also the smallest ($d = .39$) whereas that of PCK is the largest ($d = 1.75$).

Taking these results into account, the content focus seems to have an impact on the development of knowledge dimensions. Thus, the development of teachers' self-assessments is highest in the knowledge dimensions that were focused in the training courses.

7.8 Discussion and Limitations

The purpose of this article was to present the research results of two professional developments for vocational education teachers, which involve the topic of digitization. One of the professional developments included content and technological aspects on the topics of Industry 4.0 and digitized production. The other training focused on pedagogical content knowledge aspects of fault diagnosis in automation technology on a computer simulation. While the contents of the training courses were developed along the TPACK-model, the structural aspects were developed based on the offer-and-use model by Lipowsky (2014). The effectiveness of the teacher training was assessed via a self-assessment questionnaire of the teacher knowledge. The survey instrument is divided into the knowledge dimensions of the TPACK-model. Two research questions are to be answered with the help of the evaluation of the training courses.

Firstly, what are the relationships between the more closely related knowledge dimensions of the TPACK-model? Various studies (e.g. Schmidt et al., 2009; Sahin, 2001) examined the correlations between the TPACK-dimensions (see Table 2). Those studies were conducted exclusively in general education and with both pre- and in-service teachers. The evaluation of the developed further training courses shows similar relationships (see Table 5). The results of our study indicate that the findings of Schmidt et al. (2009) and others are also transferable for in-service teachers in the vocational education sector.

Secondly, which changes can be observed in the self-assessment of knowledge in the individual TPACK-dimensions? It is noticeable that the self-assessment is highest in the knowledge dimensions that were focused on in professional developments (see Section 7.2). Thus, according to the results of Garet et al. (2001) and Ingvarson et al. (2003, 2005), the content focus has an influence on the (self-assessed) teacher knowledge.

In the structural and methodological aspects of the teacher training and the research design, various limitations have arisen:

First of all, the evaluation of the effectiveness of professional development by self-assessment questionnaires on knowledge is regarded as a limitation. On the one hand, the recording of the teacher's knowledge by self-assessments is less meaningful than testing knowledge directly. In addition, further (non-) cognitive aspects, such as beliefs, motivational orientation, and self-regulation (Wuttke & Seifried, 2016), are not considered. On the other hand, a self-assessment of changes in knowledge of teachers cannot be used to draw conclusions about changes in the teaching behaviour (Level 3) or even the students learning (Level 4). However, when working with in-service teachers in a one-shot training, it seems to us rather inappropriate to record knowledge by expertise tests. Above all, the voluntary participation of in-service teachers in combination with the short duration of the further training were reasons for the use of a self-assessment questionnaire.

Secondly, the absence of a control group limits the validity of the research results. The results show that the greatest changes in both teacher training courses are assessed in the respective focused knowledge dimensions (cf. Table 6). Although there has been a change in self-assessment, it remains unclear whether this was actually caused by the professional development itself. This question is part of a dissertation project.

Thirdly, a larger sample would have been desirable for dividing the participants into an experimental and a control group. Therefore, the sample size is a further limitation of the studies.

The teacher training courses will be further expanded within the framework of follow-up projects. The aim is to counteract the limitations listed above. In the follow-up project (cf. DEFINE, 2019-2023), the effectiveness of the professional developments is recorded at the student level (Level 4). In addition, teacher training will be promoted more strongly in order to increase the number of participants. The aim is to divide the participants into experimental and control groups at both teacher and student level.

The developed and tested advanced training concepts offer first insights into pedagogical and technological content knowledge-oriented teacher training in the technical field. The content and technologically focused offer on Industry 4.0 and digitized production have met with great approval among the teachers involved. However, the professional development of the pedagogical content knowledge elements of fault diagnosis on automated systems has also met with a high level of acceptance. Feedback from practice shows great interest in further events. Vocational schools also welcome the participation of universities in the scientific evaluation of teacher training courses.

References

acatech (Ed.) (2016). Kompetenzentwicklungsstudie Industrie 4.0 – *Erste Ergebnisse und Schlussfolgerungen.* München.

Akiba, M., Murata, A., Howard, C. C., & Wilkinson, B. (2019). Lesson study design features for supporting collaborative teacher learning. *Teaching and Teacher Education 77*, 352-365.

Besser, M., Leiss, D., & Klieme, E. (2015). Wirkung von Lehrerfortbildungen auf die Expertise von Lehrkräften zu formativem Assessment im kompetenzorientierten Mathematikunterricht. *Zeitschrift für Entwicklungspsychologie und Pädagogische Psychologie, 47*(2), 110-122.

Bos, W., Eickelmann, B., & Gerick, J. (2014). Computer- und informationsbezogene Kompetenzen von Schülerinnen und Schülern der 8. Jahrgangsstufe in Deutschland im internationalen Vergleich. In Bos, Wilfried (Ed.), *ICILS 2013* –Computer- und informationsbezogene Kompetenzen von Schülerinnen und Schülern in der 8. Jahrgangsstufe im internationalen Vergleich (pp. 113-146). Münster, New York: Waxmann,

Brown, J. S., Collins, A., & Duguid, P. (1989). Situated Cognition and the Culture of Learning. *Educational Researcher, 18*(1), 32-42.

Darling-Hammond, L., Hyler, M. H., & Gardner, M. (2017). *Effective Teacher Professional Development.* Palo Alto, CA: Learning Policy Institute.

Desimone, L. M., Porter, A. C., Garet, M. S., Yoon, K. S., & Birman, B. F. (2002). Effects of Professional Development on Teachers Instruction: Results from a Three-year Longitudinal Study. *Educational Evaluation and Policy Analysis 24*(2), 81-112.

Dong, Y., Chai, C. S., Sang, G., Koh, J. H. L., & Tsai, C. (2015). Exploring the profiles and interplays of pre-service and in-service teachers' Technological Pedagogical Content Knowledge (TPACK) in China. In: *International Forum of Educational Technology & Society (IFETS), 18*(1), 158–169.

Garet, M. S., Porter, A. C., Desimone, L., Birmann, B. F., & Yoon, K. S. (2001). What Makes Professional Development Effective? Results from a National Sample of Teachers. *American Educational Research Journal 38*(4), 915-945.

Gronau, N. (2015). Der Einfluss von Cyber-Physical Systems auf die Gestaltung von Produktionssystemen. *Industrie 4.0 Management 31*(3), 16-20.

Hellmann, K. (2019). Kohärenz in der Lehrerbildung – Theoretische Konzeptionalisierung. In K. Hellmann, J. Kreutz, , M. Schwichow, & K. Zaki (Eds.), *Kohärenz in der Lehrerbildung* (pp. 9-30). Wiesbaden: Springer Fachmedien Wiesbaden.

Hohenstein, F., Köller, O., & Möller, J. (2015). Pädagogisches Wissen von Lehrkräften. *Zeitschrift für Erziehungswissenschaften ,18*(2), 183-186.

Ingvarson, L., Meiers, M., & Beavis, A. (2003). Evaluation the quality and impact of professional development programs. In Australian Council for Educational Research (Ed.). *Building Teacher Quality: What does the research tell us? Professional Development for Teachers and School Leaders* (pp. 28-34). Melbourne: ACER.

Ingvarson, L., Meiers, M., & Beavis, A. (2005). Factors Affecting the Impact of Professional Development Programs on Teachers' Knowledge, Practice, Student Outcomes & Efficacy. *Education Policy Analysis Archives*, 13(10), 1-28.

Jäger, R. S. & Bodensohn, R. (2007). *Die Situation der Lehrerfortbildung im Fach Mathematik aus Sicht der Lehrkräfte. Ergebnisse einer Befragung von Mathematiklehrern.* Bonn: Deutsche Telekomstiftung.

Kennedy, M. (1998*). Research Monograph No. 13: Form and Substance in Inservice Teacher Education.* National Institute for Science Education. University of Wisconsin-Madison.Washington, DC.

Kiemer, K., Gröschner, A., Pehmer, A.-K., & Seidel, T. (2015). Effects of a classroom discourse intervention on teachers' practice and students' motivation to learn mathematics and science. *Learning and Instruction, 35*, 94-103.

Kirkpatrick, D. L., & Kirkpatrick, J. D. (2006). *Evaluating Training Programs* (3rd Ed.). San Francisco: Berrett-Koehler Publishers.

Kleickmann, T., Tröbst, S., Jonen, A., Vehmeyer, J., & Möller, K. (2016). The effects of expert scaffolding in elementary science professional development on teachers' beliefs and motivations, instructional practices, and student achievement. *Journal of Educational Psychology 108*(1), 21-42.

Koh, J. H. L., Chai, C. S., & Tsai, C.-C. (2013). Examining practicing teachers' perceptions of technological pedagogical content knowledge (TPACK) pathways: a structural equation modelling approach. *Instructional Science, 41(*4), 793-809.

Köller, O. et al. (2016). Research Report 2015/2016. Kiel: IPN, Leibniz Institute for Science and Mathematics Education.

Konradt, U. (1992). *Analyse von Strategien bei der Störungsdiagnose in der flexibel automatisierten Fertigung.* Bochum: Universitätsverlag Dr. N. Brockmeyer.

Krille, C. (2019). *Fortbildungsmotivation von (wirtschaftspädagogischen) Lehrkräften.* Frankfurt am Main: Goethe-Universität Frankfurt.

Krille, C., Salge, B., Wuttke, E., & Seifried, J. (2017). Evaluation of a training programme to improve the professional error competence of prospective teachers. In Wutke (Ed.) *Professional Error Competence of Preservice Teachers* (pp. 75-97). Cham: Springer.

Krille, C. (2017). Prospective Teachers' Training Motivation and Its Influence on Training Success. In E. Wuttke, & J. Seifried (Eds.), *Professional Error Competence of Preservice Teachers.* (pp. 99-114) Cham: Springer.

Kulhavy, R.W. (1977). Feedback in Written Instruction. *Review of Educational Research, 47*(1), pp. 211-232.

Kunter, M., Klusmann, U., Baumert, J., & Richter, D. (2013). Professional competence of teachers: Effects on instructional quality and student development. *Journal of Educational Psychology 105*(3), 805-820.

Lin, T.C., Tsai, C., Chai, C. S., & Lee, M.H. (2013). Identifying Science Teachers' Perceptions of Technological Pedagogical and Content Knowledge (TPACK). *Journal of Science Education and Technology, 22*(3), 325-336.

Link, N., Schäfer, P., & Walker, F. (2020). *Development and Evaluation of a Teacher Training for Industry 4.0 based on the Technological Pedagogical Content Knowledge (TPACK) approach.* In preparation.

Lipowsky, F. (2014). Theoretische Perspektiven und empirische Befunde zur Wirksamkeit von Lehrerfort- und -weiterbildung. In E. Terhart, H. Bennewitz, & M. Rothland (Eds.), *Handbuch der Forschung zum Lehrerberuf* (pp. 511-541). Münster, New York: Waxmann.

Lipowsky, F. & Rzejak, D. (2015). Key features of effective professional development programmes for teachers. *Ricercazione*, 7(2), 27-51.

Mishra, P. & Koehler, M. J. (2006). Technological Pedagogical Content Knowledge: A Framework for Teacher Knowledge. *Teachers College Record, 108*(6), 1017-1054.

Narciss, S. (2008). Feedback strategies for interactive learning tasks. In J. Michael Spector (Ed.), *Handbook of research on educational communications and technology* (3rd Ed.). (pp. 125-143). New York: Erlbaum.

Pehmer, A.-K., Gröschner, A., & Seidel, T. (2015). How teacher professional development regarding classroom dialogue affects students' higher-order learning. *Teaching and Teacher Education, 47, 108-119.*

Penuel, W. R., Fishman, B. J., Yamaguchi, R., & Gallagher, L. P. (2007). What Makes Professional Development Effective? Strategies that Foster Curriculum Implementation. *American Educational Research Journal, 44*(4), 921-958.

Rasmussen, J. (1981). Models of Mental Strategies in Process Plant Diagnosis. In J. Rasmussen, & W. B. Rouse (Eds.), *Human Detection and Diagnosis of System Failures* (pp. 241-258). Boston: Springer US.

Rowold, J., Hochholdinger, S., & Schaper, N. (Eds.) (2008). *Evaluation und Transfersicherung betrieblicher Trainings. Modelle, Methoden und Befunde.* Göttingen: Hogrefe.

Sahin, I. (2011). Development of survey of Technological Pedagogical and Content Knowledge (TPACK). *The Turkish Online Journal of Educational Technology (TOJET), 10*(1), 97-105.

Schäfer, P. & Walker, F. (2018). Problemlösen im Bereich der Automatisierungstechnik: Entwicklung und Evaluation eines Lehrerfortbildungskonzepts. *Journal of Technical Education (JOTED), 6*(4), 67-85.

Schäfer, P. & Walker, F. (in press). Development of Professional Knowledge in Vocational Teacher Training in the Field of Automation Technology. In Universität Koblenz-Landau (Ed.) *Proceedings of the MoSAiK Conference from 20.-22.08.2019.*

Schäfer, P., Huber, C., & Walker, F. (2020). Eine Analyse des fachdidaktischen Lehrerfortbildungsangebots im Bereich der Automatisierungstechnik an berufsbildenden Schulen innerhalb von Deutschland. In BAK (Eds.), *Bildung 4.0 – Digitalisierung im Kontext der Lehrkräftebildung* (pp. 84-94). Baltmannsweiler: Schneider Verlag Hohengehren.

Schmidt, D. A., Baran, E., Thompson, A. D., Mishra, P. Koehler, M. J. & Shin, T. S. (2009). Technological Pedagogical Content Knowledge (TPACK): The Development and Validation of an Assessment Instrument for Preservice Teachers. *Journal of Research on Technology in Education, 42*(2), 123-149.

Seifried, J. & Wuttke, E. (2017). Der Einsatz von Videovignetten in der wirtschaftspädagogischen Forschung. Messung und Förderung von fachwissenschaftlichen und fachdidaktischen Kompetenzen angehender Lehrpersonen. In C. Gräsel, & K. Trempler (Eds.), *Entwicklung von Professionalität pädagogischen Personals: Interdisziplinäre Betrachtungen, Befunde und Perspektiven* (pp. 303–322). Wiesbaden: Springer Fachmedien Wiesbaden.

Shulman, L. S. (1986). Those Who Understand: Knowledge Growth in Teaching. *Educational Researcher, 15*(2), 4-14.

Spath, D., Ganschar, O., Gerlach, S., Hämmerle, M., Krause, T., & Schlund, S. (2013). *Produktionsarbeit der Zukunft – Industrie 4.0.* Stuttgart: Fraunhofer IAO.

Spöttl, G., Gorldt, C., Windelband, L., Grantz, T., & Richter, T. (2016). *bayme vbm Studie – Industrie 4.0 – Auswirkungen auf Aus- und Weiterbildung in der M+E Industrie.*

Tenberg, R. & Pittch, D. (2017). Ausbildung 4.0 oder nur 1.2? Analyse eines technisch-betrieblichen Wandels und dessen Implikationen für die technische Berufsausbildung. *Journal of Technical Education (JOTED), 5*(1), 27-46.

Thiel, F., Ophardt, D., & Piwowar, V. (2013). *Abschlussbericht des Projekts "Kompetenzen des Klassenmanagements (KODEK). Entwicklung und Evaluation eines Fortbildungsprogramms für Lehrkräfte zum Klassenmanagement."* Freie Universität Berlin.

Timperley, H., Wilson, A., Barrar, H., & Fung, I. (2007). *Teacher professional learning and development. Best Evidence Synthesis Iteration (BES).* Thorndon, Wellington: Education Counts.

Tröbst, S., Kleickmann, T., Depaepe, F., Heinze, A., & Kunter, M. (2019). Effects of instruction on pedagogical content knowledge about fractions in sixth-grade mathematics on content knowledge and pedagogical knowledge. *Unterrichtswissenschaft, 47*(1), 79-97.

Vigerske, S. (2017). *Transfer von Lehrerfortbildungsinhalten in die Praxis: Eine empirische Untersuchung zur Transferqualität und zu Einflussfaktoren.* Wiesbaden: Springer VS.

Voogt, J., Fisser, P., Roblin, P., Tondeur, J., & van Braak, J. (2013). Technological pedagogical content knowledge - a review of the literature. *Journal of Computer Assisted Learning, 29*(2), 109-121.

Walker, F., Kuhn, J., Hauck, B., Ulber, R., Hirth, M., Molz, A., Schäfer, M., & van Waveren, L. (2017). Erfassung von technologisch-pädagogischem Inhaltswissen in Lehrerfortbildungen zum naturwissenschaftlich-technischen Experimentieren unter Entwicklung und Verwendung neuer Smartphone-Experimente: Erste Ergebnisse einer Pilotierung. *Lehrerbildung auf dem Prüfstand, 10*(1), 1-18.

Walker, F., Link, N., Mohr, F., & Schäfer, P. (2018). Entwicklung eines Fortbildungskonzepts auf Basis des Ansatzes zum technologisch-pädagogischen Inhaltswissen zu Industrie 4.0. *Lernen & Lehren, 130*(2), 53-59.

Walker, F., Link, N., van Waveren, L., Hedrich, M., Geißel, B., & Nickolaus, R. (2016). Berufsfachliche Kompetenzen von Elektronikern für Automatisierungstechnik – Kompetenzdimensionen, Messverfahren und erzielte Leistungen (KOKO EA). In K. Beck, Langenberger, M., & F. Oser (Eds.), Technologiebasierte Kompetenzmessung in der beruflichen Bildung: Ergebnisse aus der BMBF-Förderinitiative ASCOT (pp. 139-170). Bielefeld: wbv.

Walker, F., Link, N., & Nickolaus, R. (2015). Berufsfachliche Kompetenzstrukturen bei Elektronikern für Automatisierungstechnik am Ende der Berufsausbildung. *Zeitschrift für Berufs- und Wirtschaftspädagogik, 111*, 222-241.

Wang, W., Schmidt-Crawford, D., & Jin, Y. (2018). Preservice Teachers' TPACK Development: A Review of Literature. *Journal of Digital Learning in Teacher Education, 34*(4), 234-258.

Watson, R. & Manning, A. (2008). Factors influencing the transformation of new teaching approaches from a programme of professional development to the classroom. *International Journal of Science Education, 30*(5), 689–709.

Wolf, W., Göbel-Lehnert, U., & Chroust, P. (1997). *Lehrerfortbildung in Hessen. Eine empirische Bestandsaufnahme aus Lehrersicht.* Fuldatal: Hessisches Institut für Lehrerfortbildung.

Wuttke, E., & Seifried, J. (2017). Modeling and Measurement of Teacher Competence: Old Wine in New Skins? Mulder, M. (Ed.), *Competence-based Vocational and Professional Education. Technical and Vocational Education and Training: Issues, Concerns, and Prospects.* (pp. 883-901). Cham: Springer International Publishing.

Yoon, K. S., Duncan, T., Lee, S. W, Scarloss, B., & Shapley, K. L. (2007). *Reviewing the evidence on how teacher professional development affects student achievement.* U.S: Department of Education, Institute of Educational Science, National Center for Education Evaluation and Regional Assistance, Regional Educational Laboratory Southwest. Washington (Issues & Answers Report, REL 2007-No. 033).

Section III:
Workplace Learning
in the Age of Digitization

8 Digital Competences in the Workplace: Theory, Terminology, and Training

Henrike Peiffer, Isabelle Schmidt, Thomas Ellwart, & Anna-Sophie Ulfert

8.1 Introduction

The use as well as the continuous development of digital systems, such as Information and Communications Technologies (ICT), has led to fundamental changes in education, at work, and in everyday life (e.g. Larson & DeChurch, 2020; Bergeri & Frey, 2016). Educators, business leaders, academics, and governmental agencies worldwide (e.g. the Organization for Economic Cooperation and Development [OECD]) regard the competent use of digital systems as a 21st century skill. Especially in the workplace, employees increasingly require competences in handling diverse digital systems. Thus, effective training is necessary to assist employees from different backgrounds (e.g. age, gender), to acquire and develop digital competences for successfully dealing with (new) digital systems.

Although digital systems have a central role in today's work environments key concepts regarding the use of digital systems are still insufficiently researched, particularly in the work context. For example, there is no consensus on what digital competences actually entail and what competences employees require to deal with digitalization.

In our first research question (RQ 1), the aim is to differentiate digital competences in the workplace and to gain an understanding of what they comprise. Research indicates that not only objective competences (performance-related competences) but also subjective competences (i.e. competence beliefs) are relevant in the workplace (Judge, Erez, & Bono, 1998; Stajkovic & Luthans, 1998). These theories can be transferred to the context of digital systems. In particular, competence beliefs, such as self-concept and self-efficacy, are strongly linked to how individuals interact with digital systems (Madhavan & Phillips, 2010). Although related, subjective competences (i.e. competence beliefs) should be differentiated from objective ones, as they independently influence performance, motivation, persistence, learning, and well-being (cf. Marsh, Martin, Yeung, & Craven, 2017). Moreover, it is important to differentiate between the different competence beliefs to avoid erroneous conclusions about their effects on employees' interaction with digital systems. In the context of using digital systems at work, two central outcomes are discussed and investigated: technostress and trust. In examining determinants, previous research has predominately focused on self-efficacy but not self-concept. RQ 2 examines how both competence beliefs are related to the user reactions, namely, technostress and trust, in digital systems.

Based on RQ 1 and 2, one may ask how employees can acquire and develop these digital competence beliefs that are important for work-related outcomes. Thus, RQ 3 explores how positive competence beliefs can be promoted through trainings and how effective trainings can be developed. To do so, we refer to previous studies that investigated and evaluated such training approaches.

8.2 Theoretical Background

8.2.1 Digitalization at work

In the context of work, the term *digitalization* has been used in an ambiguous manner to describe both (1) the process of digitizing work processes or work products (e.g. scanning documents) and (2) the consequences resulting from the introduction or integration of new technologies into existing work processes (Wolf & Strohschen, 2018; Hagberg, Sundstrom, & Egels-Zandén, 2016; Mertens & Wiener, 2018). Following these definitions, the present chapter focuses particularly on the changes that take place as a result of digitalization.

To understand the consequences of the digitalization of tasks and processes and to train employees regarding these changes, it is important to distinguish three influencing factors. According to the socio-technical system approach, these factors can be classified as the following (Baxter & Sommerville, 2011): (1) individual-related, (2) technology-related, and (3) environment-related factors.

First, individual-level factors describe the individual's objective and subjective competences, experiences, or characteristics (e.g. traits, cognitive and emotional factors), which impact how individuals adapt and react to digitalization. Second, technology-related factors include the characteristics of digital systems (e.g. level of automation) or system capabilities (e.g. reliability or feedback; Endsley, 2017). Third, environment-related factors describe a person's work environment, including task characteristics (e.g. task type) as well as team or organizational characteristics (e.g. team collaboration; Schaefer, Chen, Szalma, & Hancock, 2016).

Technology-related factors and environment-related factors are relatively easily adaptable. However, the influence of individual-level factors (i.e. one's objective competences to handle a system as well as one's perception of their own competence to do so [competence beliefs]) can hinder users from using digital systems in the first place (Goddard, Roudsari, & Wyatt, 2012). In the present chapter, we focus particularly on how competence beliefs (individual-level factors) influence the users' interaction with digital systems and how competence beliefs are related to work-related outcomes (e.g. technostress); we also explore how training that is targeted at competence beliefs may help improve the interaction with digital systems. Before focusing on the important role of digital competence beliefs, we look at the concept of digital competences as a whole.

In the following section, we will address RQ1 and will elucidate how two digital competences, namely, objective and subjective digital competences, which are often used interchangeably in the literature (see Laanpere, 2019), can be differentiated.

8.2.2 Digital Competences

8.2.2.1 Objective Digital Competences

Objective digital competences describe the ability to use different digital systems and can be evaluated by performance-based assessments. Given the growing importance of assessing digital competences in work and daily life, international organizations such as the OECD have been addressing the importance of digital competences. To describe the nature of digital competences and requirements as well as assessment instruments for measuring individual digital competences, these organizations have been developing theoretical frameworks, including large-scale studies, such as the International Computer and Information Literacy Study (ICILS) or the Programme for the International Assessment of Adult Competencies (PIAAC). When describing the nature of the competent use of digital systems, the international discourse is dominated by the terms ICT literacy, ICT skills, ICT fluency, digital literacy, and digital competence (e.g. Chinien & Boutin, 2011; Filzmoser, 2016). For example, ICT literacy[1] can be defined as "[...] using digital technology, communications tools, and/or networks to access, manage, integrate, evaluate, and create information in order to function in a knowledge society" (International ICT panel, 2002, 2).

Based on an intensive literature review (publications from 1997-2017) of studies with an ICT focus, Silva and Behar (2019) conclude that competent ICT use comprises a set of competences (e.g. knowledge, competences, abilities) and subjective variables (e.g. attitudes). Thereby, several competences form central prerequisites (i.e. reading skills, general cognitive skills, and basic computer skills). Next, to describe the factors relevant for a competent handling of digital systems, theoretical frameworks that try to describe the structure of digital competences (i.e. the dimensionality of competences) have been proposed. In particular, those frameworks aim to provide performance specifications that describe the knowledge and competences an individual should require to succeed in today's digitalized world (i.e. in both personal and professional life). Thus far, the European Commission has proposed one of the most integrative frameworks describing the digital competences that are useful for the working context. Identifying five competence areas for employees and consisting of 21 competences (see Table 1), the so-called European Digital Competence Framework for Citizens (DigComp; see Ferrari, 2013) and its second version *DigComp 2.1* (Carretero, Vourikari, & Punie , 2017) propose a multidimensional structure of digital competences. This framework is widely used in research and practice. For example, it is used by several international and national providers of commercial and non-commercial assessments and certifications (e.g. TOSA certifications; https://www.isograd.com/EN/index.php) (see for an overview: Laanpere, 2019).

---

[1] As the definitions of the different terms are highly comparable, we consistently use the term digital competences throughout this chapter.

Table 1: DigComp 2.1

Competence area	Competence
Information and data literacy	Browsing, searching and filtering data, information and digital content
	Evaluating data, information and digital content
	Managing data, information and digital content
Communication and collaboration	Interacting through digital technologies
	Sharing through digital technologies
	Engaging in citizenship through digital technologies
	Collaborating through digital technologies
	Netiquette
	Managing digital data
Digital content creation	Developing digital content
	Integrating and re-elaborating digital content
	Copyright and licenses
	Programming
Safety	Protecting devices
	Protecting personal data and privacy
	Protecting health and well-being
	Protecting the environment
Problem-solving	Solving technical problems
	Identifying needs and technological responses
	Creatively using digital technologies
	Identifying digital competence gaps

Source: Carretero, Vuorikari and Punie (2017)

In addition to performance-based assessments and certifications, there are several self-evaluation tools available on the market. Based on DigComp, these tools serve as analytical instruments for determining the digital competences of employees and organizations (see Kluzer et al., 2018). For example, since 2015, the Europass Curriculum Vitale has included an online tool (Digital Competence Check) that assists jobseekers in self-evaluating their digital competences. In the following, to describe digital competences, we use the DigComp 2.1 framework as it is widely used and applies to objective and subjective competences.

8.2.2.2 Subjective Digital Competences—The Critical Role of Digital Competence Beliefs

Unlike objective digital competences, subjective competences (i.e. competence beliefs) can be described as mental representations of one's own performance, competences, and abilities and can be summarized as „competence beliefs" (Marsh et al., 2017). They are usually assessed via self-reporting, which is performed by using questionnaires, rather than through performance-based assessments, which are used for evaluating objective competences. Although subjective competences are related to objective competences, some individuals show strong differences between objective and subjective competences by an over- or underestimation of their competences (e.g. Pajares & Miller, 1994). For this reason high-performing individuals do not always have high competence beliefs (cf. Trautwein & Möller, 2016). Both types of misjudgment of one's competences can impact subsequent behavior and performance (Goddard et al., 2012). For example, an underestimation of competences can be accompanied by negative effects for learning behavior and performance (cf. Trautwein & Möller, 2016). Unfortunately, with respect to digital competences, subjective and objective competences are often used interchangeably (see Laanpere, 2019). Presenting a clear differentiation between the concepts, the present chapter aims to clarify the differences.

As essential components in the fundamental theories of human motivation (see Craven & Marsh, 2008; Marsh et al., 2017), both objective competences and competence beliefs are highly relevant for learning, motivation, and performance. This is in line with previous research that indicates that performance trainings can benefit from targeting both competence beliefs and objective competences (e.g. Eden & Aviram 1993; O'Mara, Marsh, Craven, & Debus, 2006). This can be partly explained by findings from educational context-related research that indicate that objective and subjective competences are reciprocally related (cf. Marsh et al., 2017). Neglecting competence beliefs in trainings can therefore lead to a lower success of training.

In the context of education, the most investigated competence beliefs are self-concept and self-efficacy. While being closely related concepts, self-concept and self-efficacy differ in operational and conceptual aspects (e.g. Bong & Skaalvik, 2003, for details, see below) and can independently influence workplace performance and performance-related outcomes such as job satisfaction (Stajkovic & Luthans, 1998).

8.2.2.3 Digital Competence Beliefs—Self-Concept

Self-concepts describe the knowledge of one's own abilities and represent an individual's evaluation of their perceived *competence* (Brunner et al., 2010). Prior research has identified four sources of self-concepts. First, one of the most important sources are the comparisons within different frames of references (cf. Harter, 2012; Trautwein & Möller, 2016). Individuals compare their perceived performance with others (external frame of references) or with their performance in the past and across different performance domains (internal frame of reference (cf. Möller & Marsh, 2013). Second, individuals causally attribute previous success and failure to their own competences. Thus, competences influence self-concept as well as later performance attributions. Third, an individuals' self-concept is formed by reflected appraisals from significant others (e.g. positive evaluations of one's own skills) and, fourth, from mastery experiences (successful experiences in handling specific requirements) (Bong & Skaalvik, 2003).

Previous research indicates that self-concepts (i.e. academic self-concepts) are positively associated with learning behavior and academic achievement (e.g. Marsh et al., 2017). Further, self-concepts influence academic and professional choice behavior (Marsh & Yeung, 1997; Holling, Lüken, Preckel, & Stotz, 2000). Although most self-concept research has focused on an educational context, there are findings that underline the positive effects of self-concepts in the workplace (e.g. job competence self-perception, Harter, 2012). These findings indicate that a positive self-concept is related to a high level of job performance and job satisfaction (Judge et al., 1998).

Research concerning the more specific self-concepts related to the use of digital systems in the work context remains scarce. Empirical studies have thus far focused on the role of gender in differences in computer- specific or technology-specific self-concept. For example, Janneck, Vincent-Höper, and Ehrhardt (2012a) report gender differences in favor of male IT students. Additionally, they report significant correlations between computer self-concept and intrinsic career motivation for both genders. Similar results have been shown for employees in technical professions and have related self-concept to career success (Janneck, Vincent-Höper, & Othersen, 2012b). Thus, self-concepts might comprise an important resource for optimal career development (Wild & Möller, 2015; Beheshtifar & Rahimi-Nezhad, 2012). However, apart from the computer-/technology self-concept studies, there are no findings on self-concepts in the context of digital systems.

8.2.2.4   Digital Competence Beliefs – Self-Efficacy

Self-efficacy relates to the confidence of individuals to successfully perform a specific task (Bandura 1997; Bandura 2001). Sources of self-efficacy partly overlap with those of self-concept. First, successful actions that an individual attributes to their own abilities (mastery experience) have been called the most important source of self-efficacy (Britner & Pajares, 2006; Bandura, 1982). Second, by observing others successfully performing a task (vicarious experience), an individual's self-efficacy may be increased if the individual interprets the observed person to be similar to themselves (Bandura, 1977). Third, verbal persuasion and feedback from significant others influence the individuals' judgments of self-efficacy. For positive effects of feedback, the people giving feedback need to be viewed as competent, and the feedback must be judged as realistic (Bong & Skaalvik, 2003). Finally, physiological states (especially arousal or stress reactions) can impact the individual's own judgment of their confidence (Bandura, 1977).

In the work context, self-efficacy is more extensively researched than is self-concept. Previous research indicates that self-efficacy is related to multiple positive outcomes, such as higher job satisfaction, lower levels of work-related stress, and improved work performance (Judge et al., 1998; Stajkovic & Luthans, 1998). With respect to work digitalization, there is long-standing literature on self-efficacy research regarding the relationship of individuals with digital systems (computer, internet, and ICT/technology-related systems).

Computer-specific self-efficacy is a central construct in studies of how humans interact with computers. In their review of research on computer self-efficacy, Agarwal, Sambamurthy, and Stair (2000) show that computer self-efficacy is highly related to how individuals interact with and react to technology, especially when the technology is newly introduced into their work context.

Internet self-efficacy describes the individuals' confidence in interacting with the internet (e.g. using applications; Torkzadeh & van Dyke, 2002). Internet self-efficacy differs from computer self-efficacy in that individuals must already have basic computer skills in order to access and use the internet (Eastin & LaRose, 2000). Internet self-efficacy focuses on behaviours that individuals accomplish by applying skills (e.g. finding information online) rather than by applying component skills (e.g. using HTML code to program a website).

ICT and technology-related self-efficacy are broader and focus on general competence beliefs concerning the interaction with different types of technology (Rohatgi, Scherer, & Hatlevik, 2016). Similar to other types of technology-related self-efficacy, prior technology use in work or private life is a predictor of ICT self-efficacy (Rohatgi et al., 2016).

Studies on general (e.g. technology self-efficacy) as well as more specific measures of technology related self-efficacy (e.g. the differentiation of beginner and advanced skills, Torkzadeh & Koufteros, 1994) have consistently offered results indicating a strong relationship with work outcomes as well as the use of digital systems.

8.2.3 The Importance of Digital Competence Beliefs when Interacting with Digital Systems

8.2.3.1 Effects on User Reactions

Positive competence beliefs are related to multiple positive work outcomes, such as higher job satisfaction, lower levels of work-related stress, and improved work performance (Judge et al., 1998; Stajkovic & Luthans, 1998). Similarly, in the context of using digital systems, competence beliefs may play a central role in effectively interacting with these systems and influence central user reactions: stress and trust. These user reactions have previously been related to successfully interacting with digital systems; for example, they determine how likely an individual will rely on a digital system (e.g. Parasuraman & Manzey, 2010)

Stress as a reaction occurring when individuals use digital systems (i.e. technostress) is a well-studied concept (e.g. Ayyagari, Grover, & Purvis 2011; Tarafdar, Tu, Ragu-Nathan, & Ragu-Nathan, 2007; Weil & Rosen, 1997). Technostress is central to how users interact with digital systems (Ayyagari et al., 2011). It has been related to engagement with digital systems at the workplace and subsequent work behavior (Zylka, Christoph, Kroehne, Hartig, & Goldhammer, 2015). Positive competence beliefs can reduce technostress. For example, previous research indicates a strong relationship between the experience of technostress and the individual's level of self-efficacy (Shu, Tu, & Wang, 2011). Furthermore, Tarafdar, Pullins, and Ragu-Nathan (2015) argue that by enhancing technology-related self-efficacy, the levels of technostress can be decreased. Self-concepts relating to digital systems have not yet been related to technostress. However, research indicates a negative relationship with related affective reactions, such as the experience of anxiety (e.g. Zylka et al., 2015).

In addition to technostress, previous research has identified trust as a cognitive reaction that is central to how users interact with digital systems (e.g. Venkatesh, Morris, Davis, & Davis, 2003). Trust has been related to the engagement with digital systems at the workplace and subsequent work behaviour (Zylka et al., 2015). Concerning self-efficacy, the research findings indicate a positive relationship between technology-related self-efficacy and trust in newly introduced digital systems (Madhavan & Phillips, 2010; Goddard et al., 2012; Zhou, 2012). Again, there is a lack of research combining technology trust and self-concepts. In the field of human factors, however, the broader concept of self-confidence has been correlated to trust in digital systems (Goddard et al., 2012). To conclude, in digital systems in the work context, empirical findings emphasize the relation between self-efficacy and user reactions of technostress as well as trust. However, research with respect to self-concept in the digital context is still scant. Therefore, focusing on the individual factors of competence beliefs, RQ 2 examines how self-concept and self-efficacy are related to the user reactions of technostress and trust in digital systems.

8.2.3.2 Individual Differences in Promoting Digital Competence Beliefs

To develop effective trainings and to better adapt the training to group specific needs, it is important to explore individual differences in digital competence beliefs and related user reactions. Prior research has identified such differences, particularly with respect to gender, age and experiences with digital systems.

Gender. Research has shown consistent results concerning gender differences in competence beliefs (i.e. self-concept and self-efficacy). In the context of technology-related/computer-related self-concept, studies with IT-student samples point to gender differences favouring males (Janneck et al., 2012a). For example, Janneck, Vincent-Höper, and Oerthesen (2012) showed that technology-related self-concept was in general positively related to career success and that this relationship applied to a greater extent to females. Similar results were found in studies on computer self-efficacy (Cassidy & Eachus, 2002; Vekiri & Chronaki, 2008). Moreover, recent research has indicated that male students tend to overestimate their digital competences (their competence beliefs are higher than their objective competences), whereas female students tend to underestimate their competences (e.g. Litt 2013; Vekiri & Chronaki, 2008). As described in Section 8.1.2, low competence beliefs as well as an underestimation of one's competences can be detrimental for performance-related outcomes. This highlights a need for the implementation of interventions to promote competence beliefs within professional trainings in the work context, especially for females.

Age. Some studies point to the older employees' (>aged 55) problems in coping with the implementation of new technologies in the workplace (e.g. Gray & McGregor, 2003). This is due partly to a lack of competence beliefs (e.g. Marquié, Jourdan-Boddaert, & Huet 2002), the absence of which is accompanied by negative attitudes (e.g. Beas & Salanova, 2006) and anxieties relating to new technologies (e.g. Delgoulet, Marquié, & Escribe, 1997). For example, there is evidence that older workers have lower computer self-efficacy than do younger employees (Czaja & Sharit, 1998) and seem to underestimate themselves more in their digital competence than younger ones do (e.g. Marquié et al., 2002). Lower competence beliefs may be an obstacle for employees to learn and therefore to benefit from trainings. For example, results from a study with employees in the IT sector showed that positive attitudes (that are associated with self-concept) towards digital systems is positively related to training effects (Beas & Salanova, 2006). Thus, it is of particular importance to promote competence beliefs, especially those of older employees.

Experiences with digital systems. Results from a study with the German sample of the PIAAC study have shown that the adults' individual experiences with digital systems (i.e. the continued usage of digital systems at work and in everyday life) are positively related to digital competence (Wicht, Reder, & Lechner, 2019). Previous research with student samples indicates that the experience with digital systems (i.e. computers) and access to these systems are positively related to computer self-efficacy (Tondeur, Sinnaeve, van Houtte, & van Braak, 2011; Hatlevik, Throndson, Loi, & Gudmundsdottir, 2018) and objective digital competences (Fraillon, Ainley, Schulz, Friedman, & Gebhardt, 2014). Thus, a lack of access to digital technologies accompanied by a lower frequency of technology use can promote inequalities between employees in digital competences.

To summarize, females and older employees may have lower digital competence beliefs; therefore, there is a stronger need for support for these groups. It becomes clear that mainly competence beliefs or misjudgements (over-/underestimation) of competences are problematic for the success in handling digital systems. Thus, the promotion of competence beliefs should be an integral part of trainings at work (not just the promotion of only objective digital competences). In order to understand how competence beliefs can be improved through training approaches, particularly in situations involving the use of digital systems at work, we should take the competence beliefs' sources and consequences into account. Therefore, as RQ 3, we aim to explore what kind of support employees need in order to acquire and to develop digital competence beliefs and what training approaches might be effective.

8.3 Research Questions

In the present chapter, based on the aforementioned overview of the current literature and using our data from two random samples (see Section 8.3), we examine two central research questions (RQ). RQ 1 concerns the concept of digital competences as a whole (objective competences and subjective competence beliefs). We ask our participants to identify what comprises these competences at the workplace. Knowing the difference between objective and subjective competences and the importance of competence beliefs for work-related outcomes (see Section 8.1), second, we investigate if competence beliefs are related to the employee user reactions of technostress and trust in digital systems (RQ 2). Third, since digital competence beliefs at the workplace are important factors for the employees' outcomes, we explore what kind of support employees need in order to develop these competence beliefs and what training approaches could be effective in practice (RQ 3).

8.4 Methods: Samples and Study Designs

For the practitioner view, we collected quantitative (online survey) and qualitative data (semi-structured interviews) from two different samples. Sample 1 was assessed through an online survey in 2018 and comprises $N=11$ Human Resources Managers (HRMs) from different industries in Germany (e.g. banking, hospital, and public administration). The participants were asked to identify challenges and opportunities they see with the introduction of digital systems, that is, information and communication technology (ICT). Three independent coders assigned the participants' statements to the five competence areas of DigComp 2.1. With no differences between raters, the inter-rater reliability was $r = 1.00$, calculated with Krippendorf's alpha (Krippendorf, 2013) In the assignments, there were no statements that could not be assigned to a competence area. Data from Sample 1 were used to answer RQ 1.

Sample 2 was collected within an online survey conducted with German employees from different industries in 2019. The participants were acquired via social networks (e.g. Xing, Facebook) and via the mail distributor of one southwestern German university. The total number of participants (64.9% female) was $N=37$ (85.2% were under 49 years old, and 14.8% were above 50 years). The participants were asked to think about their workplace and then answer questions about the consequences of the introduction of digital systems in the context of digitalization at their workplace. In detail, participants answered self-concept questions (5 items, Cronbach's alpha (α = .97, e.g. "I am good at using digital systems"; Schauffel, 2019) and SE questions (20 items, α =.70 e.g. „I am very unsure about my abilities in dealing with computers"; Spannagel & Bescherer, 2009). In addition to the relevant constructs, the following variables were also collected: technostress (3 items, α =.95; Ayyagari et al., 2011) and trust in digital systems (3 items, α = .92; Hertel et al., 2019). Data from Sample 2 were used to answer RQ 2.

8.5 Results

8.5.1 Digital Competences

In practice as in the literature, there is an increasing interest in which competences employees must supply in the course of digitalization. According to RQ 1, the different sample 1 (N=11) statements concerning competence requirements for successfully dealing with different applications and tasks in digital work environments were collected and compared with the competence areas mentioned in DigComp 2.1 (Carretero et al., 2017). The percentage of responses in the different competence areas is presented in Figure 1.

Information and data literacy. HRMs particularly stated that employees must be able to access local or networked data storage. In line with DigComp 2.1, employees need the competence to search for data and information as well as to analyse and compare information and digital contents. Further, employees must have the competence to manage, store, and retrieve data, information, and content in different digital environments (e.g. personnel management systems), although practitioners emphasized this skill less often. The competence to critically evaluate data and sources of data was not explicitly mentioned.

Communication and collaboration. Among the practitioners, the second competence area appears to be of particular importance. For example, as a necessary competence, practitioners listed the employees' ability to use internal communication platforms, the intranet, or the share-point platforms of work groups. Employees should also be able to work with different digital communication systems, such as email programs or group drives. According to DigComp 2.1, employees should be able to use a variety of digital systems for collaborative processes, as well as for co-construction and the co-creation of data, resources, and knowledge. Additionally, some of the HRMs mentioned that in their organizations, business meetings are often coordinated via digital calendars (e.g. Microsoft Outlook) and that important documents are foremost sent digitally instead of analogously (competence to share data, information and digital content). However, as formulated in DigComp 2.1, the competences cultural and generational diversity awareness or the ability to protect one's own reputation were not listed by the HRMs. The digital competence to participate in society seems to be less relevant in practice.

Digital content creation. The third competence area is associated in practice with only few competences. Most of the practitioners mentioned that employees should have the competence to complete business results by a fixed time or to generate digital graphs and diagrams. Further, in specific organizations such as hospitals, it may be necessary to be able to create and manage digital personnel files and to develop digital shift plans. However, practitioners did not report an employee relevance for all digital competences, for example, the ability to edit digital content in different formats or as described in DigComp 2.1, the ability to understand how copyright and licenses apply to data and digital information.

Safety. The fourth competence area, which comprises the employees' competences to protect personal data and privacy, to know about safety and security measures, or to be able to protect oneself and others from possible dangers in digital environments, was only mentioned indirectly as risk management, information security, or in the context of protected accesses for teleworkers or home workers (VPN tunnel). This is surprising in view of the increasing importance of data protection regulations in society in the face of increasing digital security threats (see the EU General Data Protection Regulation 2016/679 European Union 2016).

Problem solving. The fifth competence area mentioned by practitioners was problem solving. Some noted that for all digital systems, employees must receive trainings related to the competence needed to understand where one's own digital competence needs to be improved. In DigComp 2.1., the area of problem solving combines two aspects: solving content problems with the help of digital systems and solving technical problems that occur in the use of digital systems themselves. Concerning the latter, practitioners tend to see these competences as being the responsibility of IT specialists.

To summarize, regarding RQ 1, HRMs agree that many of the digital competences mentioned in the DigComp 2.1 are relevant in the workplace. Especially in the area of communication (internal and external) as well as in the area of storage and processing of data, the practitioners report that to face the challenges of digitalization, employees need a wide range of skills mentioned in DigComp 2.1. In contrast, practitioners hardly ever mention the competence area of safety. However, the area of problem solving was only narrowly mentioned (i.e. technical problems whose solution is not the responsibility of the individual employee) and actually seems of less importance in practice.

Figure 1: Percentage of responses categorized by the competence areas mentioned in the DigComp 2.1

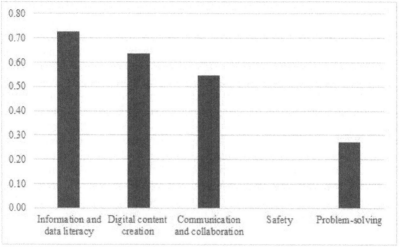

Notes. Sample 2, $N=11$; multiple answers possible.

8.5.2 The Importance of Digital Competence Beliefs regarding User Reactions

Corresponding to theoretical findings (see Section 8.1.3), in RQ 2, we examined the importance of competence beliefs amongst practitioners. Self-concept and self-efficacy were investigated in relation to user reactions, specifically technostress and trust in digital systems (Sample 2; $N=37$), Concerning technostress, our results revealed that employees who believe that they are able to handle digital systems at work (self-concept) and who believe they will successfully master challenges with digital systems (self-efficacy) experience less technostress (self-concept: $r = -.55$, $p < .001$; self-efficacy; $r = -.81$, $p < .001$). Likewise, with respect to the trust in digital systems, we found self-concept ($r = .54$, $p < .001$) and self-efficacy ($r = .40$, $p < .01$) to be positively correlated. This means that employees who feel that they are able to deal with digital systems and who experience confidence in handling digital systems also trust these systems more than do employees with lower self-concept or self-efficacy.

Both self-concept and self-efficacy are related to technostress and trust in digital systems. Interestingly, self-efficacy has a stronger relation with technostress than does self-concept, whereas with respect to trust in digital systems, the findings are the reverse. This result might be explained by the conceptual differences between the two constructs: self-concept is past-oriented, and self-efficacy is future-oriented (see Section 8.1.2). Future-orientation implies that self-efficacy is an individuals' belief that upcoming challenging situations and environmental demands (stressors) can be managed, and findings show the positive effect of a high self-efficacy on stress in diverse contexts (Bandura 1977, 1997). The higher relation between self-concept and trust may be explained by the fact that self-concept is domain-specific, and trust in digital systems is a domain (includes various digital systems). Self-efficacy however refers primarily to trust in the handling of concrete digital tasks (Agarwal et al., 2000). In sum, the findings underscore the need in future studies to consider self-concept and self-efficacy separately when investigating the reactions of users interacting with digital systems. Furthermore, if the importance of both competence beliefs for user reactions is significant, the question arises as to how these can be promoted practically.

8.5.3 Effective Trainings to Foster the Self-Concept and Self-Efficacy of Employees using Digital Systems

In the following, to answer RQ 3, we present selected results from previous research that aim to promote competence beliefs in different performance-related contexts in general and specifically concerning the use of digital systems.

Promoting competence beliefs through training has a long tradition in learning contexts, especially in education (e.g. increasing student's grades, Wilson & Linville, 1985; see also O'Mara et al., 2006; van Dinther, Dochy, & Segers, 2011), but also in the workplace in general (e.g. supporting job applicants; Latham & Budworth, 2006; Shantz & Latham, 2012). However, trainings specifically designed to promote digital competence beliefs are scarce. There is some evidence that suggests that effective trainings of digital competence beliefs should target self-concept and self-efficacy indirectly by targeting their related constructs (e.g. through skill-building interventions; Bieschke, Fouad, Collins, & Halonen, 2004) or enhance both competence beliefs by directly affecting their major sources (e.g. frames of reference and mastery experiences). This is in line with the results from studies that evaluated trainings to promote competence beliefs in more general contexts (i.e. in education and at work). We assume that effective elements of trainings in more general contexts are also valid for specific contexts such as dealing with digital systems. Furthermore, studies in educational contexts showed that interventions that aim to improve performance by promoting skills as well as competence beliefs, prove to be among the most effective interventions (see O'Mara et al., 2006). This may also apply for digital competences. The success of such interventions may be explained by the fact that due to the increased (digital or general) competences, employees have the chance to accumulate mastery experiences for example in interacting with digital systems. This engagement in turn increases their self-concept and self-efficacy (Bong & Skaalvik, 2003). However, it is important to make sure that, employees not only collect mastery experiences in handling digital systems but also attribute their successes internally (i.e. to their own competences or exercise) and attribute failure to a lack of exercise instead of a lack of competence (Dresel & Ziegler, 2006). Such an attribution style is beneficial for high but realistic competence beliefs and is, for example, the aim of the *attribution-persona-toolkit* (Niels, 2019) developed to foster computer-specific self-concept.

Another important aspect that is particularly true for handling digital systems, is the expected benefit that individuals attribute to the use of such systems, which again results in the acceptance of digital systems. As described in classical models of technology acceptance (e.g. Holden & Karsh, 2010; Venkatesh et al., 2003), if a digital system provides an employee with benefit in their work processes (e.g. time saving), this leads to a positive evaluation of the digital system and thus a higher probability of using the system. The regular use of the digital system can then again lead to mastery experiences that increase self-concept and self-efficacy. The satisfaction with digital systems can be promoted in particular by the employees' participation. We know from organizational change research that the possibility to participate (e.g. in workshops) can positively influence employees' behavioural intentions and subsequent behavior with regard to the use of changed or new digital applications and technologies (e.g. Venkatesh et al., 2003).

In sum, in today's world of the digitalized workplace, employees' competence beliefs, such as self-concept and self-efficacy, are just as important as objective competences and should be equally be encouraged by training. High but realistic competence beliefs are an important resource to cope with changing and increasingly intelligent digital systems and should therefore be an incremental component of training in the work context.

8.6 Limitations and Implications

So far, there has been a lack of research on digital competences (especially research regarding digital competence beliefs) in the work context. Our findings provide initial indications and do not represent comprehensive research. Consequently, there are some limitations, which will be briefly mentioned. To begin, our findings have limitations based on the two samples. We only collected data from German employees and HRM's. This makes it difficult to generalize the statements to other countries and work environments. Thus, future research should investigate digital competence beliefs in larger samples (e.g. employees, HRMs) in various regions and countries (e.g. across Europe) and in diverse work environments (e.g. IT industry). Concerning different English-speaking countries, the term digitalization is handled differently (Mertens & Wiener, 2018); thus, an adjustment of single items of the measurements of digital competence beliefs might be necessary.

Furthermore, the cross-sectionality of the data from Sample 2 does not allow a statement about the causal relationships between competence beliefs and technostress or trust in digital systems. Nevertheless, the findings provide initial indications of theory-compliant relationships between competence beliefs and outcomes. In future studies, the relation between competence beliefs and work-related outcomes, such as performance, satisfaction and health, should also be examined by using longitudinal designs, as done in the educational context (Bandura, 1997; Jerusalem & Schwarzer, 1992). Note that the educational and work context have several common aspects, for example, the transfer of knowledge and the possibility to experience successes and disappointments that alter one's competence beliefs. Consequently, it is plausible to generalize from the educational to the work context, the findings on the relation between competence beliefs and other factors, for example, health variables.

Other limitations are the scales used to assess the competence beliefs. The measurement of self-concept is based on a newly developed scale that has been validated in one study, and further validation studies are still ongoing (see Schauffel, 2019). Nevertheless, it should be noted that an initial development of the self-concept scale will make an important contribution to future research in the field of digital competences.

8.7 Conclusion

Based on the literature and aligned with the results from our three samples, it can be stated that employees require various digital competences in order to cope with work-related changes in the course of digitalization (e.g. OECD, 2016). This competence acquisition need makes trainings and life-long learning more important than ever (Curtarelli, Gualtieri, Jannati, & Donlevy, 2017). In many cases, however, objective and subjective competences do not coincide (e.g. Trautwein & Möller, 2016), and the fact that individuals differ in support needs has implications for trainings. As competence beliefs are associated with desirable outcomes (e.g. less technostress, Ayyagari et al., 2011; high learning and achievement motivation, Guay, Marsh, & Boivin, 2010) and as competence beliefs are malleable constructs, intervention strategies are useful to improve competence beliefs in the work contexts. To promote competence beliefs, concrete training approaches, for example, the creation of positive mastery experiences in dealing with digital systems or the provision of targeted feedback from superiors in the testing of new digital systems (van Dinther et al., 2011; Schunk, 1991), should be implemented and analysed.

References

Agarwal, R., Sambamurthy, V., & Stair, R. M. (2000). Research Report: The Evolving Relationship Between General and Specific Computer Self-Efficacy—An Empirical Assessment. *Information Systems Research, 11*(4), 418-430.

Ayyagari, R., Grover, V., & Purvis, R. L. (2011). Technostress: Technical Antecedents and Implications. *MIS Quarterly, 35*(4), 831-858.

Bandura, A. (2001). Social Cognitive Theory: An Agentic Perspective. *Annual Review of Psychology, 52*, 1-26.

Bandura, A. (1977). Self-efficacy: Toward a Unifying Theory of Behavioral Change. *Psychological Review, 84*(2), 191-215.

Bandura, A. (1982). Self-efficacy Mechanism in Human Agency. *American Psychologist, 37*(2), 122-147.

Bandura, A. (1997). *Self-efficacy: The Exercise of Control.* New York: W.H. Freeman and Company.

Baxter, G. & Sommerville, I. (2011). Socio-technical Systems: From Design Methods to Systems Engineering. *Interacting with Computers, 23*(1), 4-17.

Beas, M. I. & Salanova, M. (2006). Self-efficacy Beliefs, Computer Training and Psychological Well-being among Information and Communication Technology Workers. *Computers in Human Behavior, (22)*6, 1043-1058.

Beheshtifar, M. & Rahimi-Nezhad, Z. (2012). Role of Self-Concept in Organizations. *European Journal of Economics, Finance and Administrative Sciences 2012, Issue 44*, 159-164.

Berger, T. & Frey, C. B. (2016). *Structural Transformation in the OECD: Digitalisation, Deindustrialisation and the Future of Work.* OECD Social, Employment and Migration Working Papers, No. 193. Retrieved from https://www.oecd-ilibrary.org/social-issues-migration-health/structural-transformation-in-the-oecd_5jlr068802f7-en

Bieschke, K. J., Fouad, N. A., Collins, F. L., & Halonen, J. S. (2004). The Scientifically-minded Psychologist: Science as a Core Competency. *Journal of Clinical Psychology, 60*(7), 713–723.

Bong, M., & Skaalvik, E. M. (2003). Academic Self-Concept and Self-Efficacy: How Different Are They Really? *Educational Psychology Review, 15*, 1-40.

Britner, S. L. & Pajares, F. (2006). Sources of Science Self-efficacy Beliefs of Middle School Students. *Journal of Research in Science Teaching, 43*(5), 485-499.

Brunner, M., Keller, U., Dierendonck, C., Reichert, M., Ugen, S., Fischbach, A., & Martin, R. (2010). The Structure of Academic Self-concepts Revisited: The Nested Marsh/Shavelson Model. *Journal of Educational Psychology, 102*(4), 964-981.

Carretero, S., Vuorikari, R., & Punie, Y. (2017). *DigComp 2.1: The Digital Competence Framework for Citizens. With Eight Proficiency Levels and Examples of Use*. Luxembourg: Publications Office of the European Union.

Cassidy, S. & Eachus, P. (2002). Developing the Computer User Self-Efficacy (Cuse) Scale: Investigating the Relationship between Computer Self-Efficacy, Gender and Experience with Computers. *Journal of Educational Computing Research, 26*(2), 133-153.

Chinien, C. & Boutin, F. (2011). *Defining Essential Digital Skills in the Canadian Workplace. Final Report.* Retrieved from https://en.copian.ca/library/research/digi_es_can_workplace/digi_es_can_workplace.pdf (2020-05-02).

Chou, H. (2001). Effects of Training Method and Computer Anxiety on Learning Performance and Self-efficacy. *Computers in Human Behavior, 17*(1), 51-69.

Craven, R. G. & Marsh, H. W. (2008). The centrality of self-concept construct for psychological wellbeing and unlocking human potential: Implications for child and educational psychologists. *Educational and Child Psychology, 25*(2), 104-118.

Curtarelli, M., Gualtieri, V., Jannati, M. S., & Donlevy, V. (2017). *ICT for Work: Digital Skills in the Workplace. European Commission.* Retrieved from https://ec.europa.eu/digital-single-market/en/news/ict-work-digital-skills-workplace/ (2020-06-02).

Czaja, S. J. & Sharit, J. (1998). Age differences in Attitudes Toward Computers. *The Journals of Gerontology Series B Psychological Sciences and Social Sciences, 53*(5), 329-340.

Delgoulet, C., Marquié, J. C., & Escribe, C. (1997). Training Older Workers: Relationships between Age, Other Trainee Characteristics, and Learning Anxiety. In A. Kilbom (Ed.), *Work after 45? Proceedings from a Scientific Conference, Held in Stockholm 22-25 September 1996* (pp. 70-78). Solna: Arbetslivsinstitutet.

Dresel, M. & Ziegler, A. (2006). Langfristige Förderung von Fähigkeitsselbstkonzept und impliziter Fähigkeitstheorie durch computerbasiertes attributionales Feedback. *Zeitschrift für Pädagogische Psychologie, 20,* 49-63.

Eastin, M. S. & LaRose, R. (2000). Internet Self-Efficacy and the Psychology of the Digital Divide. *Journal of Computer-Mediated Communication, 6*(1).

Eden, D. & Aviram, A. (1993). Self-efficacy Training to Speed Reemployment: Helping People to Help Themselves. *Journal of Applied Psychology, 78*(3), 352-360.

Endsley, M. R. (2017). From Here to Autonomy. *Human Factors, 59*(1), 5-27.

European Union (2016). *Regulation (EU) 2016/679 of the European Parliament and of the Council of 27 April 2016 on the protection of natural persons with regard to the processing of personal data and on the free movement of such data, and repealing Directive 95/46/EC* (General Data Protection Regulation).

Ferrari, A. (2013). *DIGCOMP: A framework for developing and understanding digital competence in Europe. EUR, Scientific and technical research series, Vol. 26035.* Luxembourg: Publications Office of the European Union.

**Filzmoser, G. (2016). *Wie wollen wir es nennen: Computerkompetenz, Medienkompetenz oder digitale Kompetenz.* Retrieved from http://magazin. vhs.or.at/magazin/2016-2/259-november-2016/schwerpunkt-digitale-kompetenzen-medienkompetenz/wie-wollen-wir-es-nennen-computerkompetenz-medienkompetenz-oder-digitale-kompetenz/ (2020-02-05).

Fraillon, J., Ainley, J., Schulz, W., Friedman, T., & Gebhardt, E. (2014). *Preparing for Life in a Digital Age.* Cham: Springer International Publishing.

Gegenfurtner, A., Quesada-Pallarès, C., & Knogler, M. (2014). Digital Simulation-based Training: A Meta-analysis. *British Journal of Educational Technology, 45*(6), 1097-1114.

Goddard, K., Roudsari, A., & Wyatt, J. C. (2012). Automation Bias: A Systematic Review of Frequency, Effect Mediators, and Mitigators. *Journal of the American Medical Informatics Association JAMIA, 19*(1), 121-127.

Gray, L. & McGregor, J. (2003). Human Resource Development and Older Workers: Stereotypes in New Zealand. *Asia Pacific Journal of Human Resources, 41*(3), 338-353.

Guay, F., Marsh, H. W., & Boivin, M. (2003). Academic Self-concept and Academic Achievement: Developmental Perspectives on their Causal Ordering. *Journal of Educational Psychology, 95*(1), 124-136.

Hagberg, J., Sundstrom, M., & Egels-Zandén, N. (2016). The Digitalization of Retailing: An Exploratory Framework. *International Journal of Retail & Distribution Management, 44*(7), 694-712.

Harter, S. (2012). *The Construction of the Self; Developmental and Sociocultural Foundations, Second Edition.* New York: Guilford Press.

Hatlevik, O. E., Throndsen, I., Loi, M., & Gudmundsdottir, G. B. (2018). Students' ICT Self-Efficacy and Computer and Information Literacy: Determinants and Relationships. *Computers & Education, 118*, 107-119.

Hertel, G., Meeßen, S. M., Riehle, D. M., Thielsch, M. T., Nohe, C., & Becker, J. (2019). Directed Forgetting in Organisations: The Positive Effects of Decision Support Systems on Mental Resources and Well-being. *Ergonomics, 62*(5), 597-611.

Holden, R. J. & Karsh, B. (2010). The Technology Acceptance Model: Its Past and Its Future in Health Care. *Journal of Biomedical Informatics, 43*(1), 159172.

Holling, H., Lüken, K. H., Preckel, F., & Stotz, M. (2000). *Berufliche Entscheidungsfindung. Bestandsaufnahme, Evaluation und Neuentwicklung computergestützter Verfahren zur Selbsteinschätzung. Beiträge zur Arbeitsmarkt- und Berufsforschung, Band 236.* Nürnberg: Zentralamt der Bundesanst. für Arbeit.

International ICT Panel (2002). Digital Transformation: A Framework for ICT Literacy. *A Report of the International ICT Literacy Panel.* Princeton, New Jersey.

Janneck, M., Vincent-Höper, S., & Ehrhardt, J. (2012a). Das Computerbezogene Selbstkonzept: Eine Gender-sensitive Studie. In H. Reiterer, & O. Deussen, (Eds.), *Mensch & Computer 2012 – Workshopband (*pp. 243-252*).* München: Oldenbourg Verlag.

Janneck, M., Vincent-Höper, S., & Othersen, I. (2012b). Entwicklung und Validierung eines Fragebogens zum Technikbezogenen Selbstkonzept (TSK): Eine gendersensitive Studie. *Gruppendynamik und Organisationsberatung, 43*(3), 289-310.

Jerusalem, M. & Schwarzer, R. (1992). Self-efficacy as a resource factor in stress appraisal processes. In R. Schwarzer (Ed.), *Self-efficacy: Thought control of action (*pp.195-217*).* London, New York: Routledge.

Judge, T. A., Erez, A., & Bono, J. E. (1998). The Power of Being Positive: The Relation Between Positive Self-Concept and Job Performance. *Human Performance, 11*(2-3), 167-187.

Kluzer, S., Priego, L. P., Gomez, S. C., Punie, Y., Vuorikari, R., Cabrera, M. G., & O'Keeffe, W. (2018). *DigComp into Action: Get Inspired, Make it Happen. A User Guide to the European Digital Competence Framework. EUR, Scientific and Technical Research Series, Vol. 29115.* Luxembourg: Publications Office of the European Union.

Krippendorff, K. (2013). *Content analysis: An introduction to its methodology* (3rd Ed.). Thousand Oaks, CA: Sage.

Laanpere, M. (2019). Recommendations on Assessment Tools for Monitoring Digital Literacy within UNESCO's Digital Literacy Global Framework. *Information Paper No. 56.* Montreal, Canada.

Larson, L. & DeChurch, L. A. (2020). Leading Teams in the Digital Age: Four Perspectives on Technology and What They Mean for Leading Teams. *The Leadership Quarterly, 31*(1), 101377.

Latham, G. P. & Budworth, M. (2006). The Effect of Training in Verbal Self-guidance on the Self-efficacy and Performance of Native North Americans in the Selection Interview. *Journal of Vocational Behavior, 68*(3), 516-523.

Litt, E. (2013). Measuring Users' Internet Skills: A Review of Past Assessments and a Look Toward the Future. *New Media & Society, 15*(4), 612-630.

Madhavan, P. & Phillips, R. R. (2010). Effects of Computer Self-Efficacy and System Reliability on User Interaction with Decision Support Systems. *Computers in Human Behavior, 26*(2), 199-204.

Marquié, J.-C., Jourdan-Boddaert, L., & Huet, N. (2002). Do Older Adults Underestimate their Actual Computer Knowledge? *Behaviour & Information Technology, 21*(4), 273–280.

Marsh, H. W., Martin, A. J., Yeung, A. S., & Craven, R. G. (2017). Competence Self-perceptions. In A. J. Elliot, C. S. Dweck, & D. S. Yeager Eds.), *Handbook of Competence and Motivation: Theory and Application* (2nd ed.) (pp. 85-115). New York: The Guilford Press.

Marsh, H. W. & Yeung, A. S. (1997). Coursework Selection: Relations to Academic Self-Concept and Achievement. *American Educational Research Journal, 34*(4), 691-720.

Mertens, P. & Wiener, M. (2018). Riding the Digitalization Wave: Toward a Sustainable Nomenclature in Wirtschaftsinformatik – A Comment on Riedl et al. (2017). *Business & Information Systems Engineering, 60*(4), 367-372.

Möller, J. & Marsh, H. W. (2013). Dimensional Comparison Theory. *Psychological Review, 120*(3), 544–560.

Niels, A. (2019). *Attributionen in der Mensch-Computer-Interaktion: Einfluss auf die Bewertung und Gestaltung interaktiver Produkte.* Wiesbaden: Springer Fachmedien Wiesbaden.

OECD (2016). *Skills Matter: Further Results from the Survey of Adult Skills. OECD Skills Studies.* Paris: OECD Publishing.

O'Mara, A. J., Marsh, H. W., Craven, R. G., & Debus, R. L. (2006). Do Self-Concept Interventions Make a Difference? A Synergistic Blend of Construct Validation and Meta-Analysis. *Educational Psychologist, 41*(3), 181-206.

Pajares, F. & Miller, M. D. (1994). Role of Self-efficacy and Self-concept Beliefs in Mathematical Problem Solving: A Path Analysis. *Journal of Educational Psychology, 86*(2), 193-203.

Parasuraman, R. & Manzey, D. H. (2010): Complacency and bias in human use of automation: An attentional integration. *Human factors, 52*(3), 381-410.

Rohatgi, A., Scherer, R., & Hatlevik, O. E. (2016). The Role of ICT Self-efficacy for Students' ICT Use and Their Achievement in a Computer and Information Literacy Test. *Computers & Education, 102*, 103-116.

Schaefer, K. E., Chen, J. Y. C., Szalma, J. L., & Hancock, P. A. (2016). A Meta-Analysis of Factors Influencing the Development of Trust in Automation: Implications for Understanding Autonomy in Future Systems. *Human Factors, 58*(3), 377-400.

Schauffel, N. (2019). *Digitales Selbstkonzept im Arbeitskontext: Definition, Struktur, Messung sowie Förderung im Zuge der Personalentwicklung.* (Master's Thesis). Universität Trier (unpublished).

Schunk, D. H. (1991). Self-efficacy and academic motivation. *Educational psychologist, 26*(3-4), 207-231.

Shantz, A. & Latham, G. P. (2012). Transfer of Training: Written Self-guidance to Increase Self-efficacy and Interviewing Performance of Job Seekers. *Human Resource Management, 51*(5), 733-746.

Shu, Q., Tu, Q., & Wang, K. (2011). The Impact of Computer Self-Efficacy and Technology Dependence on Computer-Related Technostress: A Social Cognitive Theory Perspective. *International Journal of Human-Computer Interaction, 27* (10), 923-939.

Da Silva, K. K. A. & Behar, P. A. (2019). Competencias Digitais na Educação: Uma Discussão Acerca do Conceito. *Educação em Revista, 35.*

Spannagel, C. & Bescherer, C. (2009). Computerbezogene Selbstwirksamkeitserwartung in Lehrveranstaltungen mit Computernutzung. *Notes on Educational Informatics – Section A: Concepts and Techniques, 5*(1), 23-43.

Stajkovic, A. D. & Luthans, F. (1998). Self-efficacy and Work-related Performance: A Meta-analysis. *Psychological Bulletin, 124*(2), 240-261.

Tarafdar, M., Pullins, E. B., & Ragu-Nathan, T. S. (2015). Technostress: Negative Effect on Performance and Possible Mitigations. *Information Systems Journal, 25*(2), 103-132.

Tarafdar, M., Tu, Q., Ragu-Nathan, B. S., & Ragu-Nathan, T. S. (2007). The impact of technostress on role stress and productivity. *Journal of management information systems, 24*(1), 301-328.

Tondeur, J., Sinnaeve, I., van Houtte, M., & van Braak, J. (2011). ICT as Cultural Capital: The Relationship between Socioeconomic Status and the Computer-use Profile of Young People. *New Media & Society, 13*(1), 151-168.

Torkzadeh, G. & van Dyke, T. P. (2002). Effects of Training on Internet Self-efficacy and Computer User Attitudes. *Computers in Human Behavior, 18*(5), 479-494.

Torkzadeh, G. & Koufteros, X. (1994). Factorial validity of a computer self-efficacy scale and the impact of computer training. *Educational and psychological measurement, 54*(3), 813-821.

Trautwein, U. & Möller, J. (2016). Self-Concept: Determinants and Consequences of Academic Self-Concept in School Contexts. In A. A. Lipnevich, F. Preckel, & R. D. Roberts (Eds.), *Psychosocial Skills and School Systems in the 21st Century: Theory, Research, and Practice. The Springer Series on Human Exceptionality* (pp. 187-214). Cham: Springer International Publishing.

van Dinther, M., Dochy, F., & Segers, M. (2011). Factors Affecting Students' Self-efficacy in Higher Education. *Educational Research Review, 6*(2), 95-108.

Vekiri, I. & Chronaki, A. (2008). Gender Issues in Technology Use: Perceived Social Support, Computer Self-efficacy and Value Beliefs, and Computer Use Beyond School. *Computers & Education, 51*(3), 1392-1404.

Venkatesh, V., Morris, M. G., Davis, G. B., & Davis, F. D. (2003). User Acceptance of Information Technology: Toward a Unified View. *MIS Quarterly, 27*(3), 425-478.

Weil, M. M. & Rosen, L. D. (1997). *Technostress: Coping with technology@ work@ home@ play* (pp. 29-32). New York: Wiley.

Wicht, A., Reder, S., & Lechner, C. (Eds.) (2019). *Sources of Individual Differences in Adults' Digital Skills.* Proceedings of the Weizenbaum Conference 2019.

Wild, E. & Möller, J. (Eds.) (2015). Pädagogische Psychologie (2nd Ed.). Springer-Lehrbuch. Berlin, Heidelberg: Springer.

Wilson, T. D. & Linville, P. W. (1985). Improving the Performance of College Freshmen with Attributional Techniques. *Journal of Personality and Social Psychology, 49*(1), 287-293.

Wolf, T. & Strohschen, J.H. (2018). Digitalisierung: Definition und Reife. *Informatik-Spektrum, 41*(1), 56-64.

Zhou, T. (2012). Understanding Users' Initial Trust in Mobile Banking: An Elaboration Likelihood Perspective. *Computers in Human Behavior, 28*(4), 1518-1525.

Zylka, J., Christoph, G., Kroehne, U., Hartig, J., & Goldhammer, F. (2015). Moving Beyond Cognitive Elements of ICT Literacy: First Evidence on the Structure of ICT Engagement. *Computers in Human Behavior, 53*, 149-160.

9 Microlearning via Smartphones in VET for Professional Drivers: The Case of Securing Cargo for International Transport

Andreas Korbach & Helmut M. Niegemann

9.1 Why Microlearning in VET?

Truck drivers and other employees in the domain of international transport need periodical training in securing cargo. The topic is especially important as many truck accidents are the result of faulty loading practices. A main problem in this area is the distribution of the training, as it is difficult to foresee when groups of professional drivers will be at a specific location. Hence, mobile learning approaches are suitable for these addressees, as they need a flexible solution with regard to mobility and time constraints. One approach that meets these requirements is microlearning with microcontent. Microlearning refers to technology-based learning, mostly using portable devices (smartphones, tablets) and rather short learning units including videos, text and pictures, which make up microcontent (Hug, 2010). The goal of the project LaSiDig (Ladungssicherung im intermodalen grenzüberschreitenden Transport von Gütern: cargo securing for intermodal international transport of goods) is to develop a mobile application for microlearning with microcontent for professional truck drivers. The primary learning objective of the application is learning to properly secure cargo. Beyond learning with the microcontent developed by trainers, the drivers should additionally produce case-based microcontent on their own, using photos and videos of their own solutions to loading problems. Users can upload this case-based microcontent to the application to share it with the community of app users in order to foster collaborative knowledge construction through discussion about the solutions to loading problems. As different media competencies are required not only for the use of the app with mobile devices, but also for the production of such microcontent, the assessment and fostering of media competence is also an important part of the project. As partners of the project LaSiDig we are going to develop microcontent for the second learning objective, which is media competence, and we explore the use of microcontent accessible via a smartphone application for microlearning activities of professional drivers. To start with the development of microcontent the first question to be posed is about the definition of microcon-

tent and microlearning, followed by an analysis of appropriate design principles for self-paced learning with multimedia microcontent and considerations
for microlearning based on the DO ID model (Niegemann, 2019).

9.2 The very idea of microlearning in VET

9.2.1 A definition of microlearning?

New media offer a wide range of short contents and chunks of information.
Blogposts, tweets, podcasts, short messages and all kind of information chunks
that can be shared with social media seem to carry information in a format that
is highly accepted by the consumer. One reason for high acceptance of these
information chunks might be the lifestyle fit and the use of short contents for
daily tasks or for in-between and on-demand learning activities (Buchem &
Hamelmann, 2010). These kinds of information chunks can be classified as
microcontent that is assumed to support learning, specifically informal or
work-based learning under given time constraints and to help the learner to
build up a customized individual learning process that can be adjusted and regulated as required. Microcontent can be defined by criteria of time and content
(Hug, 2007). The content should cover a narrow topic that can be processed
within a comparatively low amount of time. Moreover, microcontent can be
used for microlearning activities that can be defined by the same criteria of
time and content whereby microlearning activity may involve more than one
chunk of microcontent (Hug, 2007). The use of microcontent is also fostered
by recent digital technologies as small chunks of information can be easily
built, consumed, shared, stored and reused, not only with desktop computers,
but also with mobile devices. These advantages increase flexibility and make
it easy to integrate the processing of up to date information for daily life or to
make a collection of relevant content with regard to individual needs and prerequisites. Following these features of microcontent, small information chunks
can support self-directed learning in many ways and in many domains (Hug,
2010). A popular example for the purpose and intention of microcontent and
microlearning activities may be video tutorials to teach someone how to use a
given software application. Although the learning objective is considerably
complex and includes in sum all functions of the application, the whole objective is chunked down to small information units that teach single functions of
the applications so that the videos are short and cover a narrow topic Thereby
it is not necessarily a prerequisite to follow a strict step-by-step sequence of
information chunks, but one can decide with regard to individual prior

knowledge where to start. Single chunks can be used as just in time information when they are needed, or one can make a collection of the videos that are most important with regard to a given task. Of course, the learner can also work out the whole learning objective but microcontent offers the possibility to do this in a highly flexible and integrated manner, at one's own speed and within given time limits. Thus the format of microcontent and microlearning activities do not only meet the pulse of time but also several considerations and principles of learning theories as the cognitive theory of multimedia learning (CTML; Mayer, 2001, 2005) , cognitive load theory (CLT; Plass, Moreno, & Brünken, 2010; Sweller, van Merriënboer, & Paas, 1998) or models of self-regulated learning (SRL; Boekaerts, 1999; Zimmerman, 2000). The relation between these theories and microlearning with regard to the design of microcontent will be discussed in the following section.

9.2.2 Microlearning and CTML

The goal of CTML (Mayer, 2014) is to explain learning with regard to information processing and to foster the cognitive processes of information selection, organization and integration. The basic assumptions of CTML are a limited working memory capacity for the processing of information and that learning is an active process that consumes working memory capacity. The essential assumption of CTML is the dual channel assumption with separate channels for the processing of visual/pictorial and auditory/verbal information. Based on the dual coding theory of Paivio (1986) and the working memory model of Baddeley (1986; Baddeley & Hitch, 1994), CTML considers two sensory modalities, that is visual or auditory, as well as two processing modalities, that is pictorial or verbal. Thereby each processing channel has its own capacity limitation and the processing modality of one channel can be transferred to the other channel via cross-channel processing, e.g. when a verbal representation is built because of pictorial information. The multimedia principle (Mayer, 2005) therefore states that information should be presented with respect to the two processing modalities as a combination of text and picture information to make use of the available processing capacity of both channels. Moreover, the modality principle (Moreno, 2006) states that verbal information should be presented auditory and pictorial information should be presented visually to make use of the two sensory modalities and to avoid unnecessary cross-channel processing. Thereby the redundancy principle (Mayer & Moreno, 2003) states that the use of two sensory modalities and both processing channels is only beneficial for corresponding verbal and pictorial information but not for redundant verbal and pictorial information.

Concerning the design of microcontent CTML suggests using combinations of verbal and pictorial information, to present verbal information in an auditory fashion and pictorial information visually. Additionally, avoiding redundancy of text and pictures presenting identical information also fits the idea of microcontent. As microcontent should be easy to process in a relatively short amount of time the combination of auditory verbal and visual pictorial information, e.g. as video format, not only fits the model of information processing but also saves time. The same is true for redundancy, e.g. a video with auditory verbal information should not present the same verbal information as subtitles. With respect to the temporal and content requirements of microcontent the suggestions of CTML can help to meet these requirements. The design of information chunks that are easy to process should pay attention to cognitive architecture of processing channels and foster most efficient information processing. However, it should also be considered that not every learning objective needs two presentation modalities or profits form multimodality, e.g. if there is no relevant pictorial information to support information integration.

CTML (Mayer, 2001) and CLT (Sweller, 1998) are closely related, share several basic assumptions, focus on similar cognitive processes and can both be used to explain the popular effects of multimedia learning. Although the multimedia principle, the modality principle and the redundancy principle are somehow more CTML, the effects can also be explained by CLT and means of cognitive load. The other way around CTML provides also explanations for effects that are more CLT, for example the split attention or the spacing effect (Mayer & Moreno, 2003) that will be described in the following section.

9.2.3 Microlearning and CLT

The goal of CLT (Sweller, van Merriënboer, & Paas ,2019) is to avoid cognitive overload with regard to information processing. Similar to CTML the basic assumptions of CLT are a limited working memory capacity for the processing of information, and that learning is an active process that consumes working memory capacity. The essential assumption of CLT is that cognitive capacity consumption is due to different factors of cognitive load with regard to active schema construction and design features of the learning instruction. The early model of CLT (Sweller, 1998) considers three distinguishable factors of cognitive load that is extraneous cognitive load (ECL), intrinsic cognitive load (ICL) and germane cognitive load (GCL). Therein ECL is the part of cognitive load that arises because of design features of the learning instruction, ICL is the part of cognitive load that arises because of task complexity and GCL is the part of cognitive load that arises because of schema construction.

ECL is seen as additional load that hinders schema construction and should therefore be reduced to a minimum. ICL can be defined by element interactivity and depends on the number of information elements that need to be integrated to a new schema within a given learning task. With regard to the assumption of limited cognitive resources and an additive relation of ECL and ICL, GCL depends on the remaining cognitive resources for schema construction. In sum, CLT suggests reducing ECL for a given ICL to save resources for GCL. However, the early model of CLT was revised (Choi, van Merriënboer, & Paas, 2014; Kalyuga, 2011) because of the close relationship of ICL and GCL, as the cognitive load that arises from schema construction depends on element interactivity. The recent model of CLT considers GCL no longer as a separate factor that adds up to total cognitive load, but as the amount of working memory resources that is actively redistributed to learning activities (Sweller et al., 2019). Most design principles that consider CLT aim on a reduction of ECL by efficient instructional designs and a resource saving presentation of information that avoids unnecessary processing. The split attention principle (Ayres & Sweller, 2014) suggest that corresponding information that needs to be integrated to a coherent mental model should also be presented in an integrated format. Spatial or temporal distance between corresponding information forces the learner to split attention with regard to the processing and integrating of information from distinct sources, e.g. from text and picture. For the process of schema construction, textual and pictorial information must be simultaneously available in working memory and spatial or temporal distance of information presentation thereby increase ECL and the demands on working memory. Another ECL effect that supports the suggestion not to split or distract the attention of the learner is the seductive details effect (Korbach, Brünken, & Park, 2016). Seductive details describe additional, highly interesting information with the intention to increase the learners' interest and motivation. Although the additional information can be related to the learning objective, the additional information is not necessary to achieve the learning goal and therefore causes unnecessary processing and an increase of ECL. With respect to learner characteristics the effect of instructional interventions to reduce ECL and to foster schema construction may also change as a function of prior knowledge. This effect is called expertise reversal effect (Kalyuga, Ayres, Chandler, & Sweller, 2003) and describes why instructional interventions that are helpful for low prior knowledge learners can hamper learning for high prior knowledge learners at the same time. In this case the design features that foster schema construction for low prior knowledge learners cause unnecessary processing for high prior knowledge learners and increase ECL, however only for high prior knowledge learners. One more effect with a strong relation to individual learner characteristics is the spacing effect (Chen, Castro-

Alonso, Paas, & Sweller, 2018) that suggests spaced information presentation instead of massed information presentation. The effect is explained by a depletion of working memory resources due to massed practice or information processing. Although this effect shows no direct relation to the distinct cognitive load factors, one can assume that segmented information processing that is interrupted by pauses is favored over massed information processing. This suggestion pays attention to individual limitations of working memory capacity and changes in available resources with regard to learning time.

Concerning the design of microcontent the split attention principle suggests that information should be presented as an integrated format. If verbal information cannot be presented auditory simultaneously to visual information as suggested by the modality principle (Moreno, 2006), the verbal information should be integrated with the pictorial information. Considering the comparatively small size of mobile devices, it can be hard to avoid temporal or spatial distance between corresponding information. Text and picture information is often presented as a sequence with text following the picture or the other way around because both pieces of information cannot be presented simultaneously on the screen, for example side by side as is common on larger displays. One possibility to reduce split attention is the format of interactive pictures that fade in additional information over a picture where and when it is needed due to an interaction with specific areas of the picture. With regard to the seductive details effect microcontent should not contain any kind of decorative pictures that may distract the learner's attention from processing important information. All information that is presented will be processed by the learners and will therefore not only increase processing time but also cognitive load. The suggestion to include only relevant information fits with the idea of microcontent and saves cognitive resources. As each chunk of microcontent should cover a narrow but complete topic, the format also pays attention to the expertise reversal effect. High prior knowledge learners can choose where to start and what to learn next with regard to their individual prerequisites. In this way the structuring of microcontent and the segmenting of the microlearning activity avoids unnecessary information processing as the learners can choose to process only necessary information with regard to the learning objective. The idea of narrow but complete topics also meets the spacing effect, and as the learners are free to decide when to pause also the assumption of working memory depletion. The format of microcontent is not only appropriate to increase flexibility, but it also pays attention to individual learner differences with regard to cognitive demands and capacity.

As one basic assumption of CTML (Mayer, 2001) and CLT (Sweller, 1998) is the limited capacity of working memory with regard to the working memory model of Baddeley (1986; Baddeley & Hitch, 1994) the functions of the central executive may establish the connection to the process of SRL (Zimmerman, 2000). Although the question if the process of SRL consumes working memory resources is currently discussed, it can be assumed that the necessity of SRL depends on an interaction of task demands and learner characteristics (Seufert, 2018) similar to the design principles of CTML and CLT.

9.2.4 Microlearning and SRL

The goal of SRL theories is to explain how learners regulate the learning process. Component models of SRL, for example the one of Boekaerts (1999), explain SRL as a function of competencies on a cognitive, metacognitive and motivational level. In contrast process models, for example the one of Zimmerman (2000), explain SRL as cyclical phases of self-regulation during the learning process. With regard to SRL as a competence and relatively enduring learner characteristic, specifically the learners' prior knowledge about cognitive, metacognitive and motivational strategies, but also the ability and willingness to use them is of importance for the process of SRL (Wirth & Leutner, 2008). Whether or not the self-regulation competence can be taught is recently discussed, nevertheless it should be assumed that SRL can be improved by practice (Sweller & Paas, 2017). In general, SRL begins with the learners' decision to learn something (de Bruin & van Merriënboer, 2017). As learning is an active process that needs effort over time for information processing and schema construction, the learners decide about the invested effort for the learning activity and finally evaluate the results with regard to their goal settings. Zimmerman's model (2000) describes this process with respect to the phase of forethought, the phase of performance and the phase of reflection. The forethought phase includes goal setting, planning the use of appropriate cognitive strategies, and strategies of self-motivation with regard to the task requirements. The performance phase includes the use of strategies and self-monitoring with regard to cognition, emotion, task demands and one's effort. The phase of self-reflection includes self-assessment with a review of strategy use and causal attribution as well as the self-reaction concerning emotional states and a revision of goal settings. With regard to the results of self-reflection the learning process can be adjusted and starts with a new cycle of self-regulation. Thereby the need and success of self-regulation might vary as a function of task demands and learner characteristics.

In contrast to the suggestions for the design of microcontent and microlearning activity that derive from CTML (Mayer, 2014) and CLT (Sweller et al., 2019) the implications from SRL (Zimmerman, 2000) are less clear. With regard to a microlearning activity that consists of more than one chunk of microcontent as a comparatively loose sequence, the forethought phase and specifically the planning of the learning activity can be quite demanding if there is no given structure with regard to the learning objective. The planning of a complex learning activity or the planning of a learning activity that has no explicit structure can be assumed to add cognitive demands to the actual task (Seufert, 2018). However, to make a selection on one's own and to generate an individual structure might also cause practice concerning SRL. For the single chunks of microcontent the process of monitoring during the performance phase should be less demanding because of the narrow but complete topic. The same might be true for the phase of self-reflection as the process of evaluation should be easy for comparatively small tasks.

9.2.5 Pros and cons of microlearning

In sum, with regard to CTML (Mayer, 2014), CLT (Sweller et al., 2019) and Zimmerman's (2000) model of SRL, microlearning with microcontent seems to be a suitable way for VET if the participants are less interested in longer text-based information. The idea of short information chunks that cover a narrow but complete topic in a way that strict sequencing is not necessary meets several theoretically founded and empirically tested design principles. It seems to be a promising approach with great potential to foster efficient information processing, to reduce cognitive load and to practice self- direction and self-regulation in the vocational context. At the same time the need for self-regulation might be a burden as SRL depends on individual self-regulation competence (Boekaerts, 1999). The motivational effect of a comparatively loose sequencing as well as the effect of a missing structure for individual goal setting, self-evaluation and causal attribution cannot be clearly estimated. Regarding the goals of the project LaSiDig and the requirements of the target group, microcontent seems to provide an adequate solution for time constraints and the need for mobility and flexibility. The character of microcontent in general supports the integration of microlearning activities to everyday life and VET. However, the effectiveness of microcontent in this vocational context needs to be tested, may depend on learners' acceptance, and recognized usability during the implementation.

9.3 Instructional Design for Microlearning

To design the learning units, we orientated towards the Decision Oriented Instructional Design Model (DO ID Model: Niegemann, 2019) as a framework model and adopted essential features from the Four Component Instructional Design (4C/ID) model (van Merriënboer & Kirschner, 2018).

Figure 1: Decision Oriented Instructional Design Model (Niegemann, 2019)

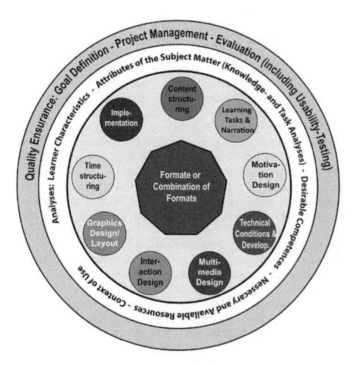

The DO ID model (Figure 1) is a framework model developed over the last 12 years (Niegemann, et al., 2008) to support instructional design by providing sound scientific information to make efficient ID decisions. The model represents three areas of instructional design: (1) A goal perspective and measures to ensure an appropriate standard of quality (external shell), (2) suitable procedures to analyze the needs, the relevant conditions and the context of the planned instructional programs (second shell) and (3) the fields of concrete decisions to be made by instructional designers.

The 4C/ID model is an instructional design model dedicated to cognitive complex content and in this domain, it is the most successful model. Main features are the differentiation between whole- and part-tasks and recurrent and non-recurrent aspects of learning tasks, the sequencing of the different kinds of tasks and the time and places to present supportive information and to provide procedural information.

In the LaSiDig project, the goals are quite clearly described (qualifying professional drivers for secure loadings and convey them appropriate competencies to use mobile devices for further education) and a well proven project management system had been established from the very beginning. Also, a plan for the evaluation, including usability testing, was set up at the start of the project. The need for load safety trainings is obvious and respective training is legally required. The attributes of the addressees (professional drivers) are well known, as the DEKRA Company (leader of the LaSiDig project consortium) is one of the biggest companies in Europe concerned with the training and further education of drivers. As analyses at the start of the projects confirmed drivers are a rather heterogeneous group concerning previous education, intellectual skills, learning motivation and affects regarding training measures. Although almost all of the potential participants own a smartphone, the need for media competency had to be determined. As it is a project proposed to and granted by the German government (BMBF, grant 01PZ16007B) all costs are calculated in advance and the budget, the time, and other resources are known. For the analysis of task structure (safe loading) and of the necessary background knowledge, experienced trainers were available and could be consulted.

Inside the two shells of the model there are ten fields representing categories of decisions to be made in any instructional design process. The field in the very middle of the model represents the decision for a format, sub-formats or a combination of formats. Formats are more or less schematic ways to convey the subject matter, e.g. e-lectures, webinars, computer supported collaborative learning, serious games, explain videos, simulations etc. As already explained above the decision for the main format was part of the core idea of the project: Microlearning units (learning nuggets) should be developed and their effectiveness and efficiency should be evaluated. The decision for a specific format, or a combination of formats, is the first decision, and many other decisions are swayed by it. The course of the further decisions is not mostly linear, many decisions and their respective consequences interact. Given the analyses of the content and the learning tasks the sequence and the segmentation have to be determined. While the sequence of the learning nuggets is not linear but depends on the learners' choices, segmentation is crucial for the format of microlearning. To allow very short units just one separable complete action or a theoretical "idea" constitute one learning nugget. If possible, these content units should be included or wrapped into authentic stories of the drivers' work-day world. Besides the informational units, a series of self-test items are offered to enable the self-assessment of the own competence level concerning the different competence areas.

A specific demanding design task refers to the question how to motivate the learners to use the learning nuggets over a longer period. Following the ARCS model (Keller & Deimann, 2018) there are specific activities to grab the attention of the target group, information to convey the relevance of the subject and feedback to ensure the confidence of the learners in the increase of their competence.

Though the decision for the distribution of the LaSiDig training program via smartphones and tablets was made before the project started, there are decisions concerning technical aspects necessary due to the different operating systems and other technical features of the devices used by the learners. Design options also depend on the choice of the authoring software: Does it allow for the use of variables to offer information rich feedback (Narciss, 2008)? What kind of learning tasks could be realized? Is it possible to implement links to other pieces of information (learning nuggets, websites, software tools)? These decisions impact the multimedia design explained above: E.g., how can important details of a loading procedure be salient enough in a video on a small display? Many principles of multimedia learning (for an overview see Mayer, 2014) have to be considered in the light of technical restrictions and opportunities, as for example the above-mentioned multimedia, modality and redundancy principle. Similar challenges come across in the field of interaction design and the design of adaptivity with regard to task-learner interaction (Niegemann & Heidig, 2019). Another category of crucial design decision is partly determined by the format decision—time related aspects. As the learning units are quite short the problem of possible depletion of the learners is neglectable in this case; nevertheless, the decision of how long a specific microlearning unit should be is not trivial (Bradbury, 2016; Wilson & Korn, 2007). As for the graphical design and the layout of the units and the website they are presented on, instructional designers need the help of graphic design specialists. A last, but not the least, field of design decisions concerns the implementation of the complete instruction. All stakeholders must be included in the implementation strategy and the information policy should be adapted to the specific needs and interests of the target group. In this case several bigger transport companies and training institutions have been included in the project from the beginning to support the project.

9.4 The Case of Fostering Media Competence for Professional Drivers

9.4.1 Description of aims and procedures in the LaSiDig Project

Media competence is one of the learning objectives in the LaSiDig project. Learners need a certain level of media competence to use e-learning, in general for further education and specifically for all functions of the LaSi-App. This includes the creation of their own content, which in turn also requires knowledge about data privacy and copyrights. However, the goal is to foster not only app related media competence, but also general media competence and vocational media competence with regard to professional apps to support daily work routines. With respect to the three goals, the majority of content is about general media competence, followed by tutorials about specific functions of the app, and examples of use concerning specific vocational features. Thereby the topics of general media competence are related to the corresponding app or vocation specific content in order to foster transfer to other applications. For the target group evaluation, a sample of 78 participants with 48 professionals and 30 vocational learners responded to a survey and answered questions concerning media competence, context issues such as availability of mobile internet or time constraints, learning preferences, motivation, and self-regulation. Following the results of the target group evaluation, microlearning with microcontent seems appropriate with regard to the prerequisites of population and context. The format of loosely structured microcontent is assumed to be appropriate as the users of the LaSi-App should be able to use exactly the kind of information that is needed to quickly solve problems in their daily routine. Therefor each chunk of microcontent covers a narrow but complete topic and can be used comparatively independent from related chunks to solve concrete problems. The concept of narrow but complete topics for each chunk also supports the integration of related chunks across general, app specific, and vocational media competence. For example, a chunk from the section general media competence about the topic data privacy can be combined with chunks for app specific data privacy as well as chunks for vocation specific data privacy. At the same time, the sum of microcontent will cover the entire learning objective with regard to the selected competence framework for general media competence. Furthermore, the single chunks of microcontent offer the possibility to follow a suggested sequence with regard to the superordinate instructional objectives. The DigComp 2.1 framework (the digital competence framework for citizens with eight proficiency levels and examples of use; Carretero, Vourikari, & Punie, 2017) was considered as the basis for an adapted media competence framework with regard to the needs and requirements of the target group. The five main competence areas: (a) information and data literacy, (b) communication and collaboration, (c) digital content creation, (d) safety, and (e) problem solving were taken from the original framework. The sub-competences were selected according to the necessary competences to use all functions of the LaSi-App and according to the useful competences with respect to the daily routine of the target group in the vocational context. For each competence area the framework suggests eight proficiency levels that reach from a foundational competence level to a highly specialized competence level, with increasing task complexity and autonomy. As the results of the target group evaluation show at least a low level of media competence for the proficiency levels one to four and because the detailed promotion of proficiency levels seven and eight would exceed the limits of the LaSiDig project, the proficiency levels were reduced with regard to the cognitive affordances: (a) remembering, (b) understanding, (c) applying, (d) evaluating, and (e) creating. Following the adapted competence framework, the development of microcontent focused on short information chunks for the selected sub-competences of the single competence areas and the adjusted proficiency levels. In accordance with the cognitive affordances of the proficiency levels, the content of each sub-competence covers microcontent to present information, to practice retention and application, to foster critical evaluation, and to support self-directed learning beyond the topics included in the LaSi-App. To meet the desired character of "just in time information" the basic information chunks do not include practice tasks. Moreover, microcontent that presents information and microcontent for practice were given unique labels to support the learners' search for appropriate content. With regard to considerations of processing time for microcontent, the single chucks include information that can be processed in approximately five minutes. That is specifically important to support the integration of chunks that present information into learners' daily routine. The time that is needed to process chunks that contain practice tasks depends on the included sub-competences and proficiency levels. The time limit for tasks that provide practice for single proficiency levels is also approximately five minutes, whereas the time needed to complete tasks that provide practice across several proficiency levels or sub-competences can be up to fifteen minutes. These kinds of superordinate practice tasks thereby follow the suggested sequence of the single information chunks. The goal of these practice tasks is to reconnect the separate chunks of the superordinate instructional objective with regard to practical application, as well as to support the learners concerning the self-regulation of their learning process (Zimmerman, 2000), specifically concerning the evaluation of the learning process. The purpose is that in this way learners can identify their competence gaps and adjust the learning process, e.g. with additional practice for single topics or with a repetition of specific information chunks. As each chunk of microcontent covers only one single topic, the learners can choose exactly the topics they need and therefor avoid unnecessary information processing. With regard to the considerations of CTML (Mayer, 2014) and CLT (Sweller et al., 2019) the information is presented as a combination of verbal and pictorial information only when both modalities provide unique and corresponding information and the use of two presentation modalities supports schema construction. As far as possible short videos are used to present the verbal information auditory and the pictorial information visually to pay attention to the processing modalities. If verbal and pictorial information both need to be presented visually, the verbal information is integrated into the pictorial information. Moreover, the integrated format of presentation pays attention to the small size of the mobile devices. To keep the time for information processing as low as possible, the information chunks contain no redundant or superfluous information. To support self-directed learning all chunks of microcontent are assigned to separate collections for competence areas, as well as for the separate sub-competences of each competence area. The collections provide an overview of the single topics, which helps the learners to make individual decisions about where to start and how to go on with regard to individual needs and prerequisites. The learners also have the possibility to build their own collections, e.g. by interest or relevance to their daily routine. The concept of automated content suggestions provides further support for self-directed learning. Although the single chunks of microcontent do not have to be used for learning in a linear sequence, all microcontent can be used in a linear sequence that follows the increasing complexity of the proficiency levels for the single sub-competences of media competence. The information about these sequences is included in the meta-data and considered for automated suggestions of microcontent that has not yet been consumed by the learner. In this way, the app suggests new content of already known competence areas. Some chunks also provide cross relations to other competence areas that are also considered for automated suggestions. In this way the automated suggestions also connect general media competence to app specific or vocational media competence and to related vocational competence areas.

9.4.2 Microcontent design example 1: Interactive pictures for app tutorials

The use of the basic functions of the LaSi-App might be obvious for users with high prior knowledge concerning the use of mobile apps, however users with low prior knowledge may need more support. To pay attention to individual differences in prior experience there is a separate tutorial for each function of the app. Each tutorial consists of screenshots that show the original screen in size and resolution of a common mobile device to explain the app usage in a realistic context. The step-by-step process information is included as a short heading for each screenshot and the information about the single areas and buttons of the app is integrated into the screenshots as interactive text information. The interactive information is visually cued by colored spots and fades in when the learner hits the spot so that only the necessary information needs to be processed with regard to the individual's support needs (Figure 2).

Figure 2: Sample screenshot from a microlearning unit on app functions. Interactive presentation including buttons for additional supportive information

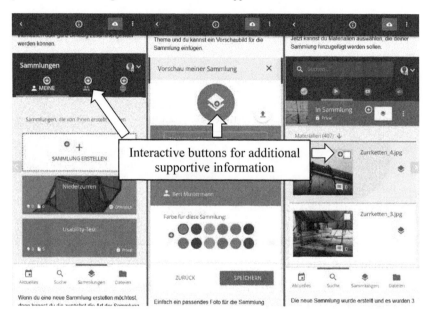

9.4.3 Microcontent design example 2: Interactive video about web search

The concept for interactive pictures also fits the format of interactive videos. For example, how to use the basic functions of a search engine might also be obvious depending on an individual's prior knowledge. The interactive video again consists of a short screen cast that demonstrates the process of a simple web search. Whenever key features of the search engine are used, a visual cue in form of a colored spot fades in at the corresponding area of the screen. If the learner hits the spot the video stops and additional text information explaining the function fades in. The video continues as soon as the learner closes the text window. In this way, the interactive video avoids unnecessary information processing as the learner can decide to stop the video and to get additional information with regard to the individual need of support (Figure 3).

Figure 3: Sample screenshot from a microlearning unit on web search. Interactive video including buttons for additional supportive information

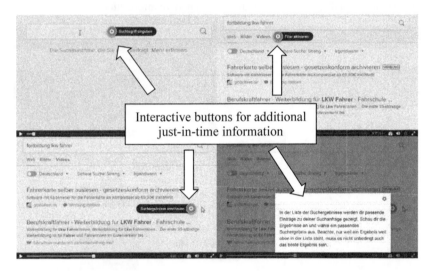

9.4.4 Microcontent design example 3: Shrinking of text information

Quite a few information chunks to foster general media competence require only text information, as the goal of these chunks is to provide essential factual knowledge in a short time. For example, to name different search engines and to know about their communalities and differences does not necessarily need additional video or picture information. To pay attention to individual needs and levels of prior knowledge with such kind of information chunks, only the general information that is true for all entities to compare is immediately present. The entity-specific information is initially hidden and fades in only when the learner selects the entity because of the decision to learn more about this entity. In this way, the format avoids unnecessary information processing with regard to individual needs and prior knowledge. In the case of the afore mentioned example of search engines, the primary learning goal is that learners know that there is more than one search engine for conducting web searches and that learners can name at least three different search engines. To evaluate the pros and contras of different search engines by comparing their communalities and differences is an optional, higher-order learning goal that is in this case is served with the same piece of microcontent. If the learner already has a favorite search engine and decides not to use an alternative search engine, the additional information about the other search engines is unnecessary with regard to the individual needs; however, the primary learning goal can still be achieved.

9.5 Conclusions and perspectives

In sum, microcontent serves several needs of microlearning in a vocational context. One of the strongest advantages of microcontent might be its high flexibility concerning individual requirements and time constraints. As discussed above the design of microcontent can pay attention to several design principles with regard to CTML (Mayer, 2014) and CLT (Sweller et al., 2019) and the idea of short information chunks meets the general idea of designs for efficient information processing. One challenge might be the loose structure, as applied for the LaSiDig project, with respect to the process of SRL (Zimmerman, 2000) and the individual competence for SRL (Boekaerts, 1999). Although automated content suggestions support the process of self-directed learning an additional structured organizer for the competence areas might be beneficial for learners with low SRL competence. Many research questions result from the context of the use of microlearning in VET: e.g. sequencing, number of units in one time period, depletion, interactivity. Some answers are to be expected by examining the results of the evaluation of the LaSiDiG project in 2020. The evaluation will be done with a pre-/post-test designed to assess the effectiveness of microcontent with regard to learning success. After a pre-test the users will work on four topics of media and professional competences over four consecutive weeks with one topic per week. For each topic specific microcontent will be suggested by a tutor. For each chunk of microcontent it will be evaluated how learners use them, how learners perform on integrated knowledge questions or problem-solving tasks, in addition to how learners rate cognitive load, practical usefulness and usability. At the end of week four, the learners will finally do the post-test and learning success will be calculated using a comparison to the pre-test results, considering the learners' activity on the suggested microcontent during the time of evaluation. The pre- and post-test will also include a questionnaire about the learners' expectations for the app usage and their learning behavior.

References

Ayres, P. & Sweller, J. (2014). The split-attention principle in multimedia learning. In R. E. Mayer (Ed.), The Cambridge Handbook of Multimedia Learning (pp. 135-146). New York: Cambridge University Press,

Baddeley, Alan D. (1986): Working Memory. Oxford: Oxford University Press.

Baddeley, A. D. & Hitch, G. J. (1994). Developments in the concept of working memory. *Neuropsychology, 8*(4), pp.485-493.

Boekaerts, M. (1999). Self-regulated learning: Where we are today. *International Journal of Educational Research, 31*(6), pp. 445-457.

Bradbury, N. A. (2016). Attention span during lectures: 8 seconds, 10 minutes, or more? *Advantages in Physiology Education, 40*, 509-513.

Brünken, R., Moreno, R., & Plass, J. (Eds.) (2010). Current issues and open questions in cognitive load research. *Cognitive Load Theory* (pp. 253–272). New York, USA: Cambridge University Press.

Buchem, I. & Hamelmann, H. (2010). Microlearning: a strategy for ongoing professional development. *eLearning Papers, 21.*

Carretero, S., Vuorikari, R., & Punie, Y. (2017). *DigComp 2.1: The digital competence framework for citizens. With eight proficiency levels and examples of use, EUR 28558 EN,* doi:10.2760/38842.

Chen, O., Castro-Alonso, J. C., Paas, F., & Sweller, J. (2018). Extending cognitive load theory to incorporate working memory resource depletion: evidence from the spacing effect. *Educational Psychology Review, 30*, 483-501.

Choi, H.-H, van Merriënboer, J. J. G., & Paas, F. (2014). Effects of the physical environment on cognitive load and learning: towards a new model of cognitive load. *Educational Psychology Review, 26*, 225-244.

De Bruin, A. B. H. & van Merriënboer, J. G. (2017). Bridging cognitive load and self-regulated learning research: A complementary approach to contemporary issues in educational research. *Learning and Instruction, 51*, 1-9.

Hug, T. (2007). Didactics of Microlearning – Introductory Note. In T. Hug (Ed.), *Didactics of Microlearning. Concepts, Discourses and Examples.* Münster: Waxmann.

Hug, T. (2010). *Mikrolernen - konzeptionelle Überlegungen und Anwendungsbeispiele. In Jahrbuch Medienpädagogik 8: Medienkompetenz und Web 2.0. (pp. 221-238).* Wiesbaden: VS Verlag.

Mayer, R. E. (2001). *Multimedia Learning.* New York: Cambridge University Press.

Mayer, R. E. (2005). *The Cambridge Handbook of Multimedia Learning.* New York: Cambridge University Press.

Mayer, R. E. (2014). *The Cambridge Handbook of Multimedia Learning.* New York: Cambridge University Press.

Mayer, R. E. & Moreno, R. (2003). Nine ways to reduce cognitive load in multimedia learning, *Educational Psychologist, 38*(1), 43-52.

Moreno, R. (2006). Does the modality principle hold for different media? A test of the method-affects-learning hypothesis. *Journal of Computer Assisted Learning, 22*, 149-158.

Kalyuga, S. (2011). Cognitive load theory: How many types of load does it really need? *Educational Psychology Review, 23*, 1-19.

Kalyuga, S., Ayres, P., Chandler, P., & Sweller, J. (2003). The expertise reversal effect. *Educational Psychologist, 38*, 23-31.

Keller, J. M. & Deimann, M. (2018). Motivation, volition, and performance. In R. A. Reiser & J. V. Dempsey (Eds.). *Trends and Issues in Instructional Design and Technology* (pp.78-86). New York: Pearson.

Korbach, A., Brünken, R., & Park, B. (2016). Learner characteristics and information processing in multimedia learning: A moderated mediation of the seductive details effect. *Learning and Individual Differences, 51*, 59-68.

Narciss, S. (2008). Feedback strategies for interactive learning tasks. In J. M. Spector, M. D. Merrill, J. van Merriënboer, & M. P. Driscoll (Eds.). *Handbook of Research on Educational Communications and Technology* (pp. 125-143). New York: Lawrence Erlbaum Associates.

Niegemann, H. M. (2019). Instructional Design. In H. M. Niegemann, A. Weinberger (Eds.). *Handbuch Bildungstechnologie.* Heidelberg: Springer Reference Psychologie. https://doi.org/10.1007/978-3-662-54373-3_8-1)

Niegemann, H. M. et al. (2008). *Kompendium multimediales Lernen.* Heidelberg, Springer.

Niegemann, H. M. & Heidig, S. (2019). Interaktivität und Adaptivität in multimedialen Lernumgebungen. In H. Niegemann, & A. Weinberger (Eds.), *Handbuch Bildungstechnologie.* Heidelberg, Springer (Retrieved from https://doi.org/ 10.1007/ 978-3-662-54373-3_33-1)

Paas, F. & Sweller, J. (2014). Implications of cognitive load theory for multimedia learning. In R. E. Mayer (Ed.), *The Cambridge Handbook of Multimedia Learning* (pp. 27-42). New York, NY, US: Cambridge University Press.

Paivio, A. (1986). *Mental Representation: A dual coding approach.* Oxford, England: Oxford University Press.

Seufert, T. (2018). The interplay between self-regulation in learning and cognitive load. *Educational Research Review, 24,* 116-129.

Sweller, J. (1989). Cognitive technology: Some procedures for facilitating learning and problem solving in mathematics and science. *Journal of Educational Psychology, 81,* 457-466.

Sweller, J., van Merriënboer, J. G., & Paas, F. (1998). Cognitive architecture and instructional design. *Educational Psychology Review, 10,* 251-296.

Sweller, J., van Merriënboer, J. G., & Paas, F. (2019). Cognitive architecture and instructional design: 20 years later. *Educational Psychology Review, 31,* 261-292.

Sweller, J., Paas, F. (2017). Should self-regulated learning be integrated with cognitive load theory? A commentary. Learning and Instruction, *51,* 85-89.

Wilson, K. & Korn, J. H. (2007). Attention During Lectures: Beyond Ten Minutes. *Teaching of Psychology, 34*(2), 85-89.

Wirth, J. & Leutner, D. (2008). Self-regulated learning as a competence: Implications of theoretical models for assessment methods. *Zeitschrift für Psychologie, 216*(2), 102–110.

Zimmerman, B. J. (2000). Attaining self-regulation: A social cognitive perspective. In M. Boekaerts, P. R. Pintrich, & M. Zeidner (Eds.), *Handbook of Self-Regulation* (pp. 13-41). San Diego: Academic Press.

Section IV:
Higher Education
in the Age of Digitization

10 Openness in MOOCs for Training and Professional Development – An Exploration of Entry and Participation Barriers

Kristina Kögler, Marc Egloffstein, & *Brigitte Schönberger*

10.1 Introduction

Massive Open Online Courses (MOOCs) constituted a high-profile phenomenon in educational technology within the last ten years and attracted a lot of attention from researchers and practitioners. Although MOOCs have not disrupted the higher education sector as profoundly as it had been propagated (Reich & Ruipérez-Valiente, 2019), a new global market for online education with commercial platform providers has emerged. By 2018, more than 900 universities had launched 11.4k MOOCs with different platform providers serving over 100 million learners. The estimated revenue of Coursera as the biggest global MOOC provider is $140 million, and a growth rate of more than 20% indicates a huge demand for online-based education and training (Shah, 2018a).

Historically, MOOCs have developed out of academia, closely related to the concepts and ideas of open education (Yuan & Powell, 2015). Openness has always been a central part of the MOOC narrative, the courses being offered at virtually no cost, without formal prerequisites and accessible from virtually everywhere. Extending the academic perspective, MOOCs have been identified as a promising option for work-related learning and professional development (Milligan & Littlejohn, 2017). Lately, MOOCs have been gaining more acceptance among employers (Hamori, 2017, 203ff.) and employees (Egloffstein & Ifenthaler, 2017), despite the fact that openness is rather uncommon in corporate contexts (Olsson, 2016). At the same time, MOOC providers are adjusting their business models after the initial years of euphoria, both for monetization and for accommodating the requirements of training and professional development. The idea of openness, meanwhile, seems to be fading into the background. More and more MOOCs are provided with entry and participation barriers at different course stages. Hence, the question arises whether openness remains a distinctive feature of MOOCs, especially with regard to training and professional development.

The aim of this contribution is to explore the openness of MOOCs for professional development and to add empirical evidence to the current discussion. This leads to the following research questions:

1. What are current notions of openness in online education and training, and how do they relate to MOOCs with respect to professional development?
2. Which types of barriers do exist in MOOCs for training and professional development?
3. Are there systematic patterns of barriers, pointing towards specific strategies of openness employed by MOOC providers?

We first discuss current notions of openness in online education and training and show possible links to generic MOOC models. We then review $N = 295$ MOOCs from nine common English-speaking providers for barriers. Based on our empirical data, we set out to characterize different types of MOOCs from the perspective of openness.

10.2   Theoretical background

10.2.1 MOOCs in post-secondary education

Broadly defined, MOOCs are "free or low-cost Internet-based university courses or near equivalents" (Waks, 2016, xiii). Following the acronym, MOOCs can be classified as "courses that are designed for large numbers of participants (*massive*), free to access (*open*), delivered entirely over the web (*online*), and structured and assessed (*courses*)" (Knox, 2015, 1372). However, there is a great variation in MOOC formats, so this broad description can only be a first conceptual consensus. Apart from MOOCs being delivered *online*, all the other defining characteristics can be questioned in one way or another. Especially how *openness* is understood seems to be a key difference of several MOOC initiatives and approaches (Knox, 2015).

As a result of two separate development paths, two generic MOOC models with different underlying pedagogical approaches have emerged (Ifenthaler, Bellin-Mularski, & Mah, 2015). cMOOCs (connectivist MOOCs), on the one hand, provide collaborative and network-oriented learning environments. They focus on learning communities and promote the autonomy of educational objectives. cMOOCs enable knowledge generation through discussions, construction and sharing of contents, and social network activities. xMOOCs (extension MOOCs), on the other hand, follow a more traditional cognitive-behaviorist approach. They focus primarily on the dissemination of contents to larger audiences. Therefore, xMOOCs enable a scalable knowledge delivery with specialized video-oriented learning platforms. Typical elements of those platforms are lecture videos, integrated quizzes and short online tests for automated assessment. With respect to instructional design criteria, the two approaches can be characterized as follows (Tu & Sujo-Montes, 2015):

cMOOCs are centred around content production, and learners are expected to create, enhance and share. Content is fragmented and not bound to a course. xMOOCs, on the other hand, follow a defined formal course structure, and learners are expected to master what they are being taught. The xMOOC teaching mode is lecture oriented, mostly implemented by instructional videos, while cMOOCs rely on distributed interactions and personal sense-making. Recently, the boundaries between the two ideal-typical MOOC models have become less clear, and the „the division has been criticized as overly simplistic in assuming particular kinds of pedagogy" (Knox, 2015, 1373). However, content delivery and scalability are still predominantly linked to xMOOCs, while pedagogical innovation has been associated with the cMOOCs model (Spector, 2017). Beyond that, the current notion of the MOOC concept predominantly relies on the xMOOCs model, so that the term MOOC has become synonymous to large-scale video-based instruction.

The MOOC trajectory can be characterized as a sequence of (1) an early experimentation phase, (2) the rise of the mainstream platforms, and (3) a current phase of redesign and consolidation aiming at sustainability (Knox, 2015). While (1) brought pedagogical innovations with cMOOCs in the light of social media from 2008 onwards, phase (2) introduced the mainstream MOOC platforms like edX, Coursera, Udacity or FutureLearn as novel players in the global education market in 2012. Since then, the inflated expectations from the hype phase have made way for a more realistic perspective on MOOCs, and more and more feasible uses cases are being developed backed by research. This includes a shift from academic education towards corporate training and digital workplace learning, a focus on competence-based education with respect to professional development, and the implementation of learning analytics. These developments require new ways of credentialing as well as new service and business models (Egloffstein, 2018, 153).

With production costs of up to 55,000 € per course (Epelboin, 2017), MOOC providers needed business models to refinance course production costs as well as the costs for managing and developing their platform right from the very beginning. Structuring the wide range of MOOC monetization efforts, three generic business models have been outlined (Patru & Balaji, 2014, 71ff): (1) freemium business models, (2) business-to-business models and (3) business models for governmental involvement. Among the current "tiers of monetization" of commercial MOOC platforms (Shah, 2018b), revenues from certificates, (micro-)credentials and full online degrees can be attributed to model (1), where a basic service is free and additional fees apply. Corporate training as a source of revenue for MOOC providers clearly follows business model (2).

10.2.2 Openness as a distinct MOOC feature

10.2.2.1 Notions of openness in online education and training

Openness is "a complex socio-political term which is deeply interwoven with technology" (Deimann, 2019, 3). In educational contexts, openness is a value-laden concept with philosophical, pedagogical and political connotations (Hug, 2017), with its respective meanings being framed by social-political worldviews (e.g., self-empowerment vs. neoliberalism). Historically, the roots of openness in education date back until the late Middle Ages, where the Gutenberg press enabled public lectures, with recent technology-driven developments from open universities in the late 20th century to open courseware and MOOCs in present times (Peter & Deimann, 2013, 11). Openness has emerged as a major paradigm for research and practice in education (Bozkurt, Koseoglu, & Singh, 2019). The literature review by Bozkurt and colleagues shows publications from the last 50 years with a dramatic increase in research output from around 2008 onwards. Thereby, open educational resources (OER), open learning, MOOCs and e-learning were identified as central concepts. Despite the growing research interest, there is still no clear understanding or common definition of openness in education. However, most of the current approaches build on three core aspects: availability, affordability and accessibility (Kopp, Gröblinger, & Zimmermann, 2017). With respect to MOOCS, different implementations of openness addressing these core aspects have to be considered.

Open Distance Learning (ODL). The concept of ODL combines two distinct ideas (Gaskell, 2015), namely open learning (in relation to access, time and place of study, and flexibility) and distance learning (distance between "teacher" and learner). ODL refers to institutions providing remote access to higher education, combined with lower entry requirements concerning academic achievements, thus bridging the gap between academia and professional development. ODL also refers to online learning, where flexibility concerning time and place is implemented via internet technology.

Open Access (OA). OA describes the free access to research outputs and materials via internet. With regard to MOOCs, two different interpretations of OA come into effect (Cronin, 2017): *Open admission* refers to the access to formal education in the shape of the elimination of entry requirements like prior knowledge or certified academic achievements. *Open as free* refers to monetary costs involved for participating in a MOOC.

Open Educational Resources (OER). OER are an extension of the ideas of OA (Cronin, 2017). Here, open means not only gratis (free of cost), but also libre (enabling legal reuse). OER thus are teaching, learning and research materials in any medium that reside in the public domain or have been released under an open license that permits no-cost access, use, adaptation and redistribution by others with no or limited restrictions. (Hewlett Foundation, 2019). OER enable the "5R activities" for open content as proposed by David Wiley (2015, 6): Retain, Reuse, Revise, Remix, Redistribute.

Open Educational Practices (OEP). OEP extend OER with a shift of focus from resources to actions. In the narrow sense, OEP describe „practices which support the (re)use and production of OER through institutional policies, promote innovative pedagogical models, and respect and empower learners as co-producers on their lifelong learning paths" (Ehlers, 2011, 4). From a wider, beyond-production perspective, OEP are "collaborative practices that include the creation, use, and reuse of OER, as well as pedagogical practices employing participatory technologies and social networks" (Cronin, 2017, 4).

10.2.2.2 Openness in MOOCs

Openness is the key criterion for defining MOOCs. How openness is implemented also seems to be the major criterion of differentiation regarding MOOC approaches. Research shows that cMOOCs and xMOOCs promote different concepts of openness (Rodriguez, 2013). Most of the described notions of openness can be found in experimental MOOCs following the cMOOCs model. These courses are often built with the intention of putting OER and OEP into practice. However, they cannot always fulfil the idea of open learning in the sense of ODL as entry barriers exist in terms of prerequisites of digital literacy and tool-related competencies. Also, flexibility and scalability might be questioned due to dependencies arising from cooperative or collaborative settings.

With respect to training and professional development, current mainstream MOOCs following the xMOOCs-model are of much greater relevance. They clearly implement openness in the sense of *ODL*, as access to learning materials is not constrained by time or place. Mainstream MOOCs also work without formal prerequisites in terms of academic qualifications. Furthermore, they implement distance learning to a very large extent: Usually the assessment is also delivered online so that no physical presence is necessary.

MOOCs only partly adhere to the idea of *OA*. On the one hand, admission to MOOCs is basically free. If not, courses are being re-labelled, for example as "SPOC" (small private online course) or as "COOC" (corporate open online course), the latter only being open within a specific corporate setting (Egloffstein, 2018). On the other hand, current MOOCs are not free of charge. Depending on the underlying business model and monetization strategy, different fees can apply.

Generally, mainstream MOOCs do not consist of *OER*. MOOC contents like videos and other learning objects usually are proprietary, and there is no option to retain, reuse, revise, remix or redistribute them. From a pure open education perspective, MOOCs thus might even be regarded as a misstep, given the apparent contradiction between the proclaimed openness and the actual concept of content ownership (Wiley, 2015). However, some providers are working on the integration of the OER concept into their platforms, with expected benefits especially on the pedagogical side (Kopp et al., 2017).

Finally, current MOOCs do not fare too well regarding *OEP*. Although "open practices would not [per se] be blocked in MOOC formats" (Czerniewicz, Deacon, Glover, & Walji, 2017, 95), there is only little evidence for OEP in mainstream MOOCs. However, a number of MOOCs has enabled new partnerships between academic and business partners, with great benefits for training and professional development purposes.

10.2.2.3 Operationalisations of openness in MOOCs

Although the interpretations of openness greatly vary, studies on MOOCs often do not present explicit conceptual descriptions of openness (Weller, Jordan, DeVries, & Rolfe, 2018). Therefore, operationalisations of openness are scarce. Economides and Perifanou (2018) developed a 19-item questionnaire for evaluating the openness of a MOOC, analysing open capabilities regarding cost, time and place as well as open capabilities regarding educational resources on the MOOC. Although the instrument leads to clear results, the approach remains rather theoretical, as it does not provide information about the course features that actually constitute openness. Rousing (2014) operationalized openness in MOOCs along five dimensions: (1) education across geographical boundaries, (2) entry barriers, (3) flexibility, (4) open pedagogy and (5) openness of resources. In a qualitative approach, the author collected and described evidence of openness (structures and policies/principles) for different providers and connected those observations to an interpretative rating. While this approach provides rich information of practical relevance, validity and reliability of the interpretations can be questioned. Hendrikx, Kreijns, and Kalz (2018) developed a classification of barriers that influence intention achievement in MOOCs. In a factor-analytical approach, they identified four distinctive barrier components: (1) technical and online learning skills, (2) social interactions, (3) course design and (4) time, support and motivation. While barrier components (1) and (4) were classified as non-MOOC-related, component (3) is directly related to MOOC design, and component (2) at least in parts. Although this approach is not directly targeted at openness, it provides rich evidence, as the lack of certain barriers related to MOOC-design can be interpreted as a sign of openness.

10.3   Analysing the openness of MOOCs for training and professional development

10.3.1   Research objectives, sample and procedure

Given the broad discussion on MOOCs and open education and the lack of empirical evidence concerning openness, we intended to analyse openness in a bottom-up approach focusing on the 'tangible' dimensions of the concept. We followed the approach of Hendrikx et al. (2018) and operationalized openness *ex negativo* through the absence of barriers. Thereby, we looked at formal aspects pertaining to the learning environment and masked out intangible learner related variables. Thus, our analysis focused on 'hard barriers' to entry and participation.

From the professional development perspective, we focused on MOOCs from the field of business and management, which represent the second largest section in the global MOOC market (Shah, 2018a) and are clearly related to training and development. As the field is rather heterogeneous, we included courses from a wide range of topics as for instance Technology and Applications, Accounting, Finance and Taxation, Marketing, Entrepreneurship, Management Skills and Leadership, Innovation Management, Project Management, Legal aspects, Human Resources and Organization or Data Analytics.

The study took place in summer 2019 and included a sample of *N*=295 different MOOCs which were hosted by nine of the biggest mainly English-speaking providers in North America, Europe and Asia. We randomly included courses that lasted no longer than twelve weeks from a starting point within the period of investigation. We analysed courses from twelve topic fields which were randomly distributed in the sample. The rating was performed by a trained rater with a background in pedagogy and instructional design over a period of ten weeks and reviewed in a process of consensual validation. The courses showed a mean length of *M*=4.76 weeks (*SD*=2.66; *Min*=1; *Max*=16) and an overall workload of *M*=20.77 hours (*SD*=16.69; *Min*=1; *Max*=120). Most of the courses were hosted by academic institutions (*n*=197) in North America, Asia and Europe. Table 1 shows the structure of the sample.

Table 1. Sample structure

Provider	(1)	(2)	(3)	(4)	(5)	(6)	(7)	(8)	(9)
Technology & Application	5	2	1	0	1	34	0	0	0
Accounting, Finance & Taxation	8	7	7	1	0	0	12	1	0
Mgt. Skills & Leadership	11	10	14	8	1	2	9	1	1
Innovation Mgt.	3	2	4	2	0	2	0	1	0
Marketing	4	5	2	0	4	1	7	0	0
Entrepreneurship	1	1	2	1	2	0	1	2	3
Project Mgt.	1	2	1	0	0	0	4	0	0
General & Strategic Mgt.	4	9	6	1	0	0	9	0	0
Data Analytics	8	4	8	0	8	4	3	0	0
Legal Aspects	1	1	0	0	0	1	0	1	1
Operations Mgt.	2	4	1	0	0	4	4	1	1
HR & Organisation	2	3	4	2	0	2	1	1	0
Total n	**50**	**50**	**50**	**15**	**16**	**50**	**50**	**8**	**6**

Note. (1) Coursera, (2) edX, (3) Future Learn, (4) iversity, (5) Udacity, (6) Open SAP, (7) NPTEL, (8) Polimi, (9) Open Learning

10.3.2 Rating scheme

The rating scheme contained 20 different types of barriers which are assigned to six categories (see Table 2). The first category comprises barriers pertaining to certain individual *prerequisites* of the participants. For instance, attending the course requires a certain previous knowledge or specific technical configurations. Additionally, in some cases, certain countries like Iran, Ukraine or Cuba were excluded from attendance. Pertaining to the *materials* there were either fees for the activation of the learning contents or access was limited temporarily. Barriers concerning the *assessments* implemented in the courses were either referring to *criterial* (a specific amount of tasks that has to be passed) or *temporal* barriers (tasks have to be completed in a certain period). In some cases, participants only had a limited number of attempts to pass the tasks successfully. When looking at barriers pertaining to the *feedback* provided in the course, some providers demanded payment for the accessibility of solutions or called for peer feedback while in other cases feedback was only provided for solutions that arrived on time. Concerning the availability of *certificates*, we differentiated between barriers which implied fees for the certificate itself or the participation in the assessments. In some cases, certification was based on a certain amount of learning contents which had to be accessed during the course, or there was no online certificate available, but the participants had to pass a local exam. In the course of consensual validation, interrater reliability was calculated by means of Cohens Kappa and reached satisfactory values from .71 to .95 for the six categories.

Table 2: Categories and types of barriers

Category	Types of Barriers
Prerequisites	0= no barriers 1= language barriers 2= specific previous knowledge 3= country of origin excluded 4= attendance of associated courses 5= technical barriers 6= several barriers at the same time
Materials	0= no barriers 1= fees for the activation of materials 2= temporal limitation of access 3= both
Assessments (criterial barriers)	0= no barriers 1= all tasks must be passed 2= share of tasks must be passed
Assessments (temporal barriers)	0= no barriers 1= tasks accomplished within deadline 2= limited number of attempts
Feedback	0= no barriers 1= fees for the accessibility of solutions 2= peer feedback necessary 3= feedback only when solution on time
Certificate	0= no barriers 1= fees for certificate 2= fees for assessment participation 3= combination of 1 and 2 4= access of material 5= no certificate available

10.4   Results

10.4.1   Entry and participation barriers in MOOCs

First, we analysed the number of barriers which were implemented in each course of the sample. The number of barriers ranged from a minimum of 1 to a maximum of 6 barriers. On average, we found approx. three barriers per course (M=2.94, SD=1.23). Six courses showed the highest number of six barriers while in 38 of the courses we only identified one barrier. The latter mainly originated from Asia (n=19) or North America (n=10). When taking a look on the categories of barriers in this subsample, there was either no online certificate available (in case of the Asian courses) or a certain previous knowledge was required. In eleven courses, the providers demanded fees for certification or access to the course materials.

In the next step, we analysed the frequency of barriers in each category of the full sample. Barriers focusing on *prerequisites* were implemented in 34.6% of the courses in the sample, most of them concerned previous knowledge (18.6%) or the attendance of associated courses being part of a specialization (8.8%). While technical barriers (2.4%) or the country of origin (0.3%) were rarely used. In 4.4% of the courses in the sample, we found more than one barrier on learners' prerequisites. When analysing barriers pertaining to the course *materials*, nearly two-thirds of the sample (65.8%) did not use any barrier while nearly a fifth of the analysed courses (16.6%) demanded fees for access to the materials and 13.9% limited access temporarily. In case of the *assessments*, we differentiated between *criterial* and temporal barriers. Most of the courses demanded for a defined share of tasks/quizzes which have to be accomplished (66.4%) while nearly a third did not implement any criterial barrier (31.2%) and in 2.4% of the courses all tasks/quizzes had to be passed successfully. *Temporal* assessment barriers mostly concerned a limited number of trials (34.9%) or a certain deadline to pass the tasks/quizzes which were implemented (13.9%). In about half of the courses in the sample (51.2%), we found no temporal barrier associated with the assessments. Barriers concerning the category of *feedback* in MOOCs were rarely found. In only 10.2% of the courses peer feedback was required, while 86.1% did not implement feedback barriers. When finally looking at barriers pertaining to the *certificates*, we identified a share of 41.7% of the courses which demanded fees for certification and 9.8% demanded fees for the participation in the assessment. 18% demanded for a certain amount of access to the course materials to get the certificate. 17.3% of the courses did not implement any barrier to certification.

10.4.2 Distinctive MOOC features and number of barriers

In the next step, we analysed systematic differences concerning the number of barriers due to several distinctive features of the MOOCs in the sample. Table 3 shows the means, standard deviations and results from variance analysis. First, we compared the nine MOOC providers concerning the mean number of implemented barriers. We found significant differences: Especially Coursera, edX and openSAP implemented significantly more barriers than the other providers. When looking at the types of barriers, we typically found monetary barriers like fees for participation or certification on the one hand. On the other hand, we also observed barriers associated with promoting learning success, namely deadlines, assignments to be passed and materials to be viewed. The lowest numbers of barriers were established by NPTEL and iversity.

Further, the assumption of systematic differences also applies to the regions from which the MOOCs originate. We found a significantly higher number of barriers in MOOCs administered by European and North American institutions, while the lowest numbers of barriers were implemented in courses from Asia. Moreover, we focused on the different course topics that were represented in this study. We found significant differences and a small effect size. Post hoc tests revealed that courses in the field of Technology and Application showed a higher number of barriers compared to courses from Management Skills and Leadership or Accounting, Finance and Taxation. Finally, a comparison of academic and non-academic institutions revealed no significant differences concerning the number of barriers in business MOOCs.

Table 3: Comparison of mean numbers of barriers

	M	*SD*	F-value/T-value; η^2 /d
Provider			
Coursera *(n=50)*	3.74	1.175	
edX *(n=50)*	3.74	1.026	
FutureLearn *(n=50)*	2.84	.997	
iversity *(n=15)*	1.87	.743	
Udacity *(n=16)*	1.94	1.289	31.23**; 0.446
openSAP *(n=50)*	3.60	.535	
NPTEL *(n=50)*	1.70	.614	
Polimi *(n=8)*	2.00	.000	
Open Learning *(n=6)*	2.94	1.234	

Table 3: Comparison of mean numbers of barriers (cont.)

	M	SD	F-value/T-value; η^2 /d
Region			
North America *(n=77)*	3.38	1.396	
Europe *(n=141)*	3.05	.973	
Asia *(n=65)*	2.22	1.231	9.545**; 0.116
Australia *(n=11)*	2.73	1.348	
Africa *(n=1)*	4.00	---	
Authoring institution			
academic *(n=197)*	2.92	1.271	
non-academic *(n=98)*	2.99	1.162	*t*=-.465; *d*= -0.057
Topics			
Technology & Applications *(n=43)*	3.58	.763	
Accounting, Finance & Taxation *(n=36)*	2.81	1.142	
Management Skills & Leadership *(n=57)*	2.56	1.225	
Innovation Management *(n=14)*	2.79	.699	
Marketing *(n=23)*	2.83	1.435	
Entrepreneurship *(n=13)*	2.15	1.214	2.78; 0.097
Project Management *(n=8)*	2.88	1.356	
General & Strategic Management *(n=29)*	2.83	1.256	
Data Analytics *(n=35)*	3.40	1.265	
Legal Aspects *(n=5)*	3.20	1.304	
Operations Management *(n=17)*	3.06	1.298	
HR & Organization *(n=15)*	2.87	1.598	

10.4.3 Barrier patterns

In order to identify specific patterns of barrier combinations, we calculated a latent class analysis following an exploratory approach. As there were six different barrier categories, in a first step, we compared six latent class models to figure out the optimal number of classes. Table 4 provides several information criteria which are the basis for the model comparison. The values lead to the assumption that the solution with two classes (highlighted in bold) probably fits the data best as it shows the lowest BIC and the highest value for entropy. The AIC, however, is somewhat ambiguous as it is even slightly lower in the three-class-solution, so the results should be interpreted with caution. The average latent class probabilities which should reach values near 1 range between 0.982 (class 2) and 0.954 (class 1) indicating a reliable model estimation.

Table 4: Model comparison

Model	AIC	BIC	adj. BIC	Entropy
1 class	1409.138	1464.442	1416.873	---
2 classes	**1248.643**	**1362.939**	**1264.629**	**0.959**
3 classes	1243.175	1416.463	1267.412	0.747
4 classes	1250.972	1483.251	1283.459	0.703
5 classes	1271.259	1562.530	1311.998	0.731
6 classes	1297.342	1647.604	1346.331	0.736

In the next step, we focused on the two-class-solution and analysed the probabilities for each category to be either assigned to class 1 or 2. We found that some categories tend to be located in both classes, while others are clearly assigned to one of the classes. Table 5 illustrates the probabilities of being part of a class for each of the categories. Probabilities beyond the value of 0.500 are highlighted in bold.

Table 5: Class assignment probabilities

Category	Class 1	Class 2
Prerequisites		
knowledge	**0.895**	0.327
country	0.000	0.016
specialization	0.105	0.344
technical	0.000	0.110
several	0.000	0.203
Materials		
activation fee	0.000	**0.521**
temporal limitation	**1.000**	0.362
both	0.000	0.117

Table 5: Class assignment probabilities (cont.)

Category	Class 1	Class 2
Assessments (criterial barriers)		
all tasks	0.026	0.037
share of tasks	**0.974**	**0.963**
Assessments (temporal barriers)		
deadline	**0.828**	0.000
limited attempts	0.172	**1.000**
Feedback		
solution fee	0.000	0.061
peer feedback	0.000	**0.909**
solution on time	**1.000**	0.030
Certificate		
certification fee	0.000	**0.737**
participation fee	0.000	0.174
combination	0.000	0.090
access material	**0.688**	0.000
no certificate	0.312	0.000

Concerning the individual *prerequisites,* the main differences between the classes is related to the previous knowledge of the participants followed by courses that are part of a specialization. When looking at the course *materials,* the providers either demand fees for the activation or limit the access temporarily. In the *assessment* categories, the classes do mainly differ by implementing a deadline to provide the solutions or limiting the number of attempts to successfully pass the assessments. Most of the courses demand for a share of tasks that have to be solved, concerning the criterial assessment category, we did not observe any clear differences. Pertaining to *feedback*, the classes differed insofar as either peer feedback was obligatory or the participants had to submit the solutions in time to receive feedback. Considering *certification* in classes 1 and 2, they differ insofar as they demand either fees for the certificate itself or a certain amount of materials and contents that have to be viewed.

In summary, class 1 contains courses that rather require a certain amount of previous knowledge, limit the access to the contents temporarily, and offer a certificate when the participants provide their solutions for a certain share of tasks and quizzes in time or prove to have viewed a certain amount of the course materials. Class 2, on the other hand, consists of courses that typically, charge fees for the activation of the course materials or for the certificates.

Consequently, it can be assumed that providers either tend to implement monetary or pedagogical barriers, the latter rather being associated with the learning process than with monetization in terms business models. However, we found no significant differences between the groups concerning the total number of barriers.

Table 6: Distribution of providers in classes

	n Class 1		*n* Class 2		
Provider	**acad.**	**non acad.**	**acad.**	**non acad.**	**Total**
Coursera	0	1	47	2	**50**
edX	0	0	44	6	**50**
Future Learn	0	0	41	9	**50**
iversity	0	0	4	11	**15**
Udacity	0	7	0	9	**16**
openSAP	0	50	0	0	**50**
NPTEL	24	0	26	0	**50**
Polimi	0	0	8	0	**8**
Open Learning	2	1	1	2	**6**
Total	**26**	**59**	**171**	**39**	**295**

Table 6 shows the structure of the latent classes concerning the distribution of providers. Class 2 is larger and includes more than 200 courses. It becomes obvious that for a majority of the providers (e.g. Coursera, edX, FutureLearn, open SAP, iversity, Polimi), the courses fall homogeneously into either one of the classes, while other provider-specific subsamples (e.g. Udacity, NPTEL, Open Learning) rather split up.

10.5   Discussion

In this study, we explored entry and participation barriers in MOOCs in order to add empirical evidence to the broad discussion about openness in online learning. First, we outlined different concepts of openness in education and reviewed corresponding operationalisations in MOOC research. Framing openness as the absence of entry and participation barriers, we developed a rating scheme which covered barriers from six dimensions. We reviewed $N=295$ business MOOCs from nine major global MOOC providers out of twelve different topic areas. When looking at the absolute numbers of barriers, we found a wide range of barriers from all of the categories reviewed. Only in a small share of courses just one barrier was observable. Concerning the importance of certain categories, we found a criterial assessment barrier in most of the courses where a certain share of tasks had to be accomplished successfully. Another significant category of barriers concerned the fees for course certificates, which were obligatory in nearly half of the sampled courses reviewed. These descriptive results support the assumption of different barrier concepts, which either come along with monetary, business-related constraints or rather stress pedagogical criteria in order to promote successful online learning.

Concerning differences between the observed numbers of barriers due to distinctive features of MOOCs, we identified systematic variance. Especially courses from Asia seem to correspond with the original notions of openness to a higher degree compared to European and North American courses. This might be due to the increased importance of online-based education in populous Asia and could be associated with a certain educational policy. In terms of business models, the vast absence of barriers in Asian courses could therefore be a sign of governmental involvement rather than providers following financial interests. Pertaining to the course topics, offerings in the field of Technology and Applications showed the highest overall number of barriers. Taking a closer look at the types of barriers implemented, we found a mixture which mainly concerned learners' prerequisites or a set of criteria regulating the learning outcomes, while only a small share of courses demanded fees. With regard to the confounding between the course topic Technology and Applications and the provider openSAP, we analysed whether certain topics were administered by certain providers but could not find any other significant patterns.

Finally, we intended to identify typical combinations of barriers by means of an exploratory latent class analysis. The two-class solution fitted the data best, indicating two groups of courses which mainly differ regarding the types of barriers implemented. In class 1, we identified higher probabilities for barriers which are related to pedagogical criteria for successful learning (e.g. deadlines, viewed contents), while in class 2, which represented large parts of our sample, we mainly found high probabilities for monetary barriers pointing towards revenue goals in terms of business-related strategies. Thereby, some providers could be clearly attributed to one of the classes, while others had courses in both classes. Hence, the majority of providers seems to concentrate on one of the barrier concepts, while others are inclined to implement a mixture of different approaches.

Considering these results, it becomes evident that the openness of MOOCs seems to be restricted to a basic accessibility of the courses. However, one has to differentiate between barriers that are associated with a meaningful structuring of learning processes, while others indicate business models in the market for professional development. Thus, not every barrier can be interpreted as an impediment for learning. It would be fruitful to shed light on the question if some of the barrier concepts we found are more successful than others in terms of course retention or instructional quality.

Evidently, our study faces some limitations. The convenience sample is a snapshot and can only cover a fraction of the global MOOC market. Due to language barriers, we had to limit our analysis to the English-speaking world and could not consider the vast number of MOOCs in other languages. From the professional development perspective, an extension towards other topics seems to be desirable for future approaches. Thus, the results may be interpreted as a first exploration of the field not yet providing representative findings. Further, the interpretation of the barriers in MOOCs depends on the period of investigation, as some providers change their barrier concepts when a course is not activated anymore.

To sum up, we found evidence for a reduced concept of openness implemented in MOOCs for business-related professional development. In light of the current findings on MOOCs refuting the widely heralded claim of education for all (Reich & Ruipérez-Valiente, 2019), this is not surprising. Van de Oudeweetering and Agirdag (2018) argue that even though privileged learners benefit more from MOOCs because of certain formal barriers, MOOCs still reach a notable share of underprivileged learners that would otherwise not participate in academic education. For training and professional development, this claim might hold in a similar way. The basic accessibility of MOOCs grants access to formal training for both employees and companies which might otherwise not have had the opportunity. Since MOOC providers have to address financial aspects and sustainability, barriers aiming at monetization are a necessary precondition for granting these opportunities.

With a focus on tangible factors like barriers and constraints, this study adds a pragmatic perspective to the discussion on openness in MOOCs. It has become clear that, in addition to a basic accessibility, differentiated entry and participation barriers aiming both at the generation of revenue and learning outcomes have to be taken into account.

References

Bozkurt, A., Koseoglu, S. & Singh, L. (2019). An analysis of peer reviewed publications on openness in education in half a century: Trends and patterns in the open hemisphere. *Australasian Journal of Educational Technology, 35*(4), 78-97.

Cronin, C. (2017). Openness and Praxis: Exploring the Use of Open Educational Practices in Higher Education. *The International Review of Research in Open and Distributed Learning, 18*(5).

Czerniewicz, L., Deacon, A., Glover, M. & Walji, S. (2017). MOOC-making and open educational practices. *Journal of Computing in Higher Education, 29*, 81-97.

Deimann, M. (2019). Openness. In I. Jung (Ed.), *Open and Distance Education Theory Revisited. Implications for the Digital Era* (pp. 39-46). Singapore: Springer.

Economides, A. A. & Perifanou, M. A. (2018). Dimensions of Openness in MOOCs & OERs. *Proceedings of EDULEARN18 Conference* (pp. 3684-3693). Palma de Mallorca: IATED.

Egloffstein, M. (2018). Massive open online courses in digital workplace learning: current state and future perspectives. In D. Ifenthaler (Ed.), *Digital workplace learning: bridging formal and informal learning with digital technologies* (pp. 149-166). Cham: Springer.

Egloffstein, M. & Ifenthaler, D. (2017). Employee Perspectives on MOOCs for Workplace Learning. *Tech Trends, 61*(1), 65-70.

Ehlers, U.-D. (2011). Extending the territory: From open educational resources to open educational practices. *Journal of Open, Flexible and Distance Learning*, 15(2).

Epelboin, Y. (2017). MOOCs: A Viable Business Model? In M. Jemni, K. Khribi, & M. Koutheair (Eds.), *Open Education: from OERs to MOOCs* (pp. 241-259). Berlin: Springer.

*Gaskell, A. (2015). Open Distance Learning. In M. A. Peters (Ed.), *Encyclopedia of Educational Philosophy and Theory* (pp. 1688-1693). Singapore: Springer.

Hamori, M. (2017). The Drivers of Employer Support for Professional Skill Development in MOOCs. In C. Delgado Kloos, P. Jermann, M. Pérez-Sanagustín, D. T. Seaton, & S. White (Eds.): *Digital Education: Out to the World and Back to the Campus. EMOOCs 2017* (pp. 203-209) Cham: Springer.

Hendrikx, M., Kreijns, K., & Kalz, M. (2018). A Classification of Barriers that Influence Intention Achievement in MOOCs. *Proceedings of EC-TEL 2018, LNCS, 11082*, 3-15.

Hewlett Foundation (2019). Open Educational Resources. Retrieved from https://hewlett.org/strategy/open-educational-resources/ (2019-29-11)

Hug, T. (2017). Defining Openness in Education. In M. A. Peters (Ed.), *Encyclopedia of Educational Philosophy and Theory* (pp. 387-392). Singapore: Springer.

Ifenthaler, D., Bellin-Mularski, N., & Mah, D.-K. (2015). Internet: Its impact and its potential for learning and instruction. In J. M. Spector (Ed.), *The SAGE encyclopedia of educational technology* (pp. 416-422). Thousand Oaks, CA: Sage.

Knox, J. (2015). Massive Open Online Courses (MOOCs). In M. A. Peters (Ed.), *Encyclopedia of Educational Philosophy and Theory* (pp. 1372-1378). Singapore: Springer.

Kopp, M., Gröblinger, O., & Zimmermann, C. (2017). Increasing Educational Value: The Transformation of MOOCs into Open Educational Resources. In C. Delgado Kloos, P. Jermann, M. Pérez-Sanagustín, D. T. Seaton, & S. White (Eds.), *Digital Education: Out to the World and Back to the Campus. EMOOCs 2017* (pp. 223-232). Cham: Springer.

Milligan, C., Littlejohn, A. (2017). Why study on a MOOC? The motives of students and professionals. *International Review of Research in Open and Distributed Learning, 18*(2).

Olsson, U. (2016). Open courses and MOOCs as professional development—is the openness hindrance? *Education + Training, 58*(2), 229-243.

Patru, M. & Balaji, V. (2016). *Making Sense of MOOCs: A Guide for Policy-Makers in Developing Countries.* Paris: UNESCO.

Peter, S. & Deimann, M. (2013). On the role of openness in education: A historical reconstruction. *Open Praxis, 5*(2), 7-14.

Reich, J. & Ruipérez-Valiente, J.A. (2019). The MOOC pivot. What happened to disruptive transformation of education? *Science, 363*(6423), 130-131.

Rodriguez, O. (2013). The concept of openness behind c- and x-MOOCs (Massive Open Online Courses). *Open Praxis, 5*(1), 67-73.

Rousing, T. (2014). *The Openness of MOOCs. A multifaceted investigation of four platforms.* Copenhagen: Business School. Retrieved from_http://hdl.handle.net/10417/4597 (2019-29-11)

Shah, D. (2018a). *By the numbers: MOOCs in 2018.* Retrieved from_https://www. classcentral.com/report/mooc-stats-2018/ (2019-29-11).

Shah, D. (2018b). *Six Tiers of MOOC Monetization.* Retrieved from https://www. classcentral.com/report/six-tiers-mooc-monetization/ (2019-29-11).

Spector, J. M. (2017). A Critical Look at MOOCs. In M. Jemni, K. Khribi, & M. Koutheair (Eds.), *Open Education: from OER to MOOCs* (pp. 135-147). Heidelberg: Springer.

Tu, C.H. & Sujo-Montes, L. E. (2015). MOOCs. In R. Papa (Ed.), *Media Rich Instruction. Connecting Curriculum To All Learners* (pp. 287-304). New York: Springer.

Van de Oudeweetering, K. & Agirdag, O. (2018). MOOCS as Accelerators of Social Mobility? A Systematic Review. *Educational Technology & Society, 21*(1), 1-11.

Waks, L. J. (2016). *The Evolution and Evaluation of Massive Open Online Courses. MOOCs in Motion.* London: Palgrave Macmillan.

Weller, M., Jordan, K., DeVries, I., & Rolfe, V. (2018). Mapping the open education landscape: citation network analysis of historical open and distance education research. *Open Praxis, 10*(2), 109-126.

Wiley, D. (2015). The MOOC Misstep and the Open Education Infrastructure. In C. J. Bonk, M. M. Lee, T. C. Reeves, & T. H. Reynolds (Eds.), *MOOCs and Open Education Around the World* (pp.3-11). New York: Routledge.

Yuan, L. & Powell, S. (2015). Partnership Model for Entrepreneurial Innovation in Open Online Learning. *eLearning Papers, 41*, 1-9.

11 The High School Career Academy as a Model for Promoting Technological Preparation: Promising Practices and Challenges in the United States

Victor M. Hernandez-Gantes and Edward C. Fletcher

11.1 Introduction

In the age of the global economy, technological development is at the core of human productivity (Gordon, 2016). As technology has become ubiquitous at work and in everyday life, it has become evident that related use requires education and training for further development and efficient application (Mokyr, 2018). In the United States (US), the role of science, technology, engineering, and mathematics (STEM) has been highly recognized to ensure global competitiveness through technological development and related preparation. As such, strategies to boost participation in STEM-related careers have become a national priority (National Science & Technology Council, 2018). The problem is that high school graduates continue to lag behind in their STEM preparation needed for success in today's high-tech and knowledge-based economy (National Science Board, 2018). In turn, inadequate student readiness often prevents youth from productive transitions to further education or work (Carnevale, Smith, & Strohl, 2010; Loera, Nakamoto, Oh, & Rueda, 2013).

Participation in the information technology (IT) industry is an example of this trend. The IT industry involves the integration of digital technology in all business operations and requires a variety of occupations such as hardware and software engineers, programmers, and systems analysts; all sharing a computer-related focus in all types of organizations (Wright, 2009). At the technician level, most employers require preparation beyond high school and in some cases certifications for entry into the IT workforce (Wright, 2009). From 2018 through 2028, the IT sector is expected to grow 12%, which is faster than the average for all occupations. Similarly, the median annual wage in 2018 ($86,320) is much higher than the median annual wage for all occupations ($36,640) (Bureau of Labor Statistics, 2019). However, despite the strong IT employment outlook, colleges and employers have challenges in finding students and workers in the pipeline (National Academies of Sciences, 2017). One reason for this trend is that students often report having difficulty understanding IT career opportunities and related preparation, which may be a contributing factor accounting for the low participation rates in related pathways (Wright, 2009).

To increase participation in technology-based programs such as IT, educators have explored alternative strategies to boost interest and preparation in related pathways in high school (Warner et al., 2016). Featuring smaller learning communities and occupational career themes, the career academy model has resulted in promising outcomes over the past two decades (Kemple, 2008; Lanford & Maruco, 2019). Career academies are small schools within a larger comprehensive school and work in partnership with employers to integrate academic and technical content and provide work-based learning experiences to students (Stern, Dayton, & Raby, 2010). With the goal to prepare students for college and careers, career academies were originally designed to help students at-risk of dropping out, but over the past two decades student enrollment has diversified attracting students who are better prepared. Presently, it has been reported that there are about 7,000 career academies in operation in the US, with an annual combined enrollment of about one million high school students (National Career Academy Coalition, 2019). Over the years, there has been consistent evidence documenting the positive impact of participation in career academies on dropout rates, attendance, academic course-taking, and labor market outcomes (Kemple, 2008; Warner et al., 2016). However, as the popularity of the career academy model has grown over the years, the quality of implementation and student technological preparation have been taken for granted. Given the positive outcomes of participation, the general assumption is that the career academy model should work anywhere if standards of practice are followed (Conchas & Clark, 2002; Lanford & Maruco, 2019).

With this frame of reference, our goal was to conduct a holistic analysis of the career academy model, featuring an IT curricular theme, when implemented under different conditions. The analysis is based on the results of a three-year study designed to explore how IT career academies with different configurations were implemented, with emphasis on the challenges and opportunities in enabling students to become college and career ready. Specifically, the study was guided by the following research questions: How are career academies, featuring a technology-oriented theme, implemented under different local conditions? What are the implementation challenges and opportunities for promoting students' technological preparation?

11.2 Conceptual Framework

The project's conceptual framework was built upon two core foundational strands informed by the academy model in the US and the role of organizational structures in educational settings.

11.2.1 The Career Academy Model

Career academies are smaller learning communities within high schools designed to help students become college and work ready (Orr, Bailey, Hughes, Karp, & Kienzl, 2004). A key design element of career academies is the integration of academic and technical content to enhance curricular relevance and students' career interests (Castellano et al., 2007; Kemple & Snipes, 2000). To that end, the model relies on the use of occupational themes (e.g., Engineering, IT, health sciences) drawing from 16 career clusters in the US (Advance CTE, 2019). Another requirement is the provision of work-based learning opportunities for students, which are typically accomplished in partnership with local employers In addition, in collaboration with postsecondary institutions, academies also afford students participation in dual enrollment to earn college-level credit (Hernandez-Gantes, 2016; Lanford & Maruco, 2018).

The benefits of participation in career academies have been well documented, including data from random-assignment studies, and have reinforced the promising premises of the model (Stern et al., 2010). Hence, participation in career academies has resulted in positive outcomes, including increased attendance and academic course-taking, higher graduation rates, and lower dropout rates (Stern et al., 2010; Warner et al., 2016). Related research has also suggested that career academy students perform as well, have a postsecondary transitional plan, and tend to earn about 11% higher compared to non-academy graduates, eight years after completing high school (Kemple, 2008; Kemple & Snipes, 2000; Silverberg, Warner, Fong, & Goodwin, 2004).

Due to the positive outcomes, the implementation of the career academy model has grown dramatically over the past decade, with some states requiring all high schools to have at least one career academy (Castellano et al., 2007; Hernandez-Gantes, 2016). However, as schools and districts have rushed to adopt the model, the quality of implementation has varied greatly. To address this issue, there have been efforts to inform related implementation with the development of standards of practice by national organizations (Stern, Dayton, & Raby, 2010). Nevertheless, implementation issues continued to linger, pointing to the role of varying local conditions and supports (Conchas & Clark, 2002; Lanford & Maruco, 2019).

11.2.2 Nature and Role of Organizational Structures

Unlike traditional academic programs, career academies require holistic approaches for their implementation. Within this model, the factors to consider are the curriculum, local conditions, and teacher/student supports. These factors form a system whereby organizational structures are complementary to each other (Hernández-Gantes, Phelps, Jones, & Holub, 1995; Newmann & Wehlage, 1995; Ryan, 2011). Specifically, the nature and role of the four structures associated with successful schools, served as part of the conceptual framework for our analysis: organizational purpose and vision, curriculum and instruction, operational supports, and external supports. First, researchers have indicated that a clear and coherent *organizational purpose and vision* is essential for effective implementation and student success (Adelman & Taylor, 2003; National Career Academy Coalition [NCAC], 2013; Newmann & Wehlage, 1995). That is, without stakeholders' agreement on a vision for implementation, it would be difficult to garner buy-in from community partners and ensure fidelity of implementation. In turn, the *curriculum design and instructional strategies* of career academies must also be aligned with research-based standards to ensure program quality. For instance, in a successful career academy, the curriculum must be organized under a coherent structure that emphasizes applied strategies aligned with the chosen occupational theme, such as IT (NCAC, 2013).

Further, career academies require complex *organizational supports* to remain viable and relevant (Lanford & Maruco, 2018). Related supports typically include student services, teacher-related assistance (e.g., professional development, planning time), and administrative supports, such as funding and appropriate equipment and facilities (Hernandez-Gantes & Brendefur, 2003; NCAC, 2013). Finally, when implementing career academies, *external supports* must be considered as well. External factors may include partnerships with local employers and other community stakeholders to provide students with work-based learning and mentorship opportunities (Lanford & Maruco, 2018, 2019; NCAC, 2013). Related research has suggested that career and technical education programs with established partnerships tend to perform better compared to sites with ineffective or no external partners (Alfeld, Charner, Johnson, & Watts, 2013; Badgett, 2016).

To date, there is extensive literature documenting outcomes of participation in career academies. However, there is limited holistic understanding of the role that local conditions and organizational structures play on the implementation and the preparation of students in career academies featuring technology-based curricular themes.

11.3 Method

We used a multi-case study design to explore the implementation of three IT career academies operating under different configurations and local conditions. We wanted to gather in depth descriptive information about the setting and strategies needed to provide students with opportunities to enhance their IT college and career readiness. According to Stake (2006), case studies allow researchers to focus on the description of ordinary relationships and practice in natural settings targeting aspects of concern. Thus, we studied IT academies (the cases) featuring different levels of implementation according to the standards of the NAF (formerly known as the National Academy Foundation). NAF is a national organization that provides curricular support, professional development, and technical assistance to a national network of high school career academies in five career themes, including IT (NAF, 2014). With an established membership of 667 academies across 38 states, the NAF network provided an ideal context to explore how the academy model might contribute to the technological preparation and career readiness leading to the pursuit of IT pathways beyond high school.

To promote college and career readiness, the NAF model emphasizes smaller learning communities using student cohorts, career-themed and sequenced coursework, common teacher planning, career-themed guidance, and ongoing professional development. A key component focuses on integrated curriculum and instruction to promote career and academic learning around a relevant theme (e.g., IT) through project-based activities involving classroom and work-based learning experiences, and internships. The work-based learning component is used to promote career awareness, exploration, and practicum opportunities for students. An advisory board, including members representing community stakeholder groups, is also required (NAF, 2014).

11.3.1 Sampling Procedure and Academy Sites

We selected three NAF career academies featuring curricular themes related to information technology (IT). IT is one of 16 career clusters serving as a broad curricular framework for career and technical education in the US. Each cluster provides the basis for developing programs of study connecting high schools and postsecondary education in a pathway of interest. In this regard, the IT cluster focuses on entry level occupations related to the design, development, support and management of hardware, software, multimedia and systems integration services (Advance CTE, 2019). Based on NAF ratings of the school's implementation, we sought the participation of IT career academies representing distinguished, model, and certified levels of efficacy for comparative purposes. According to NAF standards, a distinguished academy meets the highest level of implementation in every area of operation, while a model academy may require improvement in some aspects. In turn, a certified academy represents compliance with basic requirements, but further improvement is needed.

Cascade Academy. Cascade Academy is located in an urban area in the Southeastern region of the US and rated as distinguished according to NAF standards. Cascade is a high school academy with an enrollment of 653 students comprised of 57% White, 24% Latinx, 12% African American/Black, 4% Asian, 2% Multiracial, and 1% American Indian. The gender makeup was 31% female and 69% male. Forty-two percent of the student population were economically disadvantaged. Cascade Academy had a 98% graduation rate (within four years) for the 2017-2018 academic year. The academy has built an extensive network of partners in the community who contribute with funding, mentorship, and internship opportunities for students.

Johnson Academy. Johnson Academy is a high school that focuses on promoting the college and career readiness of students through college visits and work-based learning activities (e.g., job shadowing and internships). The academy is in an urban area within a Midwestern state, and has extensive university and corporate partnerships. The academy has a small student population of approximately 700 learners. The demographic characteristics of students in the academy are 98% African American/Black, 100% low-income, and 48% female. Johnson Academy had a 95% graduation rate (within four years) for the 2017-2018 academic year.

Victory Academy. Victory is a certified NAF-IT themed magnet academy, located in an urban area within the western region in the US. The academy enrolls approximately 325 students based on an open enrollment policy to ensure equity and inclusion of students regardless of background. The school district did not have transportation for students but encouraged students to ride public transportation (e.g., bus system). The ethnic and racial background of students at Victory Academy were as follows: 92% Latinx, 4% Asian, 2% African American/Black, and 2% White. The gender makeup was 52% female and 48% male. Eighty-nine percent of the student population was economically disadvantaged. Victory Academy had a 95% graduation rate (within four years) reported for the 2017-2018 academic year.

Career academies are typically small schools within larger comprehensive schools. In this study the academies listed above represent a variation in structural design as they operate as stand-alone schools. In the US, this type of academies is often referred to as wall-to-wall or whole-schools as they operate on their own and are not part of a larger high school. In turn, a magnet academy is designed to "attract" students beyond the neighborhood boundaries set for a traditional school. Depending on the size of a school district, magnet schools may or may not offer bus service to students.

11.3.2 Data Sources and Participants

To document how the academies operate, we conducted the study over a two-year period through a review of school data, and two site visits to interview stakeholders and students. Once academies were identified, the principals agreed to provide access to school data and assisted with the coordination of the site visits and interviews with stakeholders. Regarding school data, we collected documents assembled within an electronic binder related to the structure and implementation of the IT Career Academy. Documents included in the electronic binder were organized around four domains: academy development and structure, advisory board, curriculum and instruction, and work-based learning. Example items included in the electronic binder were videos of students, brochures with information regarding school performance, and examples of student capstone projects. In addition, data on student performance, graduation rates, and attendance was also available for review in the binders. The review of related information allowed us to learn about the academy development, organizational structure, supports, and general performance.

After a period of planning, we then conducted a five-day site visit in Year 1 to interview school and district administrators, school board members, technical and core academic teachers, school counselors, support staff, parents, postsecondary partners, business, and community partners. Interview data focused on understanding the local setting and nature of implementation based on the perspectives of contributing stakeholders. Questions we asked were about the development of the academy, motivation for participation, school climate, organizational structure, curriculum and instruction, student supports, and about external supports. During the initial visit, we also conducted classroom observations to develop insight regarding the instructional environments, teaching and learning processes, and types and levels of assessments administered in the career academies. To this end, we used a protocol involving note-taking on the role of teachers, student behaviors and interactions, and nature of instructional tasks. In addition, we conducted off-school site visits with business and industry partners for tours and interviews to learn about collaboration and contribution to work-based learning opportunities for students. Subsequently, in Year 2 of the study, we followed up with a four-day site visit to interview students and alumni to learn about their participation experiences and impact upon graduation. During this visit we asked students about the motivation to participate in a career academy instead of a traditional high school, their participation experience and supports, nature of work-based learning experiences, and preparation for transitions to further education and/or work.

Overall, during the two rounds of site visits combined, we conducted individual and group interviews with 238 stakeholders including district and school and district administrators ($n = 26$), teaching and other support staff ($n =$

49), community parties such as parents, school board members, and postsecondary partners ($n = 43$), staff ($n = 3$), postsecondary partners ($n = 4$), business and industry partners ($n = 17$), employers ($n = 30$), ($n = 3$), and students and alumni ($n = 100$). Individual and group interviews typically lasted approximately 60 minutes in duration. In all, data stemming from these multiple sources and perspectives allowed us to develop a consistent and triangulated understanding of the career academies' implementation.

11.3.3 Data Analysis

All interviews were audio-recorded and transcribed verbatim. All data (curricular documents, classroom observations, and interviews) were analyzed using thematic analysis to make sense of contextual factors underlying program implementation. Thematic analysis is a widely used method in qualitative research with a focus on identifying patterned meaning, as well as commonalties and differences across a dataset (Boyatzis, 1998). As such, we followed the method for thematic analysis using standards of practice reported in related literature for organizing, analyzing, and reporting themes found within a data set (Boyatzis, 1998; Nowell, Norris, White, & Moules, 2017). Accordingly, when conducting the analysis we used the following steps: (a) read the transcripts in their entirety to seize a sense of the whole in terms of how participants talked about the academy and related practices; (b) re-read the transcribed interviews and demarcated transitions in meaning using a lens focusing on work readiness; (c) reflected on the emerging themes for critical verification of evidence within and across transcripts; and (d) synthesized the themes into statements seeking to represent the perspectives of the participants (Boyatzis, 1998). The goal of the analysis was to identify the main patterns (i.e. themes) in the data characterizing the nature of implementation within and across career academies implementation, and used the themes to make sense of implications for opportunities and challenges for promoting students' technological preparation. To this end, data triangulation allowed for analysis within and across sources (curricular documents from the electronic binder, classroom observation notes, and individual/group interviews) to establish cross-data consistency. The research team also conducted analytical triangulation through collective reading and analyses and discussion of transcripts and themes.

The data collection and analysis phase of the project was completed upon receiving approval from our university board regarding provisions for the protection of research participants. On that note, to preserve the confidentiality and anonymity of participating sites and stakeholders, all identifiers in this manuscript were removed or modified. As such, the names of career academies and any stakeholders noted or quoted in the report are pseudonyms used in lieu of actual names.

11.4 Findings

11.4.1 Role of Shared Vision for Implementation

Across school sites, the common denominator for the adoption of the academy model was the need to respond to a crisis, which presented an opportunity to do something different. For the community at Cascade Academy, the issue was a desegregation lawsuit that culminated with the call for implementing a new vision for the local high school. At Johnson Academy, the problem was lack of resources and need to improve student performance, while at Victory Academy growing enrollment in the district created a need for new school facilities. As a result, and for different reasons, a crisis prompted a call to either re-envision an existing school or create something new. In all cases, local stakeholders agreed on three elements of a vision for a new approach to help students succeed in school upon graduation from high school. First, the career academy model was viewed as a promising alternative to the traditional high school model. Instead of pushing for another large high school with enrollment over 1,000 students, a shared agreement focused on planning for a smaller learning community in the form of a career academy. Mr. Gonzalez, [from Victory Academy] recounted how this alternative solution was seized:

That's how all these things started back then. It was seen, truly, as an alternative to the large, comprehensive high schools that we have in the district, which we had four at the time. [...] A lot of kids would get lost in big, comprehensive schools. I call it hiding in schools. That was one of the things I found in my research was a lot of faculty and students are able to hide in a large, comprehensive school.

Second, we also found a consensus about the need to promote college and career readiness, with emphasis in areas related to science, technology, engineering, and mathematics (STEM). In this regard, school and district administrators along with community stakeholders consistently recognized the importance of preparing students for the requirements of the new economy, so they could make successful transitions to college or work. On that note, the third element of a common vision for the adoption of the academy model, was the identification of technological preparation and work readiness as the keys to success in the world of work. In this regard, the view by Cascade Academy stakeholders was a recognized value of technological preparation along with employability skills (e.g. interpersonal, communication) as important. To clarify this view, Mr. Hendrick, a gaming teacher, offered the following perspective:

It's not only the hard skills, such as programming and design. It's also the soft skills. It's the communication, the interpersonal skills, being punctual, team skills, and responsibility. Our students are unique [but] we feel that we have a bit of a culture where the students lack soft skills, and that's something we focus on very heavily...

The vision that emerged at Cascade Academy was holistic with buy-in from all community partners including district and school staff, parents, employers, and other groups. In turn, the vision for Johnson Academy materialized out of a strong and charismatic district leader who believed in the value of rigorous education and technological preparation. In the case of Victory Academy, the vision emerged from the district's needs assessment and the opportunity to establish an academy using an existing facility. Over the years, the organic buy-in from the community underlying Cascade Academy has proven more stable in terms of sustaining the viability and success of the academy. In contrast, the vision for implementation in the other two sites has been revised along the way to fit evolving needs in the community.

11.4.2 Nature of Curriculum and Instruction

The choice of a curricular theme for an academy is at the core of successful implementation. At Cascade Academy, the choice was to build upon a desire to focus on technological preparation through a curricular theme featuring IT pathways. To that end, Cascade Academy offers clearly defined programs of study for students in the areas of multimedia design technology, computer programming, and network systems technology. In this regard, digitalization applications focused on all aspects related to the adoption, maintenance, and troubleshooting of digital processes and tools used in the workplace. Further, in collaboration with a local two-year college, the academy afforded students the opportunity to earn college credits through a dual enrollment program and to eventually complete an Associate of Arts degree while earning their high school diploma. In addition, Cascade students can complete national technology certifications in areas such as networking, gaming and simulations, programming, and technology support services. To complement in-school instruction, Cascade Academy partners with an extensive network of local employers (from large corporations to small businesses) who provide students with paid work-based learning experiences (e.g., internships). For each IT program of study, related coursework is clearly and coherently articulated from 9th through 12th grade with an emphasis on project- and problem-based instructional strategies. Deborah, a partner representing a global corporation explained the common goal:

We want to promote careers in STEM. We want to feed our own talent pipeline with good, well-prepared students because we have a hard time finding qualified applicants in many areas. This is an investment in an upcoming generation that really pays off for us.

In turn, at Johnson Academy, the vision for curriculum and instruction initially focused on rigorous college preparation. However, recognizing that this focus was only serving about 30% of their student population, in terms of aspirations

234

upon graduation from high school, a new vision emphasized providing students the opportunity to pursue a variety of curricular tracks. Thus, Johnson Academy students can complete programs of study in animation and digital design, business and finance, construction trades, health sciences, information technology, and STEM clubs and competitions. In this case, although teachers and counselors can help students customize their program of study based on their interests, the multiplicity of curricular tracks and courses diffuses the visibility of a coherent technology preparation in IT. As such, the focus on digitalization was reduced to applications to record, compress, and share music in different formats by a small group of students through participation in a club. The club attracts students with interest in technology also including other digitalization applications int the context of video production. Related work is considered extracurricular and informally supervised by a teacher. Thus, with many different curricular tracks available to students, it was evident that only few students concentrated in any particular track or participated in dual enrollment courses to earn college credit. Also, the only work-based learning experiences available to students were in the form of short summer camps or participation in labs for exposure and awareness of career options.

Similarly, at Victory Academy, the initial vision built upon a mathematics- and technology-based curriculum, which was revisited to emphasize film production and technology. Stakeholders believed their location, which was near a large film studio, warranted such emphasis. In this instance, the focus on technology was on integrating the arts, video production, script writing, and graphic design. Digitalization is applied in all aspects of digital filmmaking and video production including video development, live video production, and post production through filmmaking projects. Such focus was viewed as important in helping the majority of students with Latinx roots find an outlet to tell their experiences and stories. Although the curricular vision for the school was built upon broad technology preparation, the shift to filmmaking turned into an emphasis on the use of video technology and away from IT. In turn, access to film studios proved difficult and the absence of a local industry prevented the school from offering related work-based learning experiences to students. Further, like students at Johnson Academy, only few students at Victory Academy were able to earn college credit through dual enrollment as well. Dr. Santiago, school principal, summarized the challenge for curriculum and instruction:

So, I'm making films, and I need to access industry when there is no industry around us, and there is no budgeting to take my students to industry. I wish there was something right here where we could get our kids for that support. Some of our kids now getting into media technology, yeah, they've seen a movie, but they've never really been on any movie set.

In general, the role of clear and coherent pathways in IT-related areas was evident at Cascade Academy where students could articulate their interest in such tracks and were digitalization applications in the curriculum were more evident. Given the specific focus on IT, and the numerous employers of different sizes in the community who partner with the school, students can round their technological preparation through paid internships. In contrast, at the other two sites, given their choice of curricular theme it was evident that coherent technological preparation was more diffused and restricted to classroom instruction and extracurricula activities. The multiplicity of curricular tracks along with distance and access to relevant employers, also created additional sets of issues to help students develop technological preparation beyond classroom instruction.

11.4.3 Organizational Supports to Help Students Succeed

An element of career academies that is appreciated by all stakeholders is grounded on the small school size. A small school community allows staff to create an environment of support for teachers, and for students in particular. As such, all school sites have developed a reputation for providing a safe campus and individualized attention to help all students do well. A common strategy across all sites is the identification of low-performing students and the development of customized supports including tutoring, counseling, and other ancillary services. Cascade Academy provided bus transportation for all students regardless of their location in the county, and a laptop computer for individual use throughout high school. In turn, professional development for teachers was available upon request to stay abreast of technological developments in areas of interest.

At Johnson Academy, which operates in a low-income community, the limited resources prevented the school district to provide bus transportation for students. However, the district and the academy fully recognized the needs of students in the economically depressed area, and prioritized garnering and providing wraparound supports for students and parents in the community. Because of the limited resources in the community, the district applied for recognition of the academy as a trauma-informed school to make eligible for federal assistance and wraparound supports including clinical, counseling, housing, and other ancillary services. The district and school vision was to address the basic needs of students and their families, so students could focus on learning. For example, Ms. Lane, the instructional coach at the academy said:

I would say that of course our students have a great deal of barriers that would likely prevent them from being able to succeed, but we here at the district have determined some ways in which we can fill those gaps for them; [we] provide them with their necessary needs, whether it be just what I think about is just making them whole so that they can be successful in the school…so that their home life doesn't necessarily have to affect what takes place here at school, and they can be as successful as they need to be as long as we help them meet those needs.

236

Likewise, at Victory Academy, students do not have the benefit of bus transportation and the majority come from low-income families with immigrant backgrounds. At these two academies, the local conditions in the community and the needs of students required urgent additional supports beyond what a typical school provides.

Regardless of the conditions, what was common across sites was school staff who genuinely cared about the wellbeing of their students and committed to support them in any way they could. Additionally, despite the limited resources and small school size, all sites supported participation in athletic programs, clubs, and leadership organizations to complement the overall preparation of students. However, parental involvement was less evident at Johnson and Victory academies as the parents in the community did not have the resources for transportation and taking time off to attend school events.

11.4.4 External Supports

An expected component of career academies is the integration of classroom learning with relevant work-related experiences, including paid internships, job shadowing, field trips, mentorships, and guest lectures by employers. Sustained and meaningful internships and job shadowing experiences clearly connected to students' technological preparation if often reported as a challenge in the literature. This is not the case at Cascade Academy where promoting related support from local employers was part of the vision since its inception. Over the years, related planning has paid off and the academy has established an impressive network of external support including more than 60 employers in the community. The network is held together through a council structure and the work of a dedicated outreach worker at the academy whose job is to recruit new partners and ensure the viability and sustainability of the network. The result is a tight-knit community of support with a shared understanding that the external support they provide is an investment in the preparation of competent workers who could potentially join their ranks upon graduation from high school. Partners in this network include large global corporations as well as small businesses, unified in the belief that it is in their best interest to invest in paid internships for academy students and offer authentic work experiences. In collaboration with school staff, employers also participate in a program to prepare students for actual job applications, interviewing process, and provide feedback for improvement. Linda, a business partner representing a major restaurant franchise in the region, summarized the support provided for the academy:

I've tried to teach classes here for the 9th and 10th grade modules that they offer. I've assisted with the reviewing of senior portfolios, so basically anything that the academy needs from a business perspective, you know, donations, cash, food, internships, anything that they need, we try to offer from a business perspective.

Additional external support, playing a significant role in the academy success, is the availability of two full-time college instructors who teach dual enrollment courses in IT on the career academy campus. Further, to enhance the authenticity of instruction, CISCO furnished an entire lab with state-of-the-art networking technology to help students develop skills expected in the workplace. Under these conditions, the promotion of skills related to digitalization was more coherently emphasized through programming and Web and app development and a variety of other applications and certifications. In contrast, at Johnson and Victory academies, garnering external supports to boost students' career readiness is more complicated. To be sure, Johnson Academy has been successful building partnerships in the extended community. However, given the multiplicity of program tracks where students tend to take a menu of interesting courses, but not concentrate in specific technological tracks, it has been difficult to establish meaningful work-based experiences. Further, students lack transportation and due to their low-income background, prefer to engage in minimum-wage jobs to earn money in any way they can. To work around these issues, Johnson Academy staff have developed four-week summer camps to help selected students experience working with professionals in different areas of interest and get exposure to potential careers. To ensure participation, students receive stipends for transportation and meals, and rotate each week to a different setting for enhanced exposure to work settings. The academy also emphasizes participation in STEM clubs to help students engage in technology-based projects. Not surprisingly, the focus on digitalization is ancillary and reduced to student interest as they participate in STEM clubs.

At Victory Academy, external supports are even more problematic. In this instance, the choice of digital filmmaking as the featured curricular theme in the academy was built upon the notion that a thriving industry in this area exists in the larger geographical vicinity. The issue is that the filmmaking industry is not easy to access, especially for a school and students who lack transportation. Further, in the immediate community, there are no companies with filmmaking and video production needs. As a result, the best academy students can do is produce the weekly TV program for the academy and engage in independent filmmaking as part of schoolwork leading to an annual competition. A movie theater is available in the school building complex in a former shopping mall, and winners are showcased there at a film festival. In this academy, the cost of video production equipment has become an issue to keep the technology up-to-date. Dr. Santiago, school principal, elaborated on the issue related to cost as a form of external support:

Funding becomes a challenge when you're meant to be a film school, but you don't have the equipment and other resources essential to get that done. What ended up happening was after the initial pot of money dried up, what they didn't pencil in is a sustainable factor in it so the computers started getting dated right around five years, six years. There was no money for replacement because the initial money that was used was a one-time money...

From our analysis, we realized that the type of occupational theme chosen for an academy and the fit with local industry may create either opportunities or challenges for garnering external supports. The availability of work-based learning experiences is critical for the technological preparation of students, and although this is an expected component of career academies, it was obvious to us that this is a major challenge for career academies.

11.5 Discussion

In this study we conducted an analysis of three career academies featuring technology-related curriculum to explore the factors and conditions providing context for their success in promoting students' technological preparation. From an organizational system perspective, our goal was to describe underlying elements, and highlight challenges and opportunities for the implementation of the career academy model at the high school level in the US. In this regard, it is important to note that given the qualitative nature of our study, our findings are not generalizable. However, we believe that the findings derived from our analysis offer valuable insights into the efforts to advance technological preparation in the American system.

With advancements in technology and the increasing usage of it at work and in everyday life, the challenge around the world is to ensure relevant education and training to help students become ready for successful participation in the workforce. In the US, concerns about remaining competitive in technological development have fueled a movement for improving student preparation in science, technology, engineering, and mathematics (STEM) (National Science & Technology Council, 2018). However, over the past decade, it became evident that academic preparation alone is not enough to boost participation in STEM-related pathways and thus there is a call to increase work-based learning through school-business partnerships (National Science & Technology Council, 2018). At issue, is the fact that, in the US the education system is primarily classroom-based with an emphasis on academic preparation leading to college enrollment (Hernandez-Gantes, 2016). In this context, career and technical education is best positioned to promote technological preparation with the support of business partners (Rosen, Visher, & Beal, 2018). Within career and technical education, the career academy model is perhaps the best option for the promotion of coherent and focused technological preparation given its emphasis on small learning communities, the integration of academic and technical content under occupational themes, and the provision of work-based learning opportunities to students (Hernandez-Gantes, 2016; Rosen et al., 2018).

The benefits of participation in career academies have been well documented, and related growth in implementation over the past decade is not surprising (Stern et al., 2010; Warner et al., 2016). In this regard, our findings aligned with the literature on the reasons for embracing the career academy model. First and foremost, communities recognize the value of technical preparation, and technological competence, and often rally around the implementation of career academies using technology-related occupational themes (Brand, 2009; Stern, Wu, Dayton, & Maul, 2005). In our study, the communities in all academies had a consensus about the need for rigorous technological preparation and this was the primary reason for adopting the model. The common denominator across all sites was the belief that students would thrive in a small community under a relevant and challenging technology-oriented curriculum. When a community is faced with a crisis (e.g., low student performance), such an event is often taken as an opportunity to try something different and adopt the career model, instead of the large comprehensive high school approach (Hernandez-Gantes, Fletcher, & Keighobadi, 2019). The premise that the model should work anywhere, has led perhaps, to the increasing popularity in the implementation of career academies in the US (Lanford & Maruco, 2018; 2019). What we found is that implementation varies depending on the approach to adoption and local conditions. Successful implementation of the career academy model requires a systems approach whereby consensus on adoption must be matched with a curriculum that fits community conditions and supports.

Further, one of the benefits often associated with career academies is the connection between the relevance of an occupational curriculum and student motivation and engagement (Brand, 2009; Stern et al., 2005). This understanding spans across the literature on smaller cohort-oriented communities within high schools featuring rigorous curriculum such as International Baccalaureate programs and college preparatory programs (Ongaga, 2010; Saavedra, 2014). In career academies, the premise is that student outcomes are enhanced through the implementation of curriculum that integrates relevant academic and technical content leading to skill development and successful transitions to further education or work (Hernandez-Gantes & Brendefur, 2003; Stern et al., 2005). However, for this to happen, there must be a clear and coherent alignment between the vision for implementation, a technology-based theme, and the availability of work-based learning opportunities in the community. In our study, it was evident only one of the academies had a clear alignment of such conditions. Cascade Academy clearly translated the emphasis on technology preparation through three IT curricular tracks in the areas of multimedia design technology, computer programming, and network systems technology. The technological emphasis fits with the needs of an extensive network of local employers and thus the academy can offer paid internships for junior and senior high school students. Thus, the use of and applications of digital technologies was more evident in this academy. In contrast, at Johnson Academy, the curricular emphasis is broader and better aligned with wide STEM applications rather than specific programs of study related to IT. In turn, at Victory Academy, the curricular focus is on filmmaking, which is better aligned with the career cluster integrating the arts and the use of video technology, rather than on IT (Advance CTE 2019; Hernandez-Gantes et al., 2019). At these academies, their curricular emphasis allowed for relevant and rigorous academic education in school, but it prevented skill development commensurate with specific IT-related preparation as exhibited by students at Cascade Academy. In this regard, it was evident that the role of paid internships is a necessary curricular condition for the successful implementation of career academies. To be sure, the availability of paid internships that provide authentic work experiences to students are difficult to establish and sustain in the US and the experience at Cascade Academy may represent an exception rather than the rule (Hernandez-Gantes, Keighobadi, & Fletcher, 2018; Lanford & Maruco, 2018).

Our analysis of the career academies also revealed that, although technological preparation was a great selling point for parents and students, a more compelling reason for choosing academy participation was the opportunity to be part of a small and safe school. This view was consistently voiced by stakeholders, and more prominently by parents and students. As such, it became obvious to us that in many ways, technological preparation was an added bonus for enrollment in a school with a reputation for providing a safe learning environment and individualized attention. In this regard, our findings aligned squarely with related literature noting that career academies provide an enhanced sense of belonging through a family-like school culture (Brand, 2009; Fletcher, Warren, & Hernandez-Gantes, 2019; Lanford & Maruco, 2018).

The small size of career academies provides an opportunity for school staff to emphasize individual attention to students, which we observed across school sites. At the same time, it enhances the awareness of student needs and the obligation to help them succeed in school (Fletcher, Hernandez-Gantes, & Smith, 2019; Lanford & Maruco, 2019). In this case, Cascade Academy operates in a middle-income suburban community with a thriving economy. To that end, school staff were able to focus on meeting student academic needs and technological preparation. However, at Johnson and Victory academies, the majority of the student population are from low-income backgrounds and meeting basic student needs (e.g. health and counseling services) to help students succeed in school represents a higher priority. This was even more acute at Johnson Academy where a purposeful program of wraparound services for students and their parents was in place to address basic needs. As such, these competing needs may take precedence and limit school stakeholders' emphases to academic preparation and ensuring graduation over a stronger technological preparation (Conchas & Clark, 2002; Warner et al., 2016). Thus, in communities with a predominantly low-income student population, administrators and teachers may have to prioritize the provision of student supports to give students a chance to complete high school (Fletcher et al, 2019; Hernandez-Gantes et al., 2019). In such communities, as in Johnson and Victory academies, school stakeholders have to make rational choices and focus on meeting students' basic needs, ensure students graduate from high school, and promote college and career readiness based on the extent of local resources.

The role of external supports is, perhaps, the area where a holistic perspective for implementation intersects with the operational vision, the nature of the curricular theme, and related support from local employers (Alfeld et al., 2013; Badgett, 2016). A key component of career academies is the collaboration with business in the community through advisory boards (Hernandez-Gantes et al, 2018; Hernandez-Gantes, Jenkins, & Fletcher, 2017). In this case, we found that at Cascade Academy, where the operational vision was clearly aligned with technological preparation in IT and visible and coherent curricular tracks, local support from a network of employers was very strong. As a result, paid internships are commonplace for junior and senior students, and represent authentic experiences grounded in IT work. In contrast, although support from community partners was strong at Johnson Academy, it was spread to meet student basic needs and provide broader and shorter work-based learning experiences to promote career awareness rather than focused technological preparation. In this instance, the broad vision for implementation aligned with multiple course options for students but prevented concentration in technological preparation in a particular area. In turn, at Victory Academy, the misalignment of the vision, curricular theme on filmmaking, and lack of industry in the immediate area resulted in virtually no external support for work-based learning opportunities.

Our findings in this area confirm the role of varying local conditions expected in the US. On the one hand, we found evidence reinforcing the value of social capital as a framework for understanding collaboration between school staff and employers in the community (Lanford & Maruco, 2018; Hernandez-Gantes et al., 2018). On the other hand, we also discovered that support from local employers may be difficult to establish and maintain without coherent alignment of an operational vision and curricular theme (Badgett, 2016; Hernandez-Gantes et al., 2017). We also realized that, to be successful promoting external supports, the role of staff specifically dedicated to promote related bonds and bridges is critical for establishing and sustaining local partnerships (Lanford & Maruco, 2019; Hernandez-Gantes et al., 2017, 2018). This is where another issue comes about, as the resources in career academies are too limited by virtue of their small size. When successful, as in the case of Cascade Academy, we found that school-business partnerships are vital to the relevant technological preparation of students, but not easy to accomplish in other communities. In places where the vision for technological preparation and curricular theme do not match local workforce needs, external supports may be limited, authentic and paid internship opportunities may be hard to come by, and technological preparation may be restricted as well.

In conclusion, from a holistic perspective, we found that the career academy model provides promising avenues for technological preparation. When analyzed under the lens of the conceptual framework, it is clear that the nature and role of organizational vision, curriculum and instruction, operational supports, and external supports have to be coherently aligned as is in the case of Cascade Academy (Adelman & Taylor, 2003; NCAC, 2013; Newmann & Wehlage, 1995). Otherwise, without such alignment, it is difficult for academies to garner buy-in from community partners and ensure fidelity of implementation to directly support technological preparation in a particular area such as IT. Further, in a country as diverse as the United States, it is clear that in communities that are economically disadvantaged, the priorities may shift to focusing on internal organizational supports to help students succeed in school and graduate. In this regard, it was also evident that varying local conditions play an important role on the shape of organizational structures supporting academy implementation and the preparation of students in career academies featuring technology-based curricular themes.

An important finding was the fact that in all cases, the opportunity to enroll in a small career academy—also perceived as providing a safe environment for learning, represented a primary reason for enrollment. Even at Cascade Academy, parents, students, and alumni reinforced this view. The majority of students viewed technological preparation as important, but secondary to their vocational pursuits (Lanford & Maruco, 2018; Warner et al., 2016). At Cascade Academy where students were regarded as being technologically prepared and career-ready, the majority of students reported being interested in non-IT pathways beyond high school. This findings is consistent with related literature based on postsecondary transition data, noting that few students go on to pursue college pathways in the area they concentrated in high school (Stephan & Rosenbaum, 2013; Stone, 2017). In this context, success across all academies is translated into promoting high graduation rates and student academic achievement, and by all accounts they are excelling at this with nearly 100% graduation rates. As such, whether students have the opportunity to develop authentic technological preparation including work-based experiences, becomes somewhat ancillary to the academies' success. That is, individualized attention, academic mentoring, and other forms of college preparation may play a greater role in facilitating student achievement often associated with career academies regardless of the occupational theme (Fletcher et al., 2019;

Lanford & Maruco, 2018). Thus, it is not surprising that all academies have a strong emphasis on organizational supports for students, especially in economically-disadvantage communities.

Under these conditions, the challenges for boosting technological preparation in the US may be in addressing three longstanding limitations in the education system. First, while technological preparation may provide for a rewarding transition into the workforce, it is often associated with the stigma carried by participating in technical education (Hanushek, Woessmann, & Zhang, 2011; Hernandez-Gantes, 2016). Although in the US, the promotion of college and career readiness has become a top priority, this push has been often interpreted to mean college preparation (Achieve, 2016; Stone, 2017). This view has built upon a lingering societal belief that a college degree is the only credential needed for career readiness. Albeit, recent recognition of the value of specific skills for successful entry in the labor market, attaining a college degree continues to be the primary goal for youth, while technical preparation is often seen as a secondary pathway (Symonds, Schwartz, & Ferguson, 2011). This issue brings a second challenge related to limited career guidance in the education pipeline. As noted in the literature, students transitioning into postsecondary education are often ill-informed about career pathways (Holland & DeLuca, 2016; Stephan & Rosenbaum, 2013). The issue of limited career guidance in middle and high school has been well documented and it is not surprising that students in career academies often view the opportunity for enhanced individual attention and safety as the primary reasons for enrollment. In this case, the benefits of technological preparation are often valued as a bonus of participation given the potential transferability to college transitions in other areas of interest.

Another challenge is the cost of providing rigorous and focused technological preparation. As gleaned from our analysis, the successful implementation of a career academy is much more than just focusing on curriculum content featuring a technology-based theme. It requires a concerted effort from an entire community of stakeholders and heavy investment in social capital and resources to sustain small learning academies (Hernandez-Gantes et al., 2017, 2018; National Science & Technology Council, 2018). This is even more problematic in schools with a misalignment of the curriculum and local industry needs such as Victory Academy, where the recurring cost of maintaining equipment is taxing and can further weaken technological preparation when it becomes out-of-date. In other instances, the cost of providing organizational supports to students take precedence over investments in equipment and thus the choice to emphasize classroom-based instruction over work-based learning. Thus, given the underlying costs and the issues for garnering authentic work-based learning opportunities for students, the adoption of the career academy model warrants a more holistic assessment and long-term planning for successful implementation.

To be sure, the premises of the career academy model are appealing, and the general benefits of participation have cemented their popularity. However, our analysis suggested that varying local conditions provide different challenges for implementation, which may result in issues with technological preparation. Unlike some European countries with a dual system of vocational education and training, the limited availability of work-based learning experiences continues to be a challenge for promoting rigorous technological preparation in the US (Bliem, Petanovitsch, & Schmid, 2016; Gessler & Howe, 2015; Ruth & Grollmann, 2009). The best we can do as part of the mainstream system of technical education, is paid summer internships through career academies, but such instances may represent an exception rather than the rule (Hernandez-Gantes et al., 2018; Lanford & Maruco, 2018). Albeit these issues in the American system, the career academy model may still offer the best avenue for the promotion of technological preparation, even if only a small number of students end up pursuing related pathways.

References

Achieve (2016). *The college and career readiness of high school graduates*. Retrieved from https://www.achieve.org/files/CCRHSGrads-March2016.pdf

Adelman, H. S. & Taylor, L. (2003). On sustainability of project innovations as systemic change. *Journal of Educational and Psychological Consultation, 14*(1), 1-25.

Advance CTE. (2019). *Career clusters*. Retrieved from https://careertech.org/career-clusters

Alfeld, C., Charner, I., Johnson, L., & Watts, E. (2013). *Work-based learning opportunities for high school students*. Louisville, KY: National Research Center for Career and Technical Education.

Badgett, K. (2016). School-business partnerships: Understanding business perspectives. *School Community Journal, (26)*2, 83–105.

Bliem, W., Petanovitsch, A., & Schmid, K. (2016). *Dual vocational education and training in Austria, Germany, Liechtenstein and Switzerland: Comparative expert study*. Vienna: Institut für Bildungsforschung der Wirtschaft.

Boyatzis, R. (1998). *Transforming qualitative information: Thematic analysis and code development*. Thousand Oaks, CA: Sage Publications.

Brand, B. (2009). *High school career academies: A 40-year proven model for improving college and career readiness*. Nashville, TN: National Career Academy Coalition.

Bureau of Labor Statistics. (2019). *U.S. Department of Labor: Occupational Outlook Handbook, computer and information technology occupations*. Retrieved from https://www.bls.gov/ooh/computer-and-information-technology/home.htm.

Carnevale, A. P., Smith, N., & Strohl, J. (2010). *Help wanted: Projections of jobs and education requirements through 2018.* Georgetown University Center on Education and the Workforce. Retrieved from https://cew.georgetown.edu/cew-reports/help-wanted/#report

Castellano, M., Stone, J.R. III, Stringfield, S.C., Farley-Ripple, E.N., Overman, L.T., & Hussain, R. (2007). *Career-based comprehensive school reform: Serving disadvantaged youth in minority communities.* St. Paul, MN: National Research Center for Career and Technical Education. http://www.nrccte.org/

Conchas, G. Q. & Clark, P. A. (2002). Career academies and urban minority schooling: Forging optimism despite limited opportunity. *Journal of Education for Students Placed at Risk, 7*(3), 287–311.

Fletcher, E., Hernandez-Gantes, V. M., & Smith, C. (2019). This is my neighborhood: An exploration of culturally relevant agency to support high school Latinx students in an urban career academy. *The Qualitative Report, 24*(12).

Fletcher, E., Warren, N., & Hernandez-Gantes, V.M. (2019). The high school academy as a laboratory of equity, inclusion, and safety. *Computer Science Education, 29*(4), 382-406. doi: 10.1080/08993408.2019.1616457

Gessler, M. & Howe, F. (2015). From the reality of work to grounded work-based learning in German vocational education and training: Background, concept and tools. *International Journal for Research in Vocational Education and Training, 2*(3), 214-238.

Gordon, R.J. (2016). *The rise and fall of American growth.* Princeton, NJ: Princeton University Press.

Hanushek, E. A., Woessmann, L., & Zhang, L. (2011). *General education, vocational education, and labor-market outcomes over the life-cycle.* Cambridge, MA: National Bureau of Economic Research.

Hernandez-Gantes, V.M. (2016). College and career readiness for all: The role of career and technical education in the US. In Wyse, D., Hayward, L., & Pandya, J. (Eds.), *SAGE Handbook of Curriculum, Pedagogy and Assessment. Vol. 2* (674-689). London: SAGE.

Hernández-Gantes, V.M. & Brendefur, J. (2003). Developing authentic, integrated, standards-based mathematics curriculum: [More than just] an interdisciplinary collaborative approach. *Journal of Vocational Education Research, 28*(3), 259-284.

Hernandez-Gantes, V.M., Fletcher, E., & Keighobadi, S. (2019). A case study of the development of a career academy: Good intentions not enough? *Journal of Research in Technical Careers, 3*(2), 114-135.

Hernandez-Gantes, V. M., Jenkins, S., & Fletcher, E. (2017). Promoting active and sustained school-business partnerships: An exploratory case study of an IT academy. *Journal of Research in Technical Careers, 1*(2), 26-35.

Hernandez-Gantes, V. M., Keighobadi, S., & Fletcher, E. (2018). Building community bonds, bridges, and linkages to promote the career readiness of high school students in the United States. *Journal of Education and Work, 31*(2), 190-203. doi: 10.1080/13639080.2018.1434871

Hernández-Gantes, V. M., Phelps, L. A., Jones, J., & Holub, T. (1995). School climate in emerging career-oriented programs: Students' perspectives. *Journal of Vocational Education Research, 20*(2), 5-26.

Holland, M. M. & DeLuca, S. (2016). "Why wait years to become something?" Low income African American youth and the costly career search in for-profit trade schools. *Sociology of Education, 89*(4), 261–278.

Kemple, J. J. (2008). *Career academies: Long-term impacts on labor market outcomes, educational attainment, and transitions to adulthood.* New York: Manpower Demonstration Research Corporation.

Kemple, J. J. & Snipes, J. C. (2000). *Career academies: Impacts on students' engagement and performance in high school.* Retrieved from http://www.mdrc.org/publications/41/full.pdf

Lanford, M. & Maruco, T. (2019). Six conditions for successful career academies. *Phi Delta Kappan, 100*(5), 50-52. https://doi.org/10.1177/0031721719827547

Lanford, M. & Maruco, T. (2018). When job training is not enough: The cultivation of social capital in career academies. *American Educational Research Journal, 55*(3), 617-648.

Loera, G., Nakamoto, J., Oh, Y.J., & Rueda, R. (2013). Factors that promote motivation and academic engagement in a career technical education context. *Career and Technical Education Research, 38*(3), 173-190. https://doi.org/10.5328/cter38.3.173

Mokyr, J. (2018). Building taller ladders: Technology and science reinforce each other to take the global economy ever higher. *Finance & Development, 55*(2), 32-35.

National Academy Foundation. (2014). *Statistics and research: 2013-2014.* Retrieved at http://naf.org/statistics-and-research.

National Career Academy Coalition. (2013). *National standards of practice for career academies.* Nashville, TN: Author.

National Career Academy Coalition. (2019). *About career academies.* Nashville, TN: Author.

National Academies of Sciences. (2017). *Building America's skilled technical workforce.* Washington, DC: The National Academies Press.

National Science Board. (2018). *Science and engineering indicators 2018 (NSB-2018-1).* Alexandria, VA: National Science Foundation

National Science & Technology Council. (2018). *Charting a course for success: America's strategy for STEM education.* Washington, DC: Author.

Newmann, F. M. & Wehlage, G. G. (1995). *Successful school restructuring: A report to the public and educators.* Madison, WI: Center on Organization and Restructuring of Schools.

Nowell, L. S., Norris, J. M., White, D. E., & Moules, N.J. (2017). Thematic analysis: Striving to meet the trustworthiness criteria. *International Journal of Qualitative Methods, 16*, 1-13.

Ongaga, K. O. (2010). Students' learning experiences in an early college high school. *Peabody Journal of Education, 85*(3), 375–388.

Orr, M., T. Bailey, K. Hughes, M. Karp, and G. Kienzl (2004). The National Academy Foundation's career academies: Shaping postsecondary transitions. *Institute on Education and the Economy (IEE Working Paper No. 17).* Teacher's College, Columbia University.

Rosen, R., Visher, M., & Beal, K. (2018). *Career and technical education: Current policy, prominent programs, and evidence.* Washington, DC: MDRC.

Ruth, K. & Grollmann, P. (2009). *Monitoring VET systems of major EU competitor countries: The cases of Australia, Canada, U.S.A. and Japan.* Bremen, Germany: Institut Technik und Bildung (ITB), Universität Bremen.

Ryan, A. (2011). *Education for sustainable development and holistic curriculum change. A review guide.* Heslington, York, United Kingdom: The Higher Education Academy.

Saavedra, A. R. (2014). The academic impact of enrollment in international baccalaureate diploma programs: A case study of Chicago public schools. *Teachers College Record, 166*(4).

Silverberg, M., Warner, E., Fong, M., & Goodwin, D. (2004). *National assessment of vocational education: Final report to Congress.* Washington, DC: US Department of Education.

Stake, R. (2006). *Multiple case study analysis.* New York: Guilford.

Stephan, J. L. & Rosenbaum, J.E. (2013). Can high schools reduce college enrollment gaps with a new counseling model? *Educational Evaluation and Policy Analysis, 35*(2), 200-2019.

Stern, D., Wu, C., Dayton, C., & Maul, A. (2005). *Learning by doing career academies.* Berkeley, CA: Career Academy Support Network.

Stern, D., C. Dayton, & M. Raby. (2010). *Career academies: A proven strategy to prepare high school students for college and careers.* Berkeley, CA: University of California Berkeley Career Academy Support Network.

Stone, J. R. III. (2017). Introduction to pathways to a productive adulthood: The role of CTE in the American high school. *Peabody Journal of Education, 92*(2), 155-165.

Symonds, W.C., Schwartz, R., & Ferguson, R.F. (2011). *Pathways to prosperity: Meeting the challenge of preparing young Americans for the 21st century.* Cambridge, MA: Harvard University.

Warner, M. et al. (2016). *Taking stock of the California Linked Learning District Initiative. Seventh-year evaluation report.* Menlo Park, CA: SRI International.

Wright, B. (2009). Employment trends and training in information technology. *Occupational Outlook Quarterly, 53*(1), 34-41.

Conclusions and Outlook

12 Developing a Skillful and Adaptable Workforce: Reappraising Curriculum and Pedagogies for Vocational Education

Stephen Billett

12.1 Changing occupational and workplace requirements

Changes in occupational practices, such as the digitalization of work, the specific requirements for workplace performance and the needs of working life, such as available work, how work is conducted and work practices, periodically prompt reappraisals of the goals and processes of vocational education (Billett, 2006). In the contemporary era of digitalization, there is a growing governmental concern about vocational education achieving what is been referred to as 21[st]century skills: emphasizes the importance of i) complex problem-solving, ii) critical thinking, iii) creativity, iv) people management and v) coordination (Nokelainen, Nevalinen, & Niemi, 2018). Emphasized also is the development of the knowledge required to participate in work that has become increasingly digitized (Harteis, 2018a). A related change is that up until recently vocational education has primarily been concerned with developing occupational capacities and mainly assisting young people move into the world of work and specific occupations. Yet, now there is a strong focus on making those young people job ready—able to meet the requirements of the specific workplace in which they find employment, which is a different education goal. So, for instance, the use of technology and the impact and requirements for digitalizes work differs across workplaces.

Consequently, as work requirements change, then vocational education needs to respond accordingly. These changes include: i) addressing the specific requirements of workplaces as well as ii) developing occupational competence, which has been the key focus for much of vocational education; iii) learning knowledge that is difficult to directly experience (i.e. conceptual and symbolic knowledge) required for what is often referred to as 'knowledge work', and currently, digitized work (Hamalainen, Lanz, & Koskinen, 2018; Harteis, 2018a; Nokelainen et al., 2018; Schneider, 2018); iv) developing adaptive occupational capacities as the requirements for work and work performance are constantly changing; v) the importance of students to become active and intentional learners for their initial preparation, and vi) also that ongoing development across working life. All of this, and, currently, the impact of digitalization raises fresh problems for education (Harteis, 2018a).

A way forward for vocational education is to adopt curriculum and pedagogic practices that are aligned with achieving these kinds of outcomes. This includes appraising: what constitutes effective educational experiences, both within educational institutions and workplaces, ordering and reconciling these two sets of experiences, educational interventions to generate the capacities that vocational education students need to be effective in specific workplaces and preparing them to become active and intentional learners across their working lives. Achieving these outcomes includes considering what constitutes the existing and emerging requirements for occupational and workplace performance (i.e. the knowledge that needs to be learnt) and aligning these with the curriculum and pedagogic practices that vocational education institutions can advance and the kinds and quality of engagement that students need to adopt and practice.

The case made in this paper is, firstly, to set out some key changes that are occurring within contemporary workplaces. These are held to be fivefold. Firstly, as being 'job ready' on graduation is now increasingly a priority, a focus on how students can be made ready for work on graduation, as well as for occupational preparation. Secondly, educational processes need to understand and respond to specific needs of occupations in action (i.e. addressing the specific needs of workplaces) to assist students. That is, there is a need to assist students understand and respond to the specific requirements of workplaces as well as being occupationally prepared. Thirdly, with the broader use of electronic technology (i.e. digitized work), new regimes of management, production and service work are eventuating that require increasing levels of symbolic and conceptual knowledge (Schneider, 2018), appropriate educational interventions need enacting to assist students develop these kinds of knowledge (Hajkowicz et al., 2016). Fourthly, is developing adaptability within students so that they can adapt and respond in effective ways to the challenges they encounter beyond graduation (Ericsson & Lehmann, 1996). That is, preparing students to be active adaptable and interdependent learners. Fifthly, although much of this educational project is directed towards initial occupational preparation, increasingly, individuals need the capacities to engage with and continue their intentional learning—continuing education and training—across lengthening working lives (Organisation for Economic Co-operation and Development, 2006).

In response to these changes, curriculum and pedagogic practices within vocational education needs to include organizing and engaging students in authentic experiences, albeit in educational institutions or workplaces, and intentionally integrating the two kinds of experiences (Billett, 2015). Identifying pedagogic practices likely to generate adaptability within students is a related consideration. That adaptability is likely based on having effective disciplinary knowledge (Alexander & Judy, 1988; Gelman & Greeno, 1989) and familiarity with its application in different work settings. Yet, as much of the conceptual and symbolic knowledge required for contemporary digitized work cannot be experienced directly through sensory engagement (Harteis, 2018a), it may require specific kinds of interventions to promote its development (Vosniadou, Ioannides, Dimitrakopoulou, & Papademetriou, 2002). Also, across all of these considerations is the need to promote the learners' agency to be effective, outward-looking and intentional in their engagement in activities and interaction from which they learn (Goller, 2017). Finally, the changing nature of work requires most in the workforce to refresh, advance and even change their occupational, making continuing education a requirement for working adults (Billett, Dymock, & Choy, 2016). These curriculum and pedagogic responses are proposed as how to vocational education can proceed with developing skillful and adaptable workers.

Each of these issues is now addressed in sections headings those associated with: i) key changes reconfiguring the goals for and processes of vocational education and ii) responsive curriculum and pedagogic practices.

12.2 Key changes reconfiguring the goals for and processes of vocational education

As noted, there are a range of changes for occupational and workplace requirements that have direct implications for the provision of vocational education. These include a focus on job readiness as well as occupational preparation; addressing the specific needs of workplaces; accessing and learning the kinds of conceptual and symbolic knowledge required for digitized processes such as Manufacturing 4.0 (Hamalainen et al., 2018), and the need to develop adaptable skills to respond to the changing requirements for occupational practice and specific workplace performance. This leads to a consideration of the blending between initial and continuing education. Added here also is the need to engage learners and have them come to value and engage in vocational education and the occupations it serves.

Job readiness as well as occupational preparation

The traditional role of vocational education in the modern era has been to prepare people for working life and specific occupations (Billett, 2011b). This role has seen a focus on identifying occupational requirements and then working to prepare graduates to meet them. Representatives of workers, professional associations and licensing bodies for many occupations have been involved in informing national curricula measures for vocational education. Consequently, external have come to play a key role in not only informing what content should be taught, but also the kinds of assessments students will be subjected to and the need to meet occupational requirements. However, increasingly, employers, governments, community and students are expecting that vocational education graduates should be 'job ready' (Billett, 2015). That is, able to smoothly transition to and effectively perform in specific workplaces. This is a particularly tough goal for vocational education and demanding upon graduates. There are key differences between curriculum and experiences that are designed to meet the needs of occupational requirements and regulations, and those associated with addressing the requirements of specific workplaces. Moreover, there are structural difficulties because we do not know where these graduates will end up being employed, and their situated performance requirements. So, this growing emphasis and expectation that students from vocational education will be able to move smoothly into employment in a specific workplace requires a different set of educational goals and processes than those associated with readiness for an occupation. This requirement extends to knowing something of the variations of occupational practice and the rationales for those variations and their consequences for work performance. Fundamentally, it is about developing adaptive capacities within vocational education graduates. So, this change warrants a significant reconsideration of educational goals and processes.

Educational goals

Education is an intentional process. That is, it is guided and driven by specific kinds of intentions (e.g. goals, aims, objectives) that should be the product of a range of contributions and insights, balancing amongst these contributions and selecting and generating kinds of intents (Marsh, 2004). The degree of specificity for educational processes varies from being wide and open to being highly job specific. The latter often occurs in preparation for occupations as there are specific occupational requirements advanced by industry bodies that need to be met are captured as national standards, occupational competences or national curriculum documents. What electricians, nurse assistants, builders transport workers are required to perform is thereby mandated and even regulated by these requirements. Yet, to understand the relationship between these occupational requirements and those for specific workplaces, it is helpful to consider occupational preparation in terms of it comprising the canonical occupational knowledge and also the situational requirements for performance (Billett, Harteis, & Gruber, 2018). That is, firstly, the knowledge comprising what those practicing the occupations need to know, do and value. Knowing refers to factual, conceptual, propositional and causal knowledge. Being able to secure goals is achieved through procedural knowledge that ranges from being highly specific procedures (to achieve individual tasks) through to strategic procedures required for planning and evaluating work activities (Anderson, 1982; Ericsson & Lehmann, 1996). There is also a consideration of value—the dispositional qualities of interest and intentionality that is central to how individuals undertake their work. It is, together, these three forms of knowledge that underpin effective work performance, and what some referred to as expertise (Ericsson, Hoffman, & Kozbelt, 2018).

Requirements of situational performance

Yet, and secondly, beyond the canonical occupational knowledge is also what comprises the situational requirements that permit job performance in a specific workplace/work practice (Billett et al., 2018). Yet, the actual requirements for performance are not premised upon the possession of canonical knowledge alone. Instead, that performance is premised upon what individuals do circumstances in response to specific tasks in those circumstances (Brown, J. S., Collins, & Duguid, 1989; Gruber & Harteis, 2018). It is the range of situational factors, including the kinds of tasks, clients, patients, available equipment, location et cetera that shapes situational performance, even what counts as errors and their costs (Bauer, Leicherb, & Mulder, 2016; Rausch, Seifried, & Harteis, 2017). So, the ability to perform in and through work is related to the actual circumstances in which individuals practice that occupation (Billett, 2001). There is no such thing as being an occupational expert per se. Instead, it is the ability to respond to routine and nonroutine problem-solving in a situation that is relevant to individuals' work performance.

These requirements are shaped by the specific manifestations of occupational practice and to be addressed and will comprise specific kinds of educational intents and processes. So, vocational educational intents need to include experiences that can assist students come to learn something of the variations of occupational practice and diverse kinds of workplace performance associated with their occupations. Underpinning this, is the development of adaptability in students. That is, the ability to extend what they have learnt in one situation to be applied to tasks, goals and circumstances other than those in which it was learnt. Securing the adaptation of what has been learnt in educational programs and institutions is a perennial question (Lobato, 2012; Volet, 2013). Certainly, to be countenanced as 'education', what is learnt should not be restricted to the circumstances of its initial learning. This is never more the case than in vocational education were the key focus is on preparing people to apply what they have learnt in workplaces and work practices.

Consequently, challenge for vocational education is to find ways of understanding something of the diversity of situational requirements and expose students to instances of that diversity and allow them to understand something of the range of requirements arising from it. Engagements and partnerships with local employers and industry representatives, those from professional bodies are likely to clarify these requirements. Those kinds of engagements and outcomes are also hallmarking for what constitutes mature vocational education systems. That is, those outcomes that are not wholly premised upon what happens in the vocational education institution, but how what occurs outside of the 'school' is able to be engage with and be responsive.

Securing 'hard to learn' knowledge (e.g. digital knowledge)

Much existing and 'future work' is likely to be increasingly reliant on conceptual and symbolic knowledge (Barley & Batt, 1995; Hull, 1997), such as that required for digitalized work (Hamalainen et al., 2018; Schneider, 2018). That is, the knowing that must be mediated through concepts and symbols as it cannot be directly expressed or experienced. Much of this is associated with understanding is premised on knowledge that is opaque and difficult to access and, therefore, learn (Harteis, 2018a). Across human history, and increasingly, this kind of knowledge is that which we used to represent complex things that cannot be easily stated or represented. Consequently, use symbols to denote chemicals, factors such as used in mathematical calculations or physics representations and increasingly are exercised within electronic technology (Vosniadou et al., 2002). Examples here include the growing use of technologies in fields such as banking, clerical work, as well as healthcare (Hajkowicz et al., 2016). This kind of knowledge is often associated with changes in how work is conducted and how individuals come to mediate it. Earlier, Scribner (Scribner, 1985) with great prescience stated that

"hardly have we approach the problem of understanding the intellectual impact of the printing press and we are urged to confront the psychological implications of computerisation" (page 138).

She was drawn to capture and comprehend these changes through considering the cognitive consequences of the introduction of Computer Numerically Controlled (CNC) lathes (Martin & Scribner, 1991). These kinds of lathes comprised a shift away from those operated through and by human sensory processes (i.e. vibrations, noise, smell, sight) to those that integrated traditional machining knowledge with symbolic knowledge and logical skills, that were enacted computers (Martin & Scribner, 1991). These kinds of knowledge are difficult to learn because they cannot be directly experienced and engaged, nor easily represented and expressed.

What is also noteworthy is that these kinds of conceptual knowledge break with the convention that conceptual knowledge can be declared (i.e. spoken or written down). Indeed, in much of the American literature this kind of knowledge is referred to as declarative. Yet, this form of conceptual knowledge does not lend itself to either being spoken or written down. Therefore, it is difficult for individuals to generate cognitive representations of it. Yet, these forms of knowledge need to be constructed by individuals (i.e. learnt) because they become personal tools to mediate work and learning. These forms of knowledge are not restricted to considerations of electronic technology, but the shift to the use of digitalization brings this form of knowledge centre-stage and considerations of how it can be developed through vocational education. For instance, science education and educators have long struggled with identifying the most effective ways of representing this kind of knowledge for students to come to understand science and physics. Concerns about force, vectors, stress on physical components et cetera need to be understood through systems that require this kind of conceptual knowledge.

However, there is a need to identify pedagogic practices that comprise practical ways of seeking to make these forms of knowledge accessible so they can be engaged with, construed and constructed with by learners. And it is these that need to become part of the educational considerations.

Adaptability and interdependence

As the requirements for contemporary work changes, it is necessary for workers of all kinds to adapt in responding to transforming circumstances and challenges (Ericsson & Lehmann, 1996). All of this is important because as the PIAAC data indicates all classes of contemporary workers engage in extensive and frequent non-routine problem-solving and adaptability is central to the capacity to respond to non-routine problem-solving (Organisation for Economic Co-operational and Development, 2013). These are qualities that are broadly reported across countries and all classifications of workers (Australian Bureau of Statisics, 2013). Responding to occupational challenges workplaces, in addressing clients' problems and needs requires the capacities to adapt occupational knowledge to meet those requirements (Ericsson & Lehmann, 1996).

The means to respond to these changes is often associated with interdependence (Rogoff, 1990). That is, through working and learning with others and in ways in which reciprocity is commonplace. Through interaction with others, much can be gained from those interactions and shared learning arises in ways that is reliant upon the contributions of others and objects. So, rather than being based on cleverness alone (i.e. the ability to manipulate knowledge), the ability to engage with others and artefacts is required to respond to such challenges. This is because the knowledge required to effectively learn resides outside of individuals and they must gain it from the social world. As we know, the knowledge required for occupational practices does not rise within individuals. Individuals need to engage with others who possess that knowledge or artefacts that can mediate that knowledge for them. Yet, in terms of change, the interdependence between the workplace and the worker both comes to the fore. The workplace requires workers have the capacity to respond to new challenges and generate new procedures and practices to achieve the goals of the workplace (Billett, 2014a). Without the actions of the workers, the workplace would become moribund and unable to advance. Yet, workers need the workplace, the contributions it provides and its role in continuing to develop that knowledge that are so central to being able to respond to emerging and novel challenges.

Fundamentally, this means that core capacities for contemporary workers are: i) the ability to adapt to new challenges and novel circumstances, and ii) to engage interdependently to secure that knowledge. Consequently, more than possessing a body of occupational knowledge, and understandings of its need to be applied in different ways, are the attributes of adapting that knowledge to meet emerging challenges and new situations.

Continuing education and training

With the constant change of knowledge required for work it has become increasingly apparent that even the most effective initial occupational preparation will not equip individuals for lifetime of work. Instead, workers need to continue to actively learn across their working lives. Therefore, beyond vocational education being primarily concerned with initial occupational preparation is now increasingly important to consider the ongoing development of that knowledge through continuing education and training (CET) (Billett et al., 2016). There are a range of factors shaping the growing need for CET provisions within contemporary workforces. These include the: i) ageing populations in many countries requiring workers to sustain their employability over a longer period of time, ii) constant need for developing further and up skilling individuals' knowledge, iii) often quite specific requirements for responding to the changing nature of work, iv) availability of opportunities for practicing occupations and v) emergence of new occupations it is not surprising that there is a growing interest in continuing education and training.

Consequently, there is a need for appropriating existing models of CET provisions to meet these needs and, likely in ways that are quite different from provisions of initial occupational preparation. These CET provisions need also to be structured in ways that meet the needs of working adults. These needs include ease of access for adults with work and family commitments as well as CET, relevance to individuals learning requirements, and to be administratively easy. However, these models need to be effective and applicable by those who use them, and not based upon those that work for school age young people. Instead, the kinds of CET programs likely to be endorsed are those that are based in educational institutions. Increasingly, vocational education students are having access to practicum experiences and means by which these can be enriched and integrated into the students' overall program.

Together, these six sets of concerns are some of the key challenges for contemporary vocational education. In the next section, the discussion focuses on curriculum and pedagogic practices that are responsive to these sets of concerns.

12.3 Responsive curriculum and pedagogic practices

The above raise questions about the kinds of curriculum and pedagogic practices that can support occupational competence, job readiness, adaptability and sustain employability across working life. These issues are addressed in the following sections that offer seven considerations: i) institutional-based activities that insight authentic work experiences, ii) organizing and providing workplace experiences, iii) intentionally and actively integrating students' experiences; iv) educational processes promoting adaptability, v) securing hard to learn knowledge, vi) promoting learning agency, and vii) provisions of continuing education and training.

Institutional-based activities that incite authentic work experiences

The provision of experiences in educational institutions that are similar to those associated with the circumstances of their application has been long understood as being important for robust learning (Raizen, 1991). It follows that for the development of occupational capacities, it is important to provide students with authentic experiences of the occupations for which they are being prepared to participate. Below, it is been suggested that it is important to provide students with workplace experiences and then reconcile what they have learnt in workplace settings with the goals of their vocational education courses. However, it is not always possible for students to secure workplace experiences. Whereas some countries and occupations have very strong traditions of providing workplace experiences, others do not. It is very common in Germany for vocational students to engage in significant amounts of work experiences, whereas over one of their borders in the Netherlands there is not such a strong tradition of providing students with work experiences (de Bruijn, Billett, & Onstenk, 2017) and in France there is a cultural sentiment separating work from education (Veillard, 2015). Indeed, the Netherlands in their vocational education and applied science universities there is a strong emphasis on providing what is referred to as hybrid experiences within those institutions (Zitter, Hoeve, & de Bruijn, 2017). That is, students are provided with simulation or project work that is similar to the kinds of activities that comprise the occupational practice. Likewise, in Singapore were many of the postsecondary education institutions (i.e. the polytechnics and the Institute for Technical Education) also use project type activities within the institutional setting. For instance, in one of the polytechnics, the information technology students engage in the tasks of assisting other students with setting up their laptops and tablets with the polytechnics systems and then engage in a helpdesk and troubleshooting when students have problems. That is, the students are engaging in authentic activities associated with information technology tasks. Of course, with the increasing requirements for competence with digitally-enacted forms of work it becomes necessary for the educational experiences and teaching processes to encompass those requirements as (Petri Nokelainen, Nevalainen, & Niemi, 2018) propose.

There are two broad considerations here: curriculum and pedagogy. In terms of curriculum—the activities that are organized for students and their sequencing—consideration of shared or individual projects associated with the field of study, simulated activities (e.g. training restaurants, IT help desks) can provide students with educational activities that are closely linked with their intended occupation. This approach to curriculum engages students in the kinds of goal-directed activities that are associated with that occupation and, therefore, have high levels of authenticity associated with the knowledge targeted for them to learn. Also, these kind of projects and simulated activities engage students in a way that more passive forms of education are unlikely to be able to achieve. That is because the students are put in the 'driver's seat': they must make decisions and complete actions and then monitor and evaluate those actions. We know that this kind of engagement and kind of thinking and acting is what is required for developing the higher-order capacities required for many occupations.

So, these kinds of experiences are important educationally and the more they can be made authentic in terms of the kinds of activities and interactions they comprise the more likely that students will generate the understandings, procedures and dispositions associated with occupational practices. That will assist them learn that knowledge in ways encouraging utilization, recall, and are also aligned with performing occupational tasks upon graduation.

In terms of pedagogic practice, the teachers' ability of to use narratives, storytelling and verbalize the kinds of knowledge that needs to be learnt using instances from practice is likely to be tickly helpful for students to learn and recall what has been taught (Billett, 2014b). Activities that emphasize the utilization of the knowledge outside of the circumstances in which is being taught will assist students learn about the applicability of that knowledge and assist them through providing experiences which are not able to be directly engaged by them.

Organizing and providing workplace experiences

Currently, in many countries, vocational education systems are increasingly organizing and providing workplace experiences to assist students learn the kinds of knowledge that they require to effectively practice their preferred occupation. Important goals outlined above are associated with securing canonical occupational knowledge and understanding variations of that knowledge and how they apply in different workplace circumstances, the need for workplace experiences becomes pre-eminent. Workplace experiences provide access to: i) authentic activities and interactions; ii) richly contextualized experiences that engage students in multisensory ways and provides clues and cues about how they need to engage in their work; iii) purposive goal-directed activities that are aligned with the kinds of knowledge that students need to learn for their intended occupations; iv) engaging students in goal-directed activities that require them to resolve problems and through them learn; v) securing episodic experiences from which important causal and propositional links are developed; and the ability to monitor the activities in which they engage (Billett, 2015). These work-based experiences are much more than complementing those that students have within educational institutions. Instead, they make specific kinds of contributions and sources of knowledge that might not be found outside of them. Also, as the activities and interactions are authentic the cognitive consequences are likely to be of the kind that assist learners develop capacities that they can recall, utilize and further develop. Rogoff and Lave (1984) captured the cognitive consequences of such activities with the phrase that activity structures cognition.

Of course, the kinds, extent and quality of the work experiences that students secure is dependent on those activities and interactions they can engage in and how they engage in workplaces, their duration, variation and the degree by which students are guided and supported in workplace settings as they engage in occupational goal-directed activities. Moreover, there is a risk that if poor or inappropriate practices are being enacted, these are what students will be exposed to and potentially learn (Billett, 1995). So, the quality and appropriateness of these experiences may differ from setting to setting which provides uneven and potentially unhelpful experiences for students. Yet, it is difficult for educators to influence the organization and provision of workplace experiences for their students which are normally subject to the imperatives of workplaces. Yet, much can be done by vocational education institutions and their teachers to intentionally augment students' workplace experiences and integrate them effectively in students' educational program. This is discussed next.

Intentionally and actively integrating students' experiences

Workplace experiences provide learning opportunities that are often quite different than those that can be provided through vocational education institutions and can secure specific kinds of learning. But, as noted, there can be inherent limitations in those experiences. Consequently, there is a need not only to include these experiences within the provision of vocational education, but also find ways of integrating those workplace experiences and the learning derived from them into the vocational program (Cooper, Orrel, & Bowden, 2010). At one level, the concern is to organize and provide experiences in ways that helps students' development of occupational capacities. Yet, at another level, the aim is to engage students in ways that maximize their learning from them and to integrate that learning with what they is being learnt through participation in their vocational education course (Orrell, 2011). So, again, there is need to consider both curriculum (i.e. the provision of experiences) and pedagogies (i.e. utilization of those experiences). The findings of a large tertiary teaching project on the integration of workplace experiences identified some of the curriculum and pedagogic practices that could be adopted (Billett, 2011a). In Table 1, below issues associated with the intended (i.e. what is designed and planned), enacted (i.e. what occurs with implementation) and experienced (i.e. what students experience and learn) curriculum are set out. These were derived from a national project comprising studies from across a range of occupational disciplines in tertiary education institutions.

Table 1: curriculum considerations for integrating workplace experiences (Billett 2015)

Intended curriculum: *what is planned*	Enacted curriculum: *what is implemented*	Experienced curriculum: *what students experience and learn*
being clear about what is to be learnt through work-place experiences	augmenting or maximising available opportunities (e.g. appropriate settings)	Students' interest and readiness central to their engagement and learning in practice settings, and reconciling it with their coursework
aligning experiences provided for students with the intended learning outcomes	considering options other than supervised placements to secure experiences	immediate concerns (e.g. performing in practicum) focus of students' interest
aligning the duration of experiences with educational purpose (e.g. orientation vs skill development)	accounting for students' readiness (e.g. interest, capacities, confidence) when selecting and enacting experiences	early and staged engagement in practice settings boosts many students' confidence to re-engage and learn effectively
intentionally sequencing preparatory experiences to secure, consolidate and reconcile learning from practice experiences	additional or specific experiences may be needed for student cohorts (e.g. overseas students)	challenges to personal confidence and competence can be redressed by effective group processes, including sharing of experiences.

In this table, there are sets of considerations for how the intended curricula might be organized to optimize the integration of students' experiences in work settings. Also, there is a set of practices associated with the implementation of the curriculum (i.e. the enacted curriculum) that can inform practices and priorities associated with its enactment. Then, and perhaps most importantly, are a set of considerations about how students will come to understand and engage with what has been implemented and experienced by them (i.e. the experience curriculum).

Beyond these curriculum considerations are also processes associated with pedagogic practices that could be used to augment students experiences by assisting them integrate and reconcile the experience says they have had in work settings with those that comprise the curriculum being enacted. In Table 2, below are set out some suggestions that arose through the national study on what kind of pedagogic interventions might occur before, during and after workplace experiences. What can be seen here is the importance of preparatory activities prior to students engaging in work settings, and then interventions to promote student learning during their workplace experiences. It was also found that having interventions after the students have experience work practice was particularly helpful as students had experiences that they could compare, share and critically appraise with other students. These interventions also open up considerations of opportunities for students to develop understandings about the occupational practice, and variations of that practice in action. This phase also has the potential for students to develop understandings about practice in action and develop critical capacities to appraise work situations and the efficacy of kinds of practices. This latter kind of learning is important for ongoing learning that these students will require on graduation and as they continue to confront changes across their working life, and largely learn in the absence of teachers and educational programs.

Table 2: Pedagogic strategies for promoting integration of workplace learning experiences (Billett 2015)

Before workplace experience	During workplace experience	After workplace experience
orient students to requirements for effectively engaging in work practices	direct guidance by more experienced practitioners (i.e. proximal guidance)	facilitate the sharing and drawing out of students' experiences
clarify expectations about purposes of, support in and responsibilities of parties in practice settings etc.	active engagement in pedagogically rich work activities or interactions (e.g. handovers)	make explicit links to, and reconciliations between, what is taught (learnt) in the academy, and what is experienced in practice settings
prepare students to engage as agentic learners (e.g. importance of observations, engagement)	effective peer interactions (i.e. students' collaborative learning)	emphasise the active and selective qualities of students' learning through practice
develop procedural capacities required for tasks in workplace	active and purposeful engagement by the students as learners in workplace	generate students' critical perspectives on work and learning processes
prepare for contestations that might arise		

It follows from the findings of this teaching and learning grant (Billett, 2015), that there are actions that can be taken in the design and implementation of vocational education programs that can assist in the effective provision and integration of students experiences in workplaces with what they are learning in their programs. Perhaps most important, was the interventions that occurred after students had completed their work experiences as these provided opportunities for them to develop knowledge from what they had experienced and could engage with and learn from other students' experiences vicariously and critically. An element of the pedagogic practices outlined here is to assist students be able to adapt what they have learnt through these experiences to other circumstances and settings. That is, to promote their ability to adapt that knowledge. This is quite central to robust educational outcomes and specific considerations of how this adaptability might best be generated.

Educational processes promoting adaptability

As noted, a fundamental concern for the outcome of education per se is the ability of students to adapt what has been learnt within educational programs to circumstances outside of and beyond them. This is a key issue for vocational education, with its focus on preparing students to apply their knowledge in workplaces upon graduation when they secure employment beyond graduation. It is sometimes referred to as transfer (Mayer, 2001) or the development of transferable knowledge (Royer, 1979). This kind of learning is always not easily derived from direct teaching, but can be guided in its development (Brown & Palinscar, 1989; Palinscar & Brown, 1984). Instead, other kinds of experiences are often required, albeit supported by teacherly practices to promote adaptability, such as reciprocal teaching and learning (Palinscar & Brown, 1984), guided learning rather than teaching in classrooms (Brown & Palinscar, 1989; Collins, Brown, & Newman, 1989) and workplaces (Billett, 2000).

Here, a key curriculum goal is the development of understandings and practices (i.e. informed principles and practices) that promote adaptability. That is, identifying and assist in students develop understandings and procedures that will assist them adapt what they know, can do and value to changing or other circumstances. This can be realised in several ways, one of which is having students share their experiences of different work and identifying what is common across the enactment of that occupation (i.e. the canonical knowledge of the occupation) and what is to specific work settings (i.e. situational requirements). So, to take an example, student nursing assistants might experience nursing in a whole range of health care settings (i.e. different kinds of wards) and then be asked to identify those aspects of nursing practice that are common to all those settings, and those that are specific to just one or some of them. The former can be taken as being the canonical knowledge of nursing assistants, and the latter nursing practices that are peculiar to specific kinds of wards or clinical settings. What they would learn from this experience is that there are concepts, procedures and dispositions that are common to nursing and then variations of them that are relevant to specific nursing circumstances.

It is the combination of developing canonical occupational knowledge alongside the understandings of variations and situational requirements that can provide a basis for using occupational knowledge adaptively. By, engaging with other students to compare their experiences of work settings, albeit facilitated by the teacher, it opens up a range of options and possibilities that permit them to realise that there are variations in that practice, and for what reasons and how these might be accommodated within enactment of the occupation. Consequently, providing opportunities for students to engage in sharing, discussion and dialogue are likely to be important, as, if possible, students rotating through different kind of work settings and circumstances of occupational practice. Even then, those experiences alone may be insufficient unless there is the opportunity to consider, discuss and extend knowledge about those practices. Also, it may be necessary to guide that process of identifying canonical and situated instances of nursing practice. So, for instance, the teacher might provide a list of nursing competencies and asked students to appraise these against their own experiences. That is, identifying what is canonical and what is situated requirements.

This concern with adaptability is fundamental to the educational project. Education institutions and their programs have been established not just for learning that is relevant to them but need to be applicable to circumstances and activities that are distinct from those enacted in educational institutions. Consequently, focusing on strategies that seek to extend the applicability of what students come to know, do and value is likely to be a crucial consideration in vocational teaching. This is particularly relevant in the contemporary era were change in workplace and occupational requirements, occurs so frequently.

Securing 'hard-to-learn' knowledge (e.g. digital)

A growing element of contemporary work is to engage with tools and artefacts that are premised on digital knowledge (Harteis, 2018a). As indicated above, the increased use of conceptual and symbolic knowledge as part of workplace performance requirements, now extends to this kind of knowledge. It has increased with the use of electronic technology and the digital systems that shape work activities (Schneider, 2018). This kind of electronically-mediated work is lessening need for the direct use of tools that must be manipulated manually and the importance of ergonomic capacities such as deftness of hand movements (Harteis, 2018a). It is noteworthy that, however, there are three concerns associated with learning conceptual and symbolic knowledge. Firstly, they are sometimes quite difficult to capture and represent in written form (e.g. force, electronic systems, information processing). Secondly, they can be difficult to access because there is no direct engagement with them (e.g. they cannot be directly experienced). Thirdly, these kinds of knowledge are often difficult to be taught, and therefore need to be learnt through processes of guidance and, experiences that make this knowledge explicit. Science education has long struggled to address the problem of developing conceptual knowledge in school classrooms (Diakidoy & Kendeou, 2001; Novak, 1990; Vosniadou et al., 2002). That is, how can students learn concepts that they cannot directly experience. Literature from that field suggest the importance of making that knowledge explicit in some ways and able to be experienced or engage with or even visualised (i.e. represented in some way) and then having students construct meaning from those explicit representations. That is, actively engage students in the construction of the conceptual knowledge.

For vocational education, more broadly, the kinds of pedagogic divisions and practices required for developing conceptual knowledge are as follows. Firstly, consideration needs to be given to the kind of experiences and forms of learner engagement that are most likely to be able to represent that knowledge, on the one hand, and, on the other, have processes that students come to engage with it. It has been suggested (J. S. Brown et al., 1989) that students engaging in developing a conceptual model of the task is important as this provides the learner with:

- an advanced organiser for attempting to execute the task;
- bases to utilise feedback, hints and corrections during interactions;
- an internalised guide for independent practice by successive approximations; and
- a conceptual model which can be updated (Collins et al., 1989)

It is these kinds of considerations that can be particularly helpful for students to construct these 'hard to learn' kinds of knowledge that are required for digitised work. This development can also be underpinned by the provision of authentic activities that deliver concrete instances of how that knowledge needs to be utilised and for what purposes and these activities also assist with indexicality (i.e. the construction of knowledge in ways that permits its utilisation and recall). So, a key consideration is making accessible and explicit the conceptual and symbolic knowledge that is so central to digitised work and workplaces. This kind of access can be provided using stories, analogies, explanations, and illustrations by teachers drawing upon specific instances of practice that exemplify and illustrate the concepts being used.

So, these kinds of pedagogic practices that are important assisting the development of this important, but difficult to access, knowledge.

Promoting learning agency

Throughout the discussions above is the enduring focus on learner engagement. We are reminded here that education provisions are nothing more than an invitation to change. How students take up the invitation is ultimately fundamental to the effectiveness and success of educational provisions. So, student engagement and agency are central to effective vocational education, and how graduates come to adapt their knowledge on the world of work beyond that education and engage in the kind of effortful learning that is required to have a long productive working life (Goller, 2017). So, the issue of learning agency becomes quite central here. It is that agency that shapes the focus, intensity and direction of students' learning. However, there are some considerations associated with promoting learning agency that are outlined briefly here.

Firstly, student readiness (i.e. their ability to engage activities), and an awareness of their readiness is essential starting point for encouraging students to be proactive, interdependent and directed in their activities and learning. Secondly, having goals and processes that attract and sustain student engagement seem to be important. That is, having activities that are relevant, interesting and worthwhile to them. Central here is the idea of developing a strong sense of subjectivity associated with the occupation that incites students' effortful engagement in their learning. So, an important goal is to assist students come to recognize their occupation as their vocation (i.e. something that they come to associate with and engage).

Consequently, and fourthly, selecting and providing educational experiences that engage learners and they be interested in engaging effortful is likely to be required for the kinds of learning needed to become adaptable occupational practitioners. Part of that curriculum and pedagogic process is to place them in the circumstances where they must take responsibility for their thinking and acting, and learning. That is, putting them in the driver's seat, so to speak, because it is important that they engage in the thinking and acting required for the tasks set for them, rather than these being done by somebody else. Of course, guidance and support are provided by teachers, but fundamentally, the focus is on the agency and interdependence of learners. Practical consideration for developing these capacities is having students evaluating their peers' processes and outcomes and this kind of activity can develop the kinds of evaluative and critical capacities that people need to effectively monitor and evaluate their own work practices.

So, there are a set of activities that can be used to intentionally promote student learning agency, and these are central to many of the considerations raised above.

12.4 Developing a skillful and adaptable workforce in the era of digitalization

It has been proposed above that changes in occupational, workplace requirements and working life prompt a reappraisal of the goals and processes of vocational education. A broader view of curriculum and pedagogies need to be considered, engaged with and enacted to accommodate changes in educational goals for vocational education. These include addressing the specific requirements of workplaces as well as developing occupational competence; learning knowledge that is difficult to directly experience conceptual and symbolic knowledge required for digitized work and workplaces. Throughout, the importance of students to become active and intentional learners for their initial preparation, but also that ongoing development across working life. It is proposed here that a way forward is to adopt curriculum and pedagogic practices that are aligned with achieving these kinds of outcomes. This includes a consideration of what constitutes effective educational experiences (both within educational institutions and workplaces), ordering and reconciling these two sets of experiences, the use of educational interventions that can generate the kinds of capacities within vocational education students and assisting students become active and intentional learners across their working life. Educational interventions are likely to be required to address the growing elements of occupational 'hard to learn' knowledge that is required for much of contemporary work (Harteis, 2018b). Promoting learner agency and interdependence is likely to be an important educational outcome, not just for immediate employability, but for learning across working life.

To do this requires a consideration of what constitutes the existing and emerging requirements for occupational and workplace performance and then aligning these with the kinds of curriculum and pedagogic practices that vocational education institutions need to advance and the kinds and quality of engagement that students need to adopt and practice. These concerns are not just about individuals' personal learning, they extend to the efficacy of work practices, workplaces and communities and learning required for digitized work.

References

Alexander, P. A. & Judy, J. E. (1988). The interaction of domain specific and strategic knowledge in academic performance. *Review of Educational Research, 58*(4), 375-404.

Anderson, J. R. (1982). Acquisition of cognitive skill. *Psychological Review, 89*(4), 369-406.

Australian Bureau of Statisics. (2013). Programme for the International Assessment of Adult Competencies (Australia 2011-2012) In A. B. o. Statisics (Ed.), *Cat 42280.0*. Canberra.

Barley, S., & Batt, R. (1995). *The new crafts: The rise of the technical labour force and its implication for the organisation of work*. Retrieved from Philadelphia, PA: University of Philadelphia, National Center on the Education Quality of the Workforce.

Bauer, J., Leicherb, V., & Mulder, R. H. (2016). On nurses' learning from errors at work. In S. Billett, D. Dymock, & S. Choy (Eds.), *Supporting learning across working life: Models, processes and practices*. Dordrecht: Springer.

Billett, S. (1995). Workplace learning: its potential and limitations. *Education and Training, , 37* (5), 20-27.

Billett, S. (2000). Guided learning at work. *Journal of Workplace Learning, 12*(7), 272-285.

Billett, S. (2001). Knowing in practice: Re-conceptualising vocational expertise. *Learning and Instruction, 11*(6), 431-452.

Billett, S. (2006). *Work, Change and Workers*. Dordrecht: Springer.

Billett, S. (2011a). *Curriculum and pedagogic bases for effectively integrating practice-based experiences.* Strawberry Hills: Australian Learning and Teaching Council.

Billett, S. (2011b). *Vocational Education: Purposes, traditions and prospects*. Dordrecht: Springer.

Billett, S. (2014a). Interdependence on the boundaries between working and learning. In C. Harteis, A. Rausch, & J. Seifried (Eds.), *Discourses on professional learning: On the boundary between learning and working*. Dordrecht: Springer.

Billett, S. (2014b). *Mimetic learning at work: Learning in the circumstances of practice,* . Dordrecht: Springer.

Billett, S. (2015). *Integrating Practice-based Experiences into Higher Education*. Dordrecht: Springer.

Billett, S., Dymock, D., & Choy, S. (Eds.). (2016). *Supporting learning across working life*. Dordrecht: Springer.

Billett, S., Harteis, C., & Gruber, H. (2018). Developing occupational expertise through everyday work activities and interaction. In K. A. Ericsson, R. R. Hoffman, & A. Kozbelt (Eds.), *Cambridge Handbook of Expertise and Expert Performance* (2nd Ed.) (pp. 105-126). New York: Cambridge University Press.

Brown, A. L. & Palinscar, A. M. (1989). Guided, cooperative learning and individual knowledge acquisition. In L. B. Resnick (Ed.), *Knowing, learning and instruction, Essays in honour of Robert Glaser* (pp. 393-451). Hillsdale, N.J: Erlbaum & Associates.

Brown, J. S., Collins, A., & Duguid, P. (1989). Situated Cognition and the Culture of Learning. *Educational Researcher, 18*(1), 32-34.

Collins, A., Brown, J. S., & Newman, S. E. (1989). Cognitive apprenticeship: Teaching the crafts of reading, writing and mathematics. In L. B. Resnick (Ed.), *Knowing, Learning and Instruction: Essays in honour of Robert Glaser* (pp. 453-494). Hillsdale, NJ: Erlbaum & Associates.

Cooper, L., Orrel, J., & Bowden, M. (2010). *Work integrated learning: A guide to effective practice*. London: Routledge.

de Bruijn, E., Billett, S., & Onstenk, J. (Eds.). (2017). *Enhancing teaching and learning in the Dutch vocational education system: Reforms enacted.* Dordrecht: Springer.

Diakidoy, I.-A. N., & Kendeou, P. (2001). Facilitating conceptual change in astronomy: a comparison of the effectiveness of two instructional approaches. *Learning and Instruction, 11*, 1-20.

Ericsson, K. A., Hoffman, R. R., & Kozbelt, A. (Eds.). (2018). *Cambridge Handbook of Expertise and Expert Performance* (2nd Ed.). New York: Cambridge University Press.

Ericsson, K. A. & Lehmann, A. C. (1996). Expert and exceptional performance: Evidence of maximal adaptation to task constraints. *Annual Review of Psychology, 47*, 273-305.

Gelman, R. & Greeno, J. G. (1989). On the nature of competence: Principles for understanding in a domain. In L. B. Resnick (Ed.), *Knowing, learning and instruction: Essays in honor of Robert Glaser* (pp. 125-186). Hillsdale, NJ: Lawrence Erlbaum Associates.

Goller, M. (2017). *Human Agency at Work: An Active Approach towards Expertise Development*. Wiesbaden: Springer Fachmedien.

Gruber, H. & Harteis, C. (2018). *Individual and social influences on professional learning: Supporting the acquisition and maintenance of expertise*. (Professional and Practice-based Learning, Vol. 24). Cham: Springer.

Hajkowicz, S., Reeson, A., Rudd, L., Bratanova, A., Hodgers, L., Mason, C., & Boughen, N. (2016). *Tomorrow's digitally enabled workforce: Megatrends and scenarios for jobs and employment in Australia over the coming twenty years.* Canberra. Retrieved from https://data61.csiro.au/en/Our-Research/Our-Work/Future-Cities/Planning-sustainable-infrastructure/Tomorrows-Digitally-Enabled-Workforce

Hamalainen, R., Lanz, M., & Koskinen, K. T. (2018). Collaborative systems and environments for future working life: Towards the integration of workers, systems and manufacturing environments. In C. Harteis (Ed.), *The impact of digitalisation in the workplace: An educational view* (Vol. 21, pp. 25–38). Dordrecht: Springer.

Harteis, C. (2018a). Machines, change, work: An educational view on the digitalization of work In C. Harteis (Ed.), *The impact of digitalization in the workplace: an educational view* (pp. 1-10) (Professional and Practice-based Learning, Vol. 21).. Cham: Springer.

Harteis, C. (Ed.) (2018b). *The impact of digitalization in the workplace* (Professional and Practice-based Learning, Vol. 21). Cham: Springer.

Hull, G. (1997). Preface and Introduction. In G. Hull (Ed.), *Changing work, Changing workers: Critical perspectives on language, literacy and skills.* (pp. 3-39). New York: State University of New York Press.

Lobato, J. (2012). The actor-oriented transfer perspective and its contributions to educational research and practice. *Educational Psychologist, 47*(3), 232-247.

Marsh, C. J. (2004). *Key concepts for understanding curriculum*. London: RoutledgeFalmer.

Martin, L. M. W., & Scribner, S. (1991). Laboratory for cognitive studies of work: A case study of the intellectual implications of a new technology. *Teachers College Record, 92*(4), 582-602.

Mayer, C. (2001). Transfer of concepts and practices of vocational education and training from the centre to the peripheries: the case of Germany. *Journal of Education and Work, 14*(2), 189-208.

Nokelainen, P., Nevalainen, T., & Niemi, K. (2018). Mind or machine? Opportunities and limits of automation. In C. Harteis (Ed.), *The impact of digitalization in the workplace: An educational view* (pp. 13-24) (Professional and Practice-based Learning, Vol. 21). Cham: Springer.

Nokelainen, P., Nevalinen, T., & Niemi, K. (2018). Mind all machine? Opportunities and limits of automation. In C. Harteis (Ed.), *The impact of digitalisation in the workplace: An educational view* (Vol. 21, pp. 13–24). Dordrecht: Springer.

Novak, J. D. (1990). Concept maps and vee diagrams: Two metacognitive tools to facilitate meaningful learning. *Instructional Science, 19,* 29-52.

Organisation for Economic Co-operation and Development. (2006). *Live longer, work longer*. Paris: OECD.

Organisation for Economic Co-operational and Development. (2013). *OECD skills outlook 2013: first results from the Survey of Adult Skills*: OECD, Paris.

Orrell, J. (2011). *Good Practice Report: Work integrated learning*. Retrieved from https://www.voced.edu.au/content/ngv%3A51931

Palinscar, A. S. & Brown, A. L. (1984). Reciprocal teaching of comprehension-fostering and comprehension-monitoring activities. *Cognition and Instruction, 1*(2), 117-175.

Raizen, S. A. (1991). *Learning and work: The research base. Vocational Education and Training for youth: Towards coherent policy and practice*. Paris: OECD.

Rausch, A., Seifried, J., & Harteis, C. (2017). Emotions, coping and learning in error situations at work. *Journal of Workplace Learning, 29*(5), 374-393.

Rogoff, B. (1990). *Apprenticeship in thinking – cognitive development in social context*. New York: Oxford University Press.

Royer, J. (1979). Theories of the Transfer of Learning. *Educational Psychologist, 14*, 53-69.

Schneider, M. (2018). Digitalization of production, human capital, and organizational capital. In C. Harteis (Ed.), *The impact of digitalization in the workplace* (pp. 39-52). Springer.

Scribner, S. (1985). Knowledge at work. *Anthropology and Education Quarterly, 16*, 199-206.

Veillard, L. (2015). University-corporate partnerships for designing workplace curriculum: Alternance training course in tertiary education. In L. Filliettaz & S. Billett (Eds.), *Francophone perspectives of learning through work: Conceptions, traditions and practices*. Dordrecht: Springer.

Volet, S. (2013). Extending, broadening and rethinking existing research on transfer of training. *Educational Research Review, 8* (1), 90-95.

Vosniadou, S., Ioannides, C., Dimitrakopoulou, A., & Papademetriou, E. (2002). Designing learning environments to promote conceptual change in science. *Learning and Instruction, 11*(4-5), 381-419.

Zitter, I., Hoeve, A., & de Bruijn, E. (2017). A Design Perspective on the School-Work Boundary: A Hybrid Curriculum Model. *Vocations and Learning, 9*(1), 111-131.

About the Authors

Antje Barabasch
Antje Barabasch is chair of the research axe "Teaching and Learning in VET" at the Swiss Federal Institute for Vocational Education and Training (SFIVET). Her research interests include VET learning cultures at Swiss companies, creativity development in VET, teaching and learning in VET and VET policy transfer.

Contact: Eidgenössisches Hochschulinstitut für Berufsbildung (EHB), Kirchlindachstr. 79, CH-3052 Zollikofen, Switzerland.
Email: antje.barabasch@ehb.swiss

Matthias Berg
Matthias Berg studied Educational Technology at the University of Saarland. He obtained his master degree with a thesis about the use of virtual reality in vocational education and training (VET) in civil engineering professions.

Contact: matthias.berg@uni-saarland.de

Stephen Billett
Stephen Billett, Prof. dr. dr. h.c, dr. h.c, is Professor of Adult and Vocational Education in the School of Education and Professional Studies, Griffith University, Brisbane, Queensland Australia. His research interest are in learning the capacities required for paid work, through experiences in and across working life, educational institutions and their integration.

Contact: Education and Professional Studies, Griffith University, Australia.
Email: s.billett@griffith.edu.au

Marc Egloffstein
Marc Egloffstein is a member of the Learning, Design and Technology group at the University of Mannheim. His research focuses on educational technology, especially in higher education and professional learning and development.

Contact
University of Mannheim, Business School, Economics and Business Education – Learning, Design and Technology, L 4,1, 68161 Mannheim, Germany.
Email: egloffstein@uni-mannheim.de

Thomas Ellwart
Thomas Ellwart (Dr.rer.nat./Ph.D.) is a full professor of Business Psychology at the University of Trier. His research interests include socio-digital system design and evaluation with the main focus on team processes and team cognitions, the handling of information overload in digitized work environments, as well as topics of personnel and team diagnostics.

Contact: University of Trier, Department of Psychology, 54286 Trier, Germany.
Email: ellwart@uni-trier.de

Jan-Philipp Exner
Jan-Philipp Exner is Senior Digitization Professional at August-Wilhelm-Scheer-Institute for Digitized Products and Processes. With a background in Urban Planning and IoT, he does research in exploring new and innovative digital tools and approaches in the construction sector.

Contact: August-Wilhelm-Scheer-Institute for Digitized Products and Processes, Uni-Campus D 5 1, 66123 Saarbrücken, Germany.
Email: jan-philipp.exner@aws-institut.de

Andrea Faath-Becker
Andrea Faath-Becker works as a research associate at the Department of Technical Didactics at the Technical University of Kaiserslautern, Germany. Her research interest focuses on the assessment of professional competence in vocational education. She works also as a teacher trainer in pre-service teacher training for vocational schools.

Contact: Technical University of Kaiserslautern, Department of Technical Didactics, Postfach 3049, 67663 Kaiserslautern, Germany.
Email: faath-becker@mv.uni-kl.de

Silke Fischer
Silke Fischer is senior researcher in the research field "learning cultures and didactics" at the Swiss Federal Institute for Vocational Education and Training (SFIVET). Her research interests include creativity development in VET and game-based instruction.

Contact: Eidgenössisches Hochschulinstitut für Berufsbildung (EHB), Kirchlindachstr. 79, CH 3052 Zollikofen, Switzerland.
Email: silke.fischer@ehb.swiss

Edward C. Fletcher Jr.
Edward Fletcher is an EHE distinguished associate professor in the College of Education and Human Ecology (EHE) at The Ohio State University. His research interests include examining the experiences and related outcomes of students who participate in career academies within the United States.

Contact: The Ohio State University, College of Education and Human Ecology, Workforce Development and Education, 305 Annie & John Glenn Ave, A465 PAES Building, Columbus, OH, 43210, USA.
Email: fletcher.158@osu.edu

Rico Hermkes
Dr., Goethe University Frankfurt, Germany. His research interests include instructional support, interaction research and tacit knowledge.

Contact: Goethe University Frankfurt am Main, Faculty of Economics and Business, Business Ethics and Business Education, Theodor-W.-Adorno-Platz 4, 60629 Frankfurt am Main, Germany.
Email: hermkes@econ.uni-frankfurt.de

Victor M. Hernandez-Gantes
Victor M. Hernandez-Gantes is a full Professor of Career and Workforce Education at the University of South Florida. His research interests build on the examination of the successful promotion of student college and career readiness and structures of support within the context of school community systems.

Contact: University of South Florida, College of Education, 4202 E. Fowler Ave., EDU 105, Tampa, FL 33620, USA.
Email: victorh@usf.edu

Dirk Ifenthaler
Dirk Ifenthaler is Professor and Chair of Learning, Design and Technology at University of Mannheim, Germany, and UNESCO Deputy Chair of Data Science in Higher Education Learning and Teaching at Curtin University, Australia. Dirk's research focuses on the intersection of cognitive psychology, educational technology, data analytics, and organisational learning.

Contact: University of Mannheim, Business School, Economics and Business Education – Learning, Design and Technology, L 4,1, 68161 Mannheim, Germany.
Email: dirk@ifenthaler.info

Kristina Kögler
Kristina Kögler is a full professor at the Department for Vocational, Economical and Technical Education at the University of Stuttgart. Her research focuses on competence assessment in vocational education and training, emotional and motivational facets of teaching and learning as well as instructional quality of online-based learning arrangements.

Contact: University of Stuttgart, Institute of Educational Science, Department for Vocational, Economical and Technical Education, Geschwister-Scholl-Str. 24d, 70174 Stuttgart, Germany.
Email: koegler@bwt.uni-stuttgart.de

Andreas Korbach
Andreas Korbach is a postdoc at Saarland University. His research interests include the effects of cognitive load in multimedia learning as well as the evaluation and development of qualitative and quantitative methods for cognitive load measurement.

Contact: Saarland University, Faculty of Human and Business Sciences, Department of Empirical Educational Research, Campus A 4 2, 66123 Saarbrücken, Germany.
Email: a.korbach@mx.uni-saarland.de

Thomas Lachmann
Thomas Lachmann is full professor of Cognitive and Developmental Psychology and head of Center for Cognitive Science at the University of Kaiserslautern, Germany. His research interests include learning and learning disabilities and the development of cognitive functions across life span.

Contact: University of Kaiserslautern, E.-Schroedinger Street, 67663 Kaiserslautern.
Email: lachmann@rhrk.uni-kl.de

Nico Link
Nico Link is an assistant professor (with tenure track) at the Technical University of Dresden. His research interests focus on technical problem-solving, assessment of competencies and teacher training in TVET.

Contact: Technical University of Dresden, Faculty of Education, Institute of Vocational Education and Didactics, Chair of Mechatronics/ Vocational Didactics, 01062 Dresden, Germany.
Email: nico.link@tu-dresden.de

Alina Makhkamova
Alina Makhkamova is a Digitization Professional at the August-Wilhelm Scheer Institute for Digitized Products and Processes of Saarbrücken, Germany. Her research interests include human factors of Technology-enhanced learning.

Contact: AWS-Institut für digitale Produkte und Prozesse gGmbH, Uni Campus D 5 1, 66123 Saarbrücken, Germany.
Email: alina.makhkamova@aws-institut.de

Helmut M. Niegemann
Helmut M. Niegemann is a senior professor in economics and business education at the Goethe University Frankfurt. His research interests include educational technology and instructional psychology.

Contact: Goethe University Frankfurt, Economics and Business Education, Campus Westend, Th.-W.-Adorno Platz 4; 60323 Frankfurt/Main, Germany.
Email: niegemann@econ.uni-frankfurt.de; https://www.profniegemann.de

Henrike Peiffer
Dr. Henrike Peiffer is a postdoctoral researcher at Trier University, Germany. Her research interests include the structue, measurement and promotion of competence beliefs, the evalutaion of trainings and personnel selection and potential detection processes in the workplace.

Contact: Trier University, Department of Business Psychology, Universitätsring 15, 54286 Trier, Germany.
Email: peiffer@uni-trier.de

Martin Pietschmann
Martin Pietschmann worked as project manager and quality officer at the Association for the Promotion of Employment in Leonberg. His research interests include education and training, digital media, communication and knowledge management.

Contact: Kompetenzzentrum für Ausbau und Fassade, Siemensstraße 6-8, 71277 Rutesheim, Germany.
Email: pietschmann@stuck-verband.de

Michael Roll
Michael Roll is a research assistant and doctoral candidate at the Business School of the University of Mannheim. His research interests include competence development of trainees due to industry 4.0 and didactical use of learning factories 4.0 within technical vocational schools.

Contact: University of Mannheim, Business School, Area of Economics and Business Education – Learning, Design & Technology, L 4,1, 68161 Mannheim, Germany.
Email: roll@bwl.uni-mannheim.de

Daniel Rugel
Daniel Rugel works at the eBusiness - Competence Center of Kaiserslautern, Germany. He is responsible for digital processes in craft businesses.

Contact: d.rugel@ebz-kl.de

Pia Schäfer
Pia Schäfer, M.Ed., works as a research associate at the Department of Technical Didactics at the Technical University of Kaiserslautern, Germany. Her research interest focuses on the assessment of professional competence in vocational education.

Contact: Technical University of Kaiserslautern, Department of Technical Didactics, Postfach 3049, 67663 Kaiserslautern, Germany.
Email: pia.schaefer @mv.uni-kl.de

Isabelle Schmidt
Dr. Isabelle Schmidt is a senior researcher at GESIS – Leibniz Institute for the Social Sciences, Mannheim, Germany. Her research interests include structural and development aspects of competence beliefs in educational context and at the workplace, scale development, and data analysis of longitudinal data.

Contact: GESIS – Leibniz Institute for the Social Sciences, Germany B2,14, 68159 Mannheim, Germany.
Email: Isabelle.schmidt@gesis.org

Mareike Schmidt
Mareike Schmidt works as Senior Research Professional at imc in Saar-brücken. She graduated in computer science at Saarland University in 2011. Her research interests include e-learning and the use of digital media and technology in vocational education and training (VET).

Contact: imc information multimedia communication AG, Scheer Tower, Uni Campus Nord, 66123 Saarbrücken, Germany.
Email: mareike.schmidt@im-c.de

Brigitte Schönberger
Brigitte Schönberger is a research fellow at the Department for Vocational, Economical and Technical Education at the University of Stuttgart. Her research fields are item and feedback development in study ability tests, functional communication and knowledge transfer in a research campus environment as well as the quality analysis of online learning opportunities.

Contact: University of Stuttgart, Institute of Educational Science, Department for Vocational, Economical and Technical Education, Geschwister-Scholl-Str. 24d, 70174 Stuttgart, Germany.
Email: schoenberger@bwt.uni-stuttgart.de

Jürgen Seifried
Jürgen Seifried is a full professor at the Business School at the University of Mannheim. His research interests include competence development of teachers and trainers, learning at the workplace, and competence assessment in vocational education and training (VET).

Contact: University of Mannheim, Business School, Economics and Business Education – Professional Teaching and Learning, L 4,1, 68161 Mannheim, Germany.
Email: seifried@bwl.uni-mannheim.de

Christin Siegfried
Dr. Christin Siegfried is a post-doctoral researcher in the Faculty of Economics and Business at the Goethe University Frankfurt. Her research interests include the development of economic competence of teachers and students, problem-solving competence development of trainees and conditions of participation in vocational education and training (VET).

Contact: Goethe-University Frankfurt, Faculty of Economics and Business, Theodor-W.-Adorno-Platz 1, 60323 Frankfurt.
Email: siegfried@em.uni-frankfurt.de

Jan Spilski
Jan Spilski is scientific coordinator of the Center for Cognitive Science at the University of Kaiserslautern. His research interests include digital diagnostics and learning in vocational training.

Contact: University of Kaiserslautern, E.-Schroedinger Street, 67663 Kaiserslautern. Email: jan.spilski@sowi.uni-kl.de

Anna-Sophie Ulfert
Dr. Anna-Sophie Ulfert is a postdoctoral researcher at Goethe University Frankfurt. Her research interests include technology in the workplace, interaction with autonomous systems and technology related competence beliefs.

Contact: Goethe University Frankfurt, Institute of Psychology, Department of Educational Psychology, Theodor-W.-Adorno-Platz 6, 60629 Frankfurt, Germany.
Email: ulfert@psych.uni-frankfurt.de

Felix Walker
Felix Walker is full professor and the head of the Department of Technical Didactics at the Technical University of Kaiserslautern. His research interests are the assessment and promotion of vocational professional competence at different levels (e.g. apprentices, students, teachers, trainers) of the vocational training system.

Contact: Technical University of Kaiserslautern, Department of Technical Didactics, Postfach 3049, 67663 Kaiserslautern, Germany.
Email: walker@mv.uni-kl.de

Eveline Wuttke
Eveline Wuttke is a full professor at the faculty of Economics and Business Education at Goethe University Frankfurt, Germany. Her research interests include competence development of teachers, participation in continuous vocational education and training, learning at the workplace, identification through vocational education, and competence assessment in vocational education and training.

Contact: Goethe-University Frankfurt, Faculty of Economics and Business Education, Theodor-W.-Adorno-Platz 1, 60323 Frankfurt.
Email: wuttke@em.uni-frankfurt.de

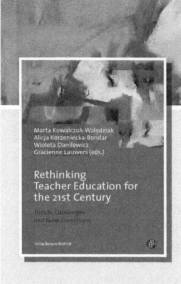

Marta Kowalczuk-Walędziak
Alicja Korzeniecka-Bondar
Wioleta Danilewicz
Gracienne Lauwers (eds.)

Rethinking Teacher Education for the 21st Century

2019 • 402 pp. • Pb. • 76,00 € (D) • US$105.00 • GBP 67.00
ISBN 978-3-8474-2241-9 • eISBN 978-3-8474-1257-1

This book focuses on current trends, potential challenges and further developments of teacher education and professional development from a theoretical, empirical and practical point of view. It intends to provide valuable and fresh insights from research studies and examples of best practices from Europe and all over the world. The authors deal with the strengths and limitations of different models, strategies, approaches and policies related to teacher education and professional development in and for changing times(digitization, multiculturalism, pressure to perform).

The book is an **Open Access** title (DOI: 10.3224/84742241) , which is free to download or can be bought as paperback.

www.barbara-budrich.net

Petra Strehmel | Johanna Heikka
Eeva Hujala | Jillian Rodd
Manjula Waniganayake (eds.)

Leadership in
Early Education in
Times of Change

Research from five Continents

2019 • 308 pp. • Pb. • 36,00 € (D) • US$50.00 • GBP 32.00
ISBN 978-3-8474-2199-3 • eISBN 978-3-8474-1224-3

The collection brings together the latest work of researchers from Australia, Africa, Asia, and Europe focusing on early childhood leadership matters.
It covers different aspects of leadership in early education: professional
education and development, identity and leadership strategies as well as
governance and leadership under different frame conditions.

The book is an **Open Access** title, which is free to download or can be
bought as paperback.

www.barbara-budrich.net